The Nashville I Knew

The Nashville I Knew

JACK NORMAN, SR.

Rutledge Hill Press
P.O. Box 140483
Nashville, Tennessee 37214

Published by Rutledge Hill Press, a Thomas Nelson Company, P. O. Box 141000, Nashville, Tennessee 37214.

Typography by ProtoType Graphics, Inc.
Jacket design by Harriette Bateman

Library of Congress Cataloging-in-Publication Data

Norman, Jack, 1904–
    The Nashville I Knew.
      p. cm.
    ISBN 1-55853-893-3 (pbk)
    Includes Index.
    1. Nashville (Tenn.)—Social life and customs—Addresses, essays, lectures. 2. Norman, Jack, 1904– —Addresses, essays, lectures. I. Title.
F444.N245N67   1984
976.8'55   84-17950
                                                       CIP

To Carrie

Contents

Illustrations

Illustrations Continued

Photo Credits

Grateful acknowledgment is given for permission to use the illustrations in this book. All photographs were provided by the *Nashville Banner* library unless indicated below.

Foreword

Jack Norman is uniquely qualified to have written the popular series "The Passing of the Nashville I Knew" in the *Banner*, which now appears in book form. In his 80 years, he came to know the city from every angle.

Born on Second Avenue in South Nashville, raised in Woodbine and on Porter Road in East Nashville, Norman graduated from Central High School and attended Vanderbilt Law School. He became one of the nation's noted criminal attorneys, a man whose face was familiar to all classes with clients ranging from the affluent to those who have known little but trouble during their lives.

Jack, at the peak of his career in the courts and in local, state and national politics, could not walk on Church Street, Fourth Avenue or the Public Square without speaking and being spoken to every few steps. And he loved it that way, in the days before Nashville became such a large city.

This ruddy man with his wavy brown hair, brisk walk and orator's voice had a feel for people and places, an appetite for history and a remarkable memory. In later years, Jack and his devoted wife, the former Carrie Sneed, traveled to every corner of the world. Rather than luxuriating in semi-retirement, Jack shared his impressions of foreign countries, his own feelings and emotions, in descriptive, in-depth articles in the *Nashville Banner.*

To make such detailed notes during busy travels and long days wasn't overtime for Jack Norman. He never knew life any other way. While attending Vanderbilt Law School's afternoon classes, he taught public speaking in the mornings at both Central High and Peabody Demonstration School and in the evenings at Watkins Institute and St. Bernard Academy. And, to be outdoors a bit, he coached the Central High track team. Later, this drummer in the Vanderbilt student band also was to win the university's Founder's Medal in Oratory.

One of Norman's very few time-saving measures was building and moving into a handsomely furnished apartment in downtown Printer's Alley, adjacent to his law office, after having lived in spacious residences and on a farm at Sycamore in Cheatham County.

After having visited 145 foreign countries, Jack Norman looked back over the years, his zest for life undiminished and reasoned that Nashville was just about the best place on earth, with some of the most vibrating chords of remembrance. THE NASHVILLE I KNEW abounds in vivid tints and clear tones of the past, wrapped in the old lavender of sentiment.

Fred Russell
Vice President
Nashville Banner

The
Nashville
I Knew

CHAPTER 1

Do You Remember?
A Medley of Memories

DO YOU REMEMBER: Charivaris on the wedding nights? The railroad "paycar"? Shouting at black revivals and river baptizings? Kites made out of cedar or "Sweet Annie" sticks, and newspapers with flour and water as paste? Cutting paper dolls and making clover ropes? Chewing gum stuck on school desks and chalked hopscotch courts on the sidewalk? Blowing up cans with wet carbide and making castles in the gutter sand?

How about walking on stilts and billy goat wagons? Smoking dry grapevine and coffee cigarettes? Green persimmons, and chewing bees' wax? Gourds at the spring and gathering watercress? Replacing palings on the fence and pulling grass out of brick sidewalks? Lace curtains, stretchers and quilting frames? Flat irons and Tiffany lights over the dining room tables? The Sears-Roebuck dollar watch (Ingersol), and the toy section of the catalog? The Indian head penny and the nickel with the "V" before the Buffalo nickel?

Can you remember the writing pen staffs and points? Rings for pigs' noses to keep them from rooting? The "Wild West" shows and medicine shows? Having your shoes half-soled? Hot oil drops and hot salt bags for the earache? Pulling a tooth with a string tied to it and the doorknob and then slamming the door shut? Rubbing chigger bites with coal oil? Darning socks? Mosquito netting and Cuticura soap?

Do you remember the water reservoir above the toilet seat and the rope you pulled to flush? Straw fans and cookie jars? Grindstones and stiles? The Seth Thomas mantel clock and the seven-day alarm clock? The fancy heater with the colored isinglass on the door? The surrey with the fringe on the top and the lap rug? The horseshoe nailed over the barn door? The "twelve o'clock whistle"?

What has become of the framed motto, "God bless our home"? The steam calliope and rock fences? Gate latches and boot-jacks? Weather vanes and lightning rods? Chicken coops and rabbit hutches? Popcorn wagons and gingerbread planks? Gingersnaps and cinnamon drops? *Collier's Weekly, Saturday Evening Post, Harper's Bazaar,* and *Woman's Home Companion?*

Do you remember the Studebaker wagons and John Deere plows? Lilac talcum powder and oil of wintergreen for the toothache? Paregoric for cramps and cheap drunks? Jacks and tiddledywinks? "O. J. number

11" canned goods and "Butter-Krust" bread? "Duck Head" overalls and canvas "leggins"? H. Boker's Tree-Brand pocket knives and Japanese paper lanterns? Brown's Mule Chewing Tobacco, and Bull Durham with free cigarette papers? "Search-light" matches and Waterman's fountain pens? Circus wagons and celluloid collars?

Do you remember Dr. Gus Dyer, John Trotwood Moore, John Cobb, Jack Price Jones, Dick McClure, Dick Lindsey, Bill Lingner, Jack Keefe, Judge A. G. Rutherford, Felix Wilson—and Clare Lovett at the Glendale Zoo?

Remember the first safety razors, flashlights, crystal set radios, zippers, automobile self-starters, electric fans, stoves and refrigerators, commercial airplanes?

Remember Joe Roller's bicycle shop, Jonte's plumbing shop, and Legler's gun store? How about St. Bernard Coal Co., McEwen's Laundry, the Gerst Brewing Company, Joe Morse and Armstrong's?

How about Weil's store on Second Avenue, and Leichhardt's drugstore on the Square? How Congressman Joe Byrns used to distribute free government seed?

Do you remember that as late as 1923, the entire fleet of the Nashville Gas Company's automobiles had solid rubber tires and that they did not roll over asphalt either? Remember the uptown traffic officers before the time of traffic lights: Dick Swint, Bob McKinstry, Enoch Shelton, Bob Leonard, and Ed Wright, etc.? Remember the oratory of Harvey Hannah, Colonel Fort, Governor McCord, Dick Atkinson, and Governor Benton McMillin?

Did you ever play golf at the Oriental Golf Club or hunt squirrels in the woods of what is now the Hobbs Road and Belle Meade sections? Did you ever park on Flag Pole Hill? Remember Sheriff Lawrence Bauman, and Luther Luton? How many of you "young things" remember Miss Annie Allison, or Miss Ludie Phillips at Phillips and Buttorff Co.? Have you ever told your grandchildren that your boyfriend used to take you to Candyland more than sixty years ago? Remember Willie, the crippled man who ran the news stand on the Church Street sidewalk at the Maxwell House corner? What has become of broom peddlers and harness makers?

Did you ever jump out of a barn loft into a pile of hay, swing out and off of a grapevine into a creek, look at pictures through a stereoscope, or go crayfish hunting?

What became of the gazebos and the trellises?

Now let's go way back,—Playing "London Bridge," "Ring Around the Roses,"mickee-saw"? Torpedo sticks at Christmas and the Fourth of July?

Davidson County Courthouse—1880.

Davidson County Courthouse—1930.

When one fastens the mind to old memories, one sometimes comes up with just a hodgepodge. One thing suggests another and that, in turn, is associated with still another. They are not necessarily linked but intriguing.

This all proves what that memory expert, Judge Albert Williams, once explained to me. The mind is the greatest computer ever created. It is a permanent storehouse of everything that is ever introduced into it by the five senses—hearing, seeing, feeling, tasting and smelling. Once the information is stored there it never leaves. Hence, one never loses a memory. We lose instead our ability to recollect. Recollection is the trigger that releases the memory. That ability to recollect is aided by the association of one thing, person or event. Once released the memory gains expression by word or action and thus we gain a review of the past. How many times have you tried hard to remember something and, try as hard as you could, you just could not reach it? However, something would happen, probably while waiting for a red light to change or maybe you woke up at four in the morning—and there it was—you remembered it completely. The memory was there—you just lost your recollection. Something associated with it later was the trigger to bring the memory out of the computer of the mind.

Let's go back to some other old memories. How about Big Ben alarm clocks, Tuxedo pipe tobacco, Manualo player pianos, Oliver typewriters, Brunswick phonographs, Easterbrook pen points, Vitali bicycles, Jewel coal ranges, Holeproof hosiery, Economy tire patches, L. C. Smith shotguns, Prest-O-Lite batteries, Paris men's garters, Litholm collars and cuffs, and Victor victrolas?

Do you remember the Case, Saxon, Franklin, Overland, Haynes, Hudson, White, Stevens, Studebaker, Reo, Garford, Nyberg and Chalmers automobiles?

Have you forgotten Robert L. Ripley, Enrico Caruso, John McCormack, Tom Mix, William S. Hart and Lionel Barrymore?

How about "cheri-cola," clabber, biscuit pudding, steamboat roustabouts, shoeshine boys and hotel call boys?

Pull these out of your memory: when cigarettes were called "fags"; Coca-Colas

Tom Mix.

were called "dopes"; cottage cheese was called "smear-case"; potatoes were called "spuds"; and baby pacifiers were called "foolers"; and when children were not called "kids" and men were not called "guys."

Remember the "One Moment Please" that flashed on the old movie screen when the film got off track or caught on fire; the turnstiles at the entrance of the first Piggly-Wiggly stores; the lunch counters at the Warner drug stores; those baskets that carried store merchandise along overhead wires to be wrapped, and the leather tubes for the money at Timothy's, Grimes' and Gilbert's?

Remember when wrist watches, zippers, ballpoint pens, electric irons, washing machines, dishwashers and electric coffee percolators came along?

Have you forgotten how housewives cleaned their pots and pans with lye soap before Octagon soap powder and Bon-Ami came on the scene—when they dried their own apples, peaches and pears?

I wonder what ever became of those long red and white striped tin horns with wooden mouthpieces that we used to get on Christmas and homemade hammocks made out of wired barrel staves?

Remember Theda Bara, Richard Cortez, Wallace Reid, Wallace Beery, Marie Dressler, Sir Harry Lauder, Geraldine Farrar and the Gish sisters? Have you forgotten the Fatty Arbuckle trial?

Did you ever cut your fingers on a nutmeg grater or receive a "chain letter"? Remember Carter and Conklin fountain pens, Iver-Johnson bicycles, Van Heusen collars and Eureka vacuum cleaners? Did you wait for the Sunday funny paper to see "The Newlyweds and Snookums," "Andy Gump and Min," "Timekiller," and "Mutt and Jeff"?

Remember "Oh Henry" candy bars?

Isn't it hard to believe that we received 52 issues of the *Saturday Evening Post* for $1.50, could buy a Steinway piano for $800, and one dozen of William Rogers 1847 silver-plated teaspoons for $3.50?

Did you ever have an automobile crank to fly out of your hand? Do you remember Jim Williams, the "Old Dirt Dobber" (and what Max Benson did to him once)?

You real oldies—do you remember the Spout Springs School in East Nashville and Ms. Katie Robinson and Ms. Edna Davis? How about Squire Jim Allen, Frank Stull,

"Buttermilk" Shelton, "Daddy" Chadwell, Paul Treanor, Sam Borum, Ted Vaughan and Dick Taylor?

Did your home have a tin or a granite water dipper—or a gourd? Did your water cooler drip? Remember when girls used to plait each other's hair—and those old-time hair curlers that looked like a pair of wire pliers that they would heat with the lamps?

Have you forgotten the old Nashville telephone prefixes—Main, Walnut, Hemlock, etc., the Johnny J. Jones midways at the old Tennessee State Fairs, and kewpie dolls?

Remember moonshiner's "rigs" during Prohibition—the "Hoptown Special" and "blockade runners"? How about "cowboy" gloves with leather fringe on the cuffs? Did your mother have a turkey feather duster, a hall rack or a trunk?

Do you remember what traces, hacking straps, kruppers, reins, belly bands and lines were? How about fifth wheels, single trees and tailgates? Or how about magneto keys? Did you have a hand tire pump clamped on the frame of your bicycle—and a leather tool kit? Have you forgotten those fancy and elaborate baby buggies—"perambulators" to the sophisticated—when all containers were made of paper, clay, cloth, wood, metal or glass?

Remember railroad fuzees, lamp wicks, Ouija boards, and pink coral necklaces?

When the well digger was locating the stream of water in your yard did he use a divining rod or just a forked peachtree limb?

We older Nashvillians inherited a language of colloquialisms and slang and we added some to the list. A review of them will indicate some of the differences of life in our earlier years and that of today.

They related to a more placid life, a less violent attitude, less belligerence, more patience and a greater appreciation and acceptance of social limitations and discipline.

Some may have indicated positive differences, but not rebellion. Some may seem to have bordered on the irreligious, but not blasphemy. Some may have denoted indignation but not castigation. They represented surprise, alarm, questioning, approval or disapproval or enthusiam for what they saw or heard in the actions and words of their neighbors, friends or relatives.

Sometimes they could be penetrating but hardly ever cruel. Some were hostile but carried no hate. Some were a little vicious but never vulgar. Some were critical but never offensive.

They were expletive, colorful, descriptive and emphatic. They flowed from lips innocently and impulsively and were intended to represent instant reaction and initial impressions. They were seldom spoken in a serious or vindictive manner.

Do you remember when the following just came natural: Gee-whiz! Doggone it! Dad blame it! Golly gee! Good gracious! Gol darned! Golly Moses! Great guns! My goodness! I'll be darned! I declare! Well, I'll be! Good night! Good golly! By golly! My, oh, my! Good granny! My stars! Well, I'm a monkey's uncle! Land sakes! By Jiminy! By Jove! By George! Dad gum! Great Jehosophat! Do tell! You don't say! I'll be dad blamed! Aw shucks! To heck with it! Aw heck! Boy, oh boy!

How about: Sakes alive! What in the world! Me oh my! Man oh man! I'll say! Do tell! You don't say! Land o' Goshen! Well, I'll be! Oh, no! You bet your boots! You are mighty right! You bet your life! To a darn certainty! As sure as heck! You really think so! To a gnat's eyebrow! Just as sure as living! Holy smokes! Holy catfish! What in the tarnation! Whowee! Be dogged! Saints preserve us! How in the world! Is that a fact! You don't say! What in the name of goodness! Don't tell me! Bless my soul!

Have you forgotten these expressions: Oh you kid; Sweet patutie; poo poo padoop; You rascal, you; Tutti fruiti; Ishkabibble; toodledoo; whammy; toot toot Tootsie; Smiggle-Fritz; cutie pie; humdinger; hot shot; whiffle diffle; cuttin' the mustard; smart alec; punch-drunk; let her rip; shimmy up; go to it; in a pig's eye; PDQ; bustin' out; souped up; goofy; gadfly; high falutin; hootenanny; dumb Dora.

Do you remember the "sour puss," the "kill joy"; the "crape hanger" and "gloomy Gus"? How about "Indian giver"; "laughing hyena"; "dudes"; "jelly bean"; the "flirt" and "stuck up"?

Evidently these became too tame, too "square" and did not give the tongue the liberty "to do its thing." Most have now given way to "four letter words" and profane expressions to announce hard opinion, mean difference and naked description. Their association with vulgarity is an evident attempt at emphasis and evidence of mental and moral license.

Had we used the language of today, we would still be unable to sit down or to get the soap out of our mouths.

Many of our old words and phrases, mentioned above, were current locally and without recognition in standard English speech. Slang, of course, is commonly only a substitute for originality. Therefore, some of them will only be found in the *Unabridged Dictionary of Varmint Town* and its old *Flat Rock Supplement,* or perhaps in an old volume of the *Billy Goat Hill* and *Crappy Shute Encyclopedia.*

Do you remember: Nat King Cole singing "Blueberry Hill," Eddie Duchin playing the piano; Rudy Vallee singing the Yale "Stein Song"? Al Jolson singing "Mammy" and the big-eyed Eddie Cantor?

I'll bet you have forgotten the old windmill at Shelby Park, blotters, street car transfer tickets, the old city dump dwellers, the shanty boats on the Cumberland River, horseflies and chicken mites.

Did you ever see the Hagenbach-Wallace Circus? the original Tom Thumb and the Siamese twins? and Al G. Fields' minstrel show when they played here? How about "Lasses" White's minstrel show? Did you ever go on an excursion up the river on the old steamboat, *Jo Horton Fall*? Remember the calliope? Remember the immaculately dressed and very polite Pullman porters and waiters? Did you ever "beat" the carpet hanging on a clothesline? Do you remember the sound of horses eating grain at "feed time" in the barn on a rainy day? Did you ever smoke coffee cigarettes—or grapevine? Did you ever catch a ride on the "perch pole" of a wagon? Remember the "poll" tax and the "road" tax? Remember the grand stairway in the old Maxwell House Hotel?

You oldies who lived in the rural sections of Old Nashville—do you recall putting bluestone in the chickens' water to keep them from the "droop," building hens' nests, pouring pine tar on pigs to kill the lice, putting axle grease on cuts on horses, putting rings in the noses of pigs to keep them from rooting, cutting off the tails of little bull puppies, giving the hogs some coal to eat, chickens roosting in trees, ducks messing up the yard, getting chased by a gander, your frustration when at milking time the cow would not "give her milk down," or when she swished you with her tail or kicked you off the stool, when the horse would not open her mouth to take the bit, feeding a baby calf from a bottle, when you moved the newborn kittens and the mother cat took them right back when you turned your back, the strutting of a bantam rooster, the noise of dogs when they had treed a coon or possum, running from a skunk, the noise of scared guineas, the flights of wild geese with the coming of winter, and chiggers? Remember Herefords, Jerseys, Holsteins, Guernseys, Angus and Shorthorns?

Remember those crazy buckles on canvas bookstraps, the cork handles on pen staffs, tracing paper and Page's white paste?

Have you forgotten the backyard grape arbors, round tree benches, clotheslines and props, back gates, ash pits, grindstones, mint beds, cellars and those rose trellises?

Remember lawn swings, hammocks, rope swings, croquet courts, porch swings, bannisters, transoms, iron front fences, and porch settees?

Did you ever operate a soda water or lemonade stand?

Marshall & Bruce Company locations.

Girls, remember bandeaux, ribbon headbands, sachets, and snoods?

Remember the old banana cellars on Third Avenue, North? That good smell of coffee roasting at the old H. G. Hill warehouse and the cooking of chocolate at the old Standard Candy Company?

Remember: Leo Boles, Morris Lebeck, John P. Brown, Monty Ross, Dr. Sam Bloomstein, Morris Barr, J. Wharton Allen, Herbert Carson, D. Marvin Cullum, Jed Apperson, Tyree Fain, Lipe Henslee, Gerald Howard, Phil Kerrigan, J. O. Kirkpatrick, Dave Morse, Hooper Love, M. I. Lusky, Ed McCarthy, A. V. McLane and Rhoton Clift?

How about Rottero's grocery, Tinsley's millinery, Troy Laundry, Herbrick & Lawrence, Huggins Candies, Bell's Booteries, Dorris-Karsch, Ellis Shoe Co., Fish Brothers, Gibson Auto Repair Co., A. L. Goldberg & Sons, Gregory Blackboard Co., and Phillips-Trawick Co.?

A few days ago, one of my grandchildren asked me what we did for music before organized country music, pop and rock, and before television. My reply, "Music—I'll tell you about real music." I told them about music in Nashville before radio, and then, before television.

Do you remember the old Victor graphophone with cylinder records—Enrico Caruso and John McCormack? The old music box; the banjo and the mandolin? The Fisk Jubilee Singers? Billy Church with Al G. Fields' minstrels, singing "Silver Threads Among the Gold," and "I'll Take You Home Again, Kathleen"? The music of Irving Berlin, Cole Porter and Victor Herbert? The Irish tenors and barber shop quartets? Kenneth Rose and his violin? Tony Rose's band and Prof. Simmon's Randall School band? The neighborhood piano teachers and recitals? The Princess Theatre orchestra? The sheet music departments of Kress's and Woolworth's? Nick Lucas singing "Tip-Toe Through the Tulips" at the Princess? Bill Perry and his mother singing at the high schools? Vito Peleteri and Katherine Guthrie playing dinner music at the Manhattan Restaurant on Sixth Avenue? Galli-Curci and Rosa Ponselle in concert at the Ryman? The music and songs of school graduation? Jimmy Melton, Joe McPherson and Snooky Lanson? The DeLuca School of Music on West End? The black boys' string band at the Sulphur Dell gate? The church choirs and those at the Gypsy Smith and Billy Sunday meetings at the Ryman? The band concerts in the park? The player piano and the rolls? When all children knew all the stanzas to "The Star-Spangled Banner," and "America"? The upright piano, the old piano stool, and the seat where the sheet music was kept? The old family pump organ?

Ask your grandmother if she remembers: The World War songs—"Tipperary," "Goodby Broadway, Hello France," "Red Cross Nurse," "White Cliffs of Dover," and "Over There"? The bands at the State Fairs—remember Thaivus' band, and the Royal Scots band? The piano player at the early movies? Leon Cole at the organ? The ukelele craze? The beautiful spirituals of the black churches? The great voices of the early Jewish cantors? The music of the light operas, "The Student Prince," "Katinka," "Cat and the Fiddle," "Damn Yankees," and others? Nelson Eddy and Jeanette MacDonald singing, "The Indian Love Call," and the "Desert Song"?

And then, with radio came the big bands—Paul Whiteman, Guy Lombardo, Sigmund Romberg, Tommy Dorsey, Glenn Miller and others. Al Jolson and "Mammy," and Eddie Cantor with "Toot, Toot, Tootsie"; the college bands with their "fight songs." What about Beesley Smith and Francis Craig at the Hermitage Hotel—and Bob Lamb, the blind singer? Grace Moore and Dinah Shore; "Tom, Joe and Jack," (Mooney, Combs and Keefe) with Margaret Shannon at WSM before the Opry; morning music from WDAD?

Yes, we had music before television, real music—the music of love, soothing music, music that expressed faith in God and love of country, music of joy, happiness—and clean music. Yes, we had our music and kept our eardrums and sacroiliac joints. Yes, we had country music—pure country music, natural, undiluted, untainted, unblemished and unsoiled by the taint and temptation of big money.

Yes, we had good country music here before television—we had Roy Acuff, Eddy Arnold, Uncle Dave Macon, Fred Rose, and these were before male musicians started to wear bracelets, necklaces, lockets, lavaliers and lace—and their hats in the house.

You oldies of Nashville, shake up the cobwebs and try to remember the words and tunes of these: "I'm forever blowing bubbles, pretty bubbles in the air. They rise so high, they nearly reach the sky. Then, like my dreams, they fall and die . . ."

"There's a long, long trail a winding, into the land of my dreams, where the nightingales are singing and a white moon beams . . ."

"Darling, I am growing old, silver threads among the gold . . ."

"Across my heart, the shadow of your smile . . ."

"I'll be seeing you . . ."

"Tonight, you belong to me . . ."

"Til we meet again . . ."

"Among my souvenirs . . ."

Battle of Nashville Monument at Thompson Lane and Woodmont Boulevard—1949.

"Listen to the mockingbird . . ."

"I'll take you home again, Kathleen, across the ocean wide, To where your heart has ever been, since first you were my bonny bride . . ."

"On the trail of the lonesome pine . . ."

"Red sails in the sunset . . ."

"When it's springtime in the Rockies . . ."

"Beautiful Ohio . . ."

"California, here I come . . ."

"I'll see you in my dreams . . ."

"Love letters in the sand . . ."

"Down by the old mill stream . . ."

"School days, school days, dear old golden rule days . . ."

"Up a lazy river . . ."

"Take me out to the ballgame . . ."

"Daisy, Daisy, give me your promise true . . ."

"The sidewalks of New York . . ."

"Come away with me, Lucille, in my merry Oldsmobile . . ."

"Georgia, Georgia, Georgia on my mind . . ."

"Three o'clock in the morning . . ."

"I found a million dollar baby in a five-and-ten-cent store . . ."

"You must have been a beautiful baby . . ."

"Memories . . ."

"Oh! You beautiful doll . . ."

"Billy Boy . . ."

"Put your arms around me honey, hold me tight. Love me tonight. Hold me honey, hug me honey, squeeze me tight . . ."

"Waiting for the Robert E. Lee . . ."

"Casey Jones . . ."

"Under a silvery moon . . ."

"Naughty baby . . ."

"What do you want to make those eyes at me for when they don't mean what they say . . .?"

And when we started to get jazzy and discovered the beats:

"Toot, toot, Tootsie, goodbye, Toot, toot, Tootsie don't cry . . ."

"Icky, yicky, yakey, you . . ."

"Jada, Jada, jing, jing, jing . . ."

"Pony-boy, pony-boy, won't you be my pony-boy . . .?"

"Barney Google, with the goo, goo, googley eyes . . ."

"Pretty Baby . . ."

"Yes, we have no bananas . . ."

"Margie, I'm always thinking of you, Margie . . ."

"I'm Alabamy bound, there'll be no heebie-jeebies hanging 'round . . ."

"Steamboat Bill . . ."

"In the good old summer time . . ."

"When you wore a tulip, and I wore a red, red rose . . ."

"All alone, by the telephone . . ."

"I don't want to play in your back yard, 'cause I don't like you anymore. You're going to be sorry, when you see me sliding down my cellar door . . ."

Do you recall: "That Old Gang of Mine"; "Has Anybody Seen My Gal"; "Back Home In Indiana"? And the old harmony songs: "Adeline," "How Dry I Am," "Show Me the Way to Go Home," "Tea for Two," "Down By the Old Mill Stream."

Then came World War I: "Tipperary," "K-K-K-Katy," "Over There," "Goodbye Broadway, Hello France," "Red Cross Nurse," "Mademoiselle From Armentiéres," "The White Cliffs of Dover" and "My Buddy".

And the girls' songs: "Mary," "Rose Marie," "Waltzing Matilda," "I Wonder What's Become of Sally," "I Want a Girl Just Like the Girl Who Married Dear Old Dad," "I Dream of Jeannie With the Light Brown Hair," "Paddlin' Madelin Home," "Wait 'Til the Sun Shines, Nellie," "Peg O' My Heart," "Diane," "Rose of Washington Square."

How many of the old hymns do you remember—and spirituals?

And at the end of all singing—"After the Ball is Over," "Good Night, Ladies" and "The Party's Over."

Don't blame me if you keep searching your mind as these pop up for sometime to come.

And, you know, we sang quietly—and didn't jump around or wear funny "get-ups."

Many letters ask that I list some more things of the older days of Nashville.

Do you remember: The photographers who came through the neighborhoods with a billy goat and wagon to take children's pictures? Blowing smoke in the ear for earache? Playing baseball in vacant lots? The old ice cream wagons, with their bells, selling one-cent and five-cent ice cream cones? "Double-decker" sleds? Making chow-chow from green tomatoes? Corn-shucking parties? When door keys were made of brass? Using Irish potatoes on the spouts of coal-oil cans? Sunday school buttons? The woodpile, ax and hatchet? Clotheslines?

Back then we called glasses "spectacles," suspenders were "galluses," and hose were "stockings." Topcoats were "overcoats" and shorts were "B.V.D.'s."

Do you recall when mothers knitted "mittens"?

How about "Crackerjacks," with a prize in every box? Caps with attached earmuffs, tie clasps and mufflers?

Did you ever "turpentine" or tie tin cans on a dog's tail, or tie a paper sack on a cat's tail, or catch the ring while riding on the "flying jinny" for a free ride? Get caught chewing gum in school? String red peppers on a string? Spread your walnuts out in the sun after hulling them? Get chestnut burr needles in your fingers? Have you forgotten slate pencils and the sponge to clear your slate? Rags for kite tails? When cigar boxes were made of wood? When girls had vaccination scars on their arms? The shoemaker's "last"? When necklaces were called "lavalieres"; lockets with pictures in them?

Do you remember "milestones" along the pikes? Masquerade parties? Mint beds around outdoor hydrants? Pone cornbread, crackling bread and dumplings? Pongee shirts and dresses, men's puttees, twisted ribbon stick candy, and whetstones? Do you recall Boy Scouts' semaphore flags, the "shimmy," zinc washboards and gaslight carbons?

Could you tie a "cat's cradle"?

Remember Favorite cigarettes, toll gates, "human flies," water coolers, "Cat's Paw" rubber heels, the Dixie Tabernacle, Weinberger's ladies shop, Doc Keim's Ramblers, the Y.M.H.A. Peps, Tanlac, shoeshine parlors, smokehouses, side saddles, children's "rompers," auto cranks and "all-day" candy suckers?

Remember getting souvenirs—palm-leaf fans, shoe buttoners, aluminum covers for folding match pads, and those small pocket mirrors?

Did you have one of those early little black box Kodaks? Remember the little whips which we bought at the fair or at the carnivals?

Remember the first typewriter you ever saw, or the Waterman fountain pen? How about old Bowen School? The school bells which rang every morning? Collecting broken china for the playhouse? Making mud pies?

Do you remember how buzzards would hover in the air over dead animals? The Hillsboro Theatre? Winton automobiles? 'Possum and sweet potatoes? Green River and muscadine punch? United Cigar stores? The movie, *Birth of a Nation*? Those little flag holders on auto radiator caps? Tool boxes on the step boards of automobiles?

Collecting cigar bands? Automobile tire "boots"? Braids on

dresses? Broom peddlers? Fingerbowls? Daisy B.B. guns? Gold teeth? Chamois skins? When you bought those little chameleons which would change their colors? Ministrel shows and end men?

Remember the little sample boxes of Kellogg's cornflakes, "Magic Lanterns," and counterpanes? Did you ever own bantam chickens? Did you ever put your ear down on a railroad rail to see if you could hear a train coming from a distance? What became of shooting galleries, tailor shops, penny postcards and barber poles?

Remember the round bars of shaving soap that fit into the bottom of your father's shaving mug, and his razor strop? When, before electricity was introduced to appliances, we had to manually operate by turning cranks to start autos, operate cash registers, pump coal oil from tanks, grind coffee, ring the bell on telephones, churn milk, draw water from wells, freeze ice cream, operate streetcar brakes, operate food grinders, to pump gasoline?

I miss licorice plugs, Pepsin gum, ambrosia and old-fashioned souse.

Remember when girls wore sashes?

Do you recall Joe Roller's bicycle shop on College Street, Jungerman & Rust's bakery, Theo Taffel's on the corner of Cherry and Church Streets, D. Lowenhein's on Union Street, Leichardt's on the Square, Early-Cain harness store on Market Street, Lowenstein's on Cherry and Deaderick Streets, Wright's drugstore at Market and Broad, Skalowski's, The Ocean, Shacklett's, Jennings' pharmacy, The Maxwell House Coffee Shop and the Log Cabin Theatre?

Remember the Exchange Club's "Sunshine Special," the Elks' Club's Christmas parties for children at the old clubhouse on Sixth Avenue, the "Banner Good Fellers" baskets, the Shriners' parties for the children of the Protestant Orphanage, Masonic Orphanage, and Junior League Home? The Knights of Columbus' parties for St. Mary's Orphanage and those old Salvation Army stalwarts of mercy and compassion?

Whatever became of pince-nez eyeglasses, garter belts, spats, ladies' vests, nightshirts and nightcaps? Did you ever carry one of those pocket notebooks which Beasley Sash and Door Company gave away as souvenirs, which carried all the streetcar passenger stations in the city?

Do you remember "Steamboat" Johnson in Sulphur Dell?

Did you know that popular and good-natured Tom Springfield, that effervescent "Slick" Welsh, little Sid Gross? pleasant and accommodating Leon Womble; fun-loving Jonas Redelsheimer, Chris Krieg, Phelps Smith, "Sister" Sykes, "Dutch" Morrisey, Jack Minton, "Slim"

Nashville Gas and Heating Co., 901 Harrison Street—1933.

*Noel Corner,
3rd and Church.*

Embry, Red Bransford, Pete Stumb, "Skinny" Stumb, and Red Cook? They were all friends of everybody and each was a part of the personality of an older Nashville.

Did you ever go to a picnic at Knapp Farm, and do you remember the Delaval cream separator?

Someone asked me recently what I missed most about the old days of Nashville. I have thought about this and these are some of the things and people.

I miss hearing boys and girls saying "Yes sir" and "No sir" and "Yes ma'am" to older people. When women were proud to be known as ladies. When men were glad to be regarded as gentlemen. When "thank you" came naturally. When people were grateful for what they had. When families gathered around the family dinner table. When ladies did not walk around in public with a cigarette hanging from their lips or with a cocktail in their hands.

When fat women did not wear tight pants. When auto drivers were courteous. When dancing was to real music and with rhythm. When people did not litter. When there were no credit cards. When literature did not center on sex.

I miss the time when people planted flowers in their yards. When people loved real music. When we walked on the right side of sidewalks. When there were no paper napkins or cellophane wrappings. When sugar was kept in sugar jars, and mustard and catsup in bottles.

I miss leaving Union Station on a train. Tramping through the woods of Overton Hills. Old time barbecues, fish fries, lawn festivals and monthly poker clubs. When people really dressed up for the uptown Easter Parade. Uptown stores and streets decorated in red, white and blue bunting, flags and banners when we had distinguished visitors or conventions. Train whistles, fire engine and streetcar bells and the clatter of horses' hoofs on the streets. The old Market House, City Hall and Courthouse on the Square and the crowds in the Transfer Station.

Remember the popular fruit stand of H. G. Hill's store at the corner of Deaderick Street and Third Avenue? The pawn shops and the J. P. courts upstairs?

I miss Mitchell's candy, spice round and Paradise Ridge grape wine. Tony Rose's band and Francis Craig's orchestra. Jack Keefe and Herman Grizzard on early radio. Coffee at John and Paul Stumb's on Fourth Avenue, hamburgers at Hudson Coomb's pie wagon, and noon time at Pete Stumb's in the Stahlman Building. Harness racing at the

Fairgrounds, baseball at Sulphur Dell, and watching steamboats unload at the wharf.

Remember Al G. Fields' minstrels, matinees at the Princess and stage shows at the Orpheum Theatre?

Remember when it was fun to sit on the front porch after supper? When neighbors were friendly, close and helpful? When school children could walk to their neighborhood schools? When it was fun to go to picnics?

I miss being thrilled when we saw soldiers marching behind the flag as the band played Sousa's "Stars and Stripes Forever." When they gave complete respect and attention to the playing of the "Star-Spangled Banner," when most people loved our country and there were no demonstrations organized by professional activists and trouble makers.

Remember when only women went to hairdressers? When children were taught to save? When men did not wear hats in the house or appear at dinner in public in shirt sleeves? When 10:00 P.M. was bedtime? When we ate a real breakfast at home?

I miss being able to cross an uptown street and not having to duck anything—except horse manure. When milk came in bottles instead of these hard to open boxes. When cats ate table scraps and mice instead of 45 cent-per-can cat food.

Remember when "slackers" were ostracized by the American people? When young married couples were afraid of debt? When high school graduates knew the multiplication tables and could spell? When people knew that alcohol and gasoline did not mix? When baseball was the American pastime and was for fun and not money?

I miss the time when one could walk the streets of Nashville at night in safety—and did not have to lock their doors. When there was plenty of clean fresh air.

Remember the distinguished and handsome men on the local streets like General Frank Bass, governors Benton McMillin and Austin Peay, Joseph W. Byrns, Cordell Hull, Clyde Shropshire, Judge John A. Pitts, K. T. McConnico, General Jeff McCarn, Dr. W. D. Haggard, Joe Morgan, Judge John Aust, Jet Potter, Joe Werthan, Doug Binns, Frank Berry, Tony Sudekum, James Cayce, Paul Davis, James E. Caldwell, Colonel Luke Lea, Judge Grafton Green, Dr. James T. Vance, John Bell Keeble, Norman Farrell, Percy Maddin, Dr. Bruce Payne, H. G. Hill, Judge J. B. D. DeBow and Major E. B. Stahlman—all of whom shared their good fortunes with our community.

I miss hot chili at Tony the Chili King's on Deaderick Street on a cold winter day. Breakfast at Frank Underwood's on the Square. Supper at

Hettie Ray's on Nine Mile Hill or at the Manhattan on Sixth Avenue. Lunch at McFadden's Grotto and the noon time conversations at Mickey Baine's in Printers Alley.

Remember "Parson" Prentice Pugh, Dr. George Stoves, Dr. Genert, Dr. Powell, and Bishop Adrian.

The political meetings and rallies at the Ryman and Maxwell House? T. Allison's camp on the Harpeth? Hammocks, homemade fruit cake and ice cream, shoe shine parlors, and the T. C. train ride to Horn Springs? Remember when doctors made house calls, hog killing time, porch swings, railroad excursions, large comfortable hotel lobbies and nickel baseballs?

Remember when candidates for the legislature, congress, senate, mayor and governor did not accept hundreds of thousands of dollars as

Duncan Hotel, Church Street.

campaign contributions from people and businesses which would be interested in matters before them?

I miss Ralph McGill, "Blinkey" Horn, Tom Little, Joe Hatcher, the Haymarket carnivals, Gilbert's-on-the-Square, Louie Monroe, Harold Shyer, Wiley Embry, Bud Minton, Judge Hickman, Alf Rutherford, Hugh Freeman, Judge Charles Gilbert. The Arcade—like it used to be, the Utopia, Tulane and Andrew Jackson hotels. Merten's bath house. Elks' Club on Sixth Avenue and the old Maxwell House.

I miss men like Seth Walker, John Hooker Sr., Charles Rolfe, Hugh Smith, Lee Bissinger, Ira Parker, Paul DeWitt, Charles Kempkau, Tom Joy, Oren Oliver, Lucien McConnell, Clark Akers, Sr., S. N. Allen, Elmer Baulch, T. Graham Hall, Charles Nelson, Pink Lawrence and John Todd, all of whom meant so much to our community.

I miss the activities and contributions to the city by Silliman Evans Sr., and James G. Stahlman. The Barnum-Bailey, Ringling Brothers cir-

Jack Norman, Silliman Evans, J. Carlton Loser, Judge Charles Gilbert—1944.

cus tents across from Centennial Park, the Glendale Zoo and the Shakespearian plays at the old Vendome theatre.

Finally, I miss the fifteen lawyers who, over the years, were my office associates, all of whom are now deceased. And, I miss so many old Nashvillians who were so kind to me over all these years.

P.S. I also miss "a nickel's worth of cheese crackers," and eight "chocolate drops" for a penny.

Maxwell House Hotel, Cherry (4th Avenue) and Church Streets—1864.

CHAPTER 2

Down Memory Lane
Nashville Streets and Environs

AFTER MOVING UP THE HILL from the area of Fort Nashboro, on the river, Nashville started out with Water Street, later Main Street, and then Market Street running north and south. Facing it, even as late as 1804, there were only six buildings on each side. Six were stores, two were homes, one was a shop and one a livery stable. At the north end was the original square with a courthouse, jail, market, the stocks, the Nashville and Talbot inns. It was not until 1791 that Nashville's first church, Methodist, was built on the Square.

Cedar Street

Since Granny White Pike was the only road leading to the west from the city, the need for a direct route west led to the construction of Cedar Street which started from the Square. It first led to the knob where the Capitol was to be built later. One T. Napier lived up there and his house was surrounded by a grove of cedar trees. This was evidently responsible for the name of the new street. This is perhaps the reason that as the young city later moved south the streets were named for trees—Cherry, Spruce, Oak, Mulberry, Elm, Chestnut, Laurel, Ash, Tulip, etc.

By 1809 the city had a population of about 17,000. Most of the population was in the surrounding countryside. Most business was confined to the two original streets—Market and Cedar—and to the south side of the square. However, the first post office was on the east of the square and the city expanded northward towards Sulphur Springs. By this time, many of the first families had homes along Cedar Street. The establishment of St. Mary's Church in 1830 and the building of the State Capitol in 1847–49 were to enhance the influence of the street.

It is said that an early settler, George Campbell, had sold a cow and a calf to another who later decided to leave the country before he was able to pay Campbell, and that he gave Campbell the Capitol Hill property and a rifle for the debt. Campbell later sold the City of Nashville the Capitol property for $30,000 and a part of the remainder to Ephriam Foster who gave St. Mary's Church the property where the church still stands. The city gave the "knob" to the state for the building of the Capitol.

As the city grew and prospered, Cedar Street became an important business section. The city then turned north and the streets were named for presidents—Jefferson, Monroe, Buchanan, Adams, Jackson, Harrison, Van Buren, Garfield, etc. Cedar Street was to have one of the first streetcar lines and Van Blackum Station was to carry it farther west.

As old Cedar had nurtured a great part of the early business life of the young city, it was later to nurture the beginning of the business life of the black citizens of Nashville. The influence of the First Baptist Church (now of Capitol Hill)—which came out of an original mission provided the early blacks by the First Baptist Church of Nashville in 1830 and became a church in 1852—had drawn many blacks to the community. The present church was built in 1873. The first black man came to this section with James Robertson and his group in 1779. "Black Bob," another, had operated a successful business as a tavern and hotel for whites near the river about 1788.

By 1915 Cedar Street was the thriving black business section of Nashville. As enterprising, hard-working, and substantial blacks entered local business they found old Cedar Street their focal point. The McKissacks, Napiers, Kennedys, Taylors, Boyds, Gardners and their families were to make great contributions to the growth of the importance of the area.

Do you remember the Washington Hotel, Holmes Brothers and the Kennedy taxi companies, National Benefit Insurance Co., Nick Coment's and DeGrafenreid's restaurants and George Aldridge's barbershop? Have you forgotten Deem's Medicines Co., Noah King's and Ed Meneese's billiard parlors; and lawyer Walter Walker? How about Doctor Townsend, Dr. Bowman, the Green Rose Restaurant and Cantrell's Barber College?

Do you remember the Frierson Realty Co., the Keystone Store, the Soldier's and Sailor's Club, the Porters' and Waiters' Club, and the Model Steam Laundry? How about the Napier Court Apartments, W. H. McGavock; the Boston Cafe and People's Drugstore?

Can you recall the shows at the old Bijou Theatre? Doctor Napier's office and when Kossie Gardner ran a ladies-wear store? Did you ever eat at Briggs' or McGee's restaurants, have your hair cut at Williams' barbershop—"shave and a haircut for two bits"? Remember Will Latham?

Did you ever spend any time with Jim Pillow or Moland Wilson, or stand out in front of Mooney's restaurant watching the girls go by? Remember the crowds that used to walk by on their way to Sulphur Dell? Did you ever bet the numbers with Bill James?

Remember Mike Riadon, the councilman, and the old Fourth Ward voting precinct?

In the years that followed, the blacks, too, would move westward toward Fisk, Meharry and old A. & I. University. As their numbers grew and they became successful they sought better residential sectors in all sections of the city. None of the old homes and few of the old business houses remain today. Most of the white and black residents and business people who knew old Cedar Street in her prime, have long since died. Some of us who still remember when Cedar was alive and kicking, will remember how well she served the city.

It, too, was to move into the modern age with many changes. It was to accommodate state office buildings, The War Memorial Building, Supreme Court Building, motels, bank buildings, the Tennessee Performing Arts Center, American General (National Life) Building, the new university buildings, and others, important to the demands of another day. "The Old Lady on the Hill," St. Mary's and the old First Baptist Church, continue as her link to the past.

Her old gas lights are now modern beamers. Her old streetcar tracks are now buried beneath layers of asphalt. Her old coal shutes are now air-conditioning units. From her early terminal at the "Cedar Knob," she now extends for miles as a main thoroughfare.

They dressed up the old gal, and Cedar Street is now Charlotte Avenue.

Old Sulphur Dell

On my way home from the Farmer's Market, I stopped on Fifth Avenue alongside the huge grave of old Sulphur Dell. As I pulled up I am sure that I heard the crack of a bat, the roar of the crowd, and, "Steamboat" Johnson calling a man "out" at home plate.

In memory, I walked over to the old "pass-gate" to take a look inside.

There was Mike Burke climbing the rightfield dump, like a goat, to catch the "fly" of a Memphis Chick. The batboy in knickers, called Mickey Kreitner, was hustling a foul ball that had gotten by "Gabby" Street.

There they all were, cheering and joking in the home "dug-out"— "Poco" Tait, "Kiki" Cuyler, "Buster" Brown, Lance Richbourg, Phil Weintraub, Al Cucinallo, Chuck Dressen, Red Lucas, "Smoky" Burgess—and many others.

Up high in the back seats, overlooking the park, "Blinkey" Horn

Aerial view of Sulphur Dell—1962.

and Ralph McGill were arguing with Roy Elam, Jimmy Hamilton, and Larry Gilbert. Fay Murray was looking on from the office window.

"Rubber" and Willie White were busy smoothing the dirt around home plate.

Down at the far side were Paul Goldberg, Julian Silverfield and Joe Frank, trying to outguess each other on hits and strikes.

The game halted a few minutes so John Mihalic could chase a stray dog off the diamond. As "Bruno" Jones yelled at the umpire, I instinctively reached in my pocket for a nickel to buy a bag of popcorn.

As I was leaving I noticed six or eight men in blue uniforms watching the game from outside through the open gate. They were the motormen and conductors of the streetcars waiting to take the crowd back to the Transfer Station.

A lone man was walking south along the brick sidewalk carrying two jugs of sulphur water from Morgan Park. Willie Wilkie was turning the lights off in the corner ticket office. A stream of mule carts was slowly making its way to the old city dump.

As I snapped back into reality, I started my car and turned on the radio in time to hear that Reggie Jackson was demanding three million dollars to play baseball for two more years. I turned it off and my mind went back to Sulphur Dell.

What a great part the old park had played in the entertainment and pleasure of Nashville. How it had helped to relieve the strains and pressures of a young city just beginning to flex its muscles. How its benefits were available to even those with small incomes. How clean and wholesome were its contributions. How satisfied we were with such simple things. As the buffalo and deer had gone there for the pleasure of sulphur and salt, Nashville had gone there for the pleasure and relaxation of our national pastime.

To break the dreams again, I turned on the radio just in time to catch the latest news about the strike of the football players.

I stepped on the gas to run out from under the march of time.

Lower Broadway

She runs down to the river, and she is taking so much punishment, one wonders why she doesn't jump in. But she had her day. One of the first municipal streets of such width in the South, Lower Broadway once accommodated an important segment of the business, social and religious life of Nashville. Some of her splendid architecture housed the early success of our merchant community.

Today, that architecture cries out for help—at least a modest facelift—and a renewed recognition of its past contribution to the growing city and its potential for the present.

In former days her first four blocks, west from the river, provided twenty-one furniture stores, five hardware stores, six wholesale stores, six restaurants, four feed stores, four drugstores, four bakery shops, three plumbing supply stores, two banks, eight tire and auto stores, two leather houses, three shoe shops and various other business establishments. In the next blocks—"up the hill"—were a livery stable, pawnshops, restaurants, three hotels, the U.S. Customs House, the busy Hume-Fogg High School, the gateway to the Ryman Auditorium, Royal Cafe, Baptist Church, Union Station, NC&St.L Office Building, Vauxhall Apartments, the freight houses, Cummins Station and a large number of miscellaneous businesses. From the river to the viaduct, she was the busiest stretch of street in the city. There was not a vacant lot nor a vacant building. Her streets were crowded with transportation and her sidewalks, with people. She was free and safe in the daytime and in the night.

Do you remember:

The crowds on their way to and from the Ryman to hear Billy Sun-

day and Gypsy Smith or to hear Senators Borah, Glass, Reed, Lodge
and Owen debate the League of Nations?

The Sunday baptisms at the edge of the river?

The Hay Market farmers and livestock traders coming up before
the Sparkman Street Bridge was built?

The entire lower area under water when the Cumberland flooded?

The cannon in front of the Customs House?

The old "two horse" furniture wagons?

Lower Broadway.

Anderson's Fish House?

Streetcars turning north at College, crossing Cherry and going both ways across at Spruce?

The horsedrawn hacks and hearses housed at the McFarland Livery Stable, which later became one of Nashville's first bus stations?

Hume-Fogg R.O.T.C. boys drilling on Lower Broad Street?

The "skiffs," flat boats and "shanty boats" pulled up along the upper wharf?

The steamboats, *H.G. Hill, Jo Horton Fall* unloading bales of cotton, lumber and freight?

The stevedores singing as they worked?

Almost anything of the day could be bought at some place along the street. It was all business, no room for places of entertainment. Merchants, bankers, tradesmen, farmers, laborers, church people and citizens in general filled the sidewalks in business necessities and pleasant society. At the noon lunchtime they found opportunity for leisurely and genial contact.

Do you remember:

Squire Ed Holt, Mayor William Gupton, Andrew Clark, Glenn Briley, Mr. Hardison, Mr. Beesley, Mr. Brown, Mr. Quarles and others passing the time of the day with Mr. Potter at the Broadway National Bank?

Upper Nashville Wharf—1916.

Jim Cox, George Linebaugh, Joe Cook, Jim Williams, Mr. Manas, Mr. Pilsk, Mr. Carter, and others laughing and joking at the old Broadway Barber Shop.

"Hurry-on-Blackwood," Harry Connors, Charles Kalamoris, J. B. Hill, Fitzgerald Hall, and Prentice Pugh lunching at the Royal Cafe?

The "Railroaders" eating lunch at the Underwood Hotel?

Mr. Vernon Sharp, L. G. Durr, Judge Hickman, Frank Carr arguing politics at the Lillard Foutch Drug Store—the Hilary Howse side, of course?

Can you recall:

The trains backing into the T.C. depot?

The Nashville Boosters boarding one of the steamboats for their annual trips?

The horse drawn lumber wagons pulling out from the Norvell-Wallace Lumber Company?

An occasional country horse frightened at the oncoming of a streetcar?

Let us go back a little further—do you remember:

When Broad Street was partially paved with cobblestones?

The change from the old gas street lights to the new iron posts with each of its four arms supporting a large, white, globe electric light?

The large watering trough for horses at Broad and Front Streets?

Wagon wheel rims getting caught in the streetcar tracks?

The Silver Dollar Saloon before prohibition?

Merchandise displayed on the sidewalks in front of the business houses?

Today old lower Broadway suffers bedsores as the result of years of endured sickness. Her past dignity looks down on her ugly transformation. Substantial businessmen struggle to hold on to the business houses of their fathers and beg for rescue. They justly rebel at the fact that their customers and friends have to make their way through an unwholesome atmosphere to reach their doors. The entire city bemoans the fact that so many of our visitors and tourists see this as their introduction to Nashville. Churchmen suffer in silence as they see the paths to their sanctuaries challenged by molestation and danger; business shuts its doors at sunset. Old facades are covered with gaudy signs and blazing neon. Old and handsome doorways have been replaced with those "peep-holes." Legitimate business tries to hold its head above the "red-light," "flesh pots," drug users and sellers, drunks and panhandlers—and the thugs with which and whom their area has been invaded.

Sadly this once proud part of Old Nashville holds no immediate promise of its former importance. That can be seen now, only in memory, and that is available only to an ever-decreasing number of us.

When finally everything is closed in the late hours of the morning, one can almost hear her pleading:

"Won't someone help me, please!"

South Nashville

Early Nashville first moved south as it began to grow. The reasons must have been because of its access to the river, because the first road and turnpike led to Murfreesboro, because it was the route to the Hermitage, the environs of which were then regarded as the best land. This movement south lasted until early in this century. By 1900 South Nashville was the most prominent section for homes and business. It came to accommodate many of our earlier institutions, public utilities, churches, schools, and early commercial enterprises.

Located south of Broad Street, between the old Lebanon and Franklin roads, it extended to the railroad and the Tennessee State Fairgrounds. It was later traversed by the Wharf Avenue and Fairfield, Nolensville, South High Street, Kane Avenue and Waverly streetcar tracks. The Lebanon, Murfreesboro, Nolensville and Franklin pikes started there. These pikes accommodated most of the wagon traffic bringing agricultural and dairy products to the young city. The City Cemetery, the City Waterworks, the City Sanitation Dept., the City Hospital, the busy Hay Market, the State Fairgrounds, the old Cumberland Race Track, the City Reservoir, the Blind School, Industrial School (Randall Cole)—all located there. It had The Gerst Brewery, the only one in Tennessee, the cotton oil mill, the flour mill, cannery, lumber yards, the barrel and hoop shop, May Hosiery Mill and other businesses along both the NC&St.L and Tennessee Central Railway lines, which ran through South Nashville. It had been a center for the early universities and colleges. The first streetcar (pulled by mules) ran out the South Nashville line in 1866.

Remember Thalman's garage on Cherry—one of the first in the city? Vincent's livery stable, Anderson's Fish and Oyster House, Zucarello's, Hackman's and Pomeroy's saloons; the Stacey Block, College Street Primitive Baptist Church, Grace Cumberland Presbyterian Church, South Side Nazarene Church, Little Gem Grocery, Jackson's grocery on Cherry Street, the Church of the Holy Trinity on Lafayette, St. Patrick's on Market, Elm Street Methodist, Meharry Medical College and Hubbard Hospital on First Avenue, South.

Remember Phillip Schmitt, the cigar maker at 907 Cherry Street?

William Gerst Brewing Company—1953.

Remember the old Fairfield streetcars that carried people to Mt. Olivet and Mt. Calvary cemeteries? The beautiful old homes on Carroll, College, Summer, High and Market streets? The Hardisons, Howells, Timothys, Captain Sadler's, Welches, Gersts, Dr. Altman's, and Tankards? Remember the old home of Captain Ryman and the stone and iron fence around it? Major's barbershop, Peach's drugstore, Howard and Trimble schools?

Remember when the Vanderbilt Medical and Dental schools were located on Summer Street? The Tennessee Central crossing as the city limit on the old Lebanon Pike?

Remember Mrs. Haslock, who lived at the corner of College Street and Cameron Avenue and her pigeons—the mother of Mrs. George Mayfield? All the activities around old St. Patrick's Church? Trimble Bottom? Black Bottom? Corinnel, Clarendon apartments, Raleigh and Ivanhoe apartments?

Remember the great Gerst brothers, George Holle, Mr. Vaupel, Edwin Miller, the Pursleys, Beidermans, Felts, Engles and others among the brewery employees?

Remember "Polly" Woodfin at the Fourteenth Ward polling place on Wharf Avenue on election day—"Titsy" Carter at the Thirteenth Ward polling place at the Market Street firehall—Branch McConnell at the Fifteenth Ward polling place on Chestnut Street?

Remember Major Hilary Howse speaking at these places during his campaigns for mayor?

Did you ever buy a ginger cake plank from Mrs. Klein at her bakery on Carroll Street?

Remember Ike Karnarsky's store, Kleiser's drugstores, Andrew Martin's drugstore, Booth Furniture Store, Tankard and Woodall's coal yard, Fox's meat market, Mrs. DeLee's and Mrs. Minnie Starr's, Gotto's and Dahlinger's grocery stores? Old Hill's Alley? The horse water trough on Chestnut Street?

Remember when they changed Cherry Street from cobblestone to brick—and later to asphalt? When the Nolensville streetcars went out Cherry and came back on College? The unsuccessful streetcar operation out Summer Street?

Remember the railroad watchman's tower and the gates at the Tutwiler railroad crossing on Cherry Street?

Remember when they started to build the Galloway Memorial Hospital on Market Street, laid the foundation and started the walls, then gave out of money, and it was never finished but stood there for years before the city finally took the property to build the city building now located there?

South Nashville was inhabited by a strong, sturdy, hard working and responsible citizenship. It furnished many of our early leaders. It had an intense pride in the community but it jokingly referred to itself as "Varmint Town." It took a great interest in the city's political life. It was charitable to its unfortunate and proud of its homes. Its labor force worked in every type of business and it furnished many of the leading doctors, lawyers, engineers, and merchants of the city.

By 1920 the city was well on its way west. South Nashville had started to lose its most affluent homes and many of its leaders along with the most prominent citizens. Commercialism was invading the section. Many were moving to the rural sections of Flat Rock, Radnor, Antioch, Una, Glencliff, and Donelson, leaving it to the steady creep of business. Today it is a vital part of the inner city. Few of its old landmarks remain to tell the story of its once proud residential section. It has been in the forefront of the passing of the Nashville I knew.

West End Avenue

By 1831 the young Nashville was requiring road outlets to and from the city. As the west was not yet settled the demand was mainly for travel to the east, north and south.

In that year the turnpike to Franklin was built. Then came the Murfreesboro turnpike in 1838; the Gallatin in 1839; the Nolensville in 1841; the Charlotte in 1842; the Lebanon in 1842; and the White's Creek in 1845. Others followed in the fifties and by then they all led in these directions accommodating passenger stages, freight wagons, farm carts, horseback riders and cattle herds. They were rough, dirty and all were toll roads.

In the early days a dirt road was extended west from the end of Broad Street only to reach the plantations west of the city. Chief of these was the plantation of John Harding, who owned the 3,500-acre plantation known as Belle Meade. It was during the last half of the century, as the city started moving west, that West End Avenue came to be the extension of Broad Street and the gateway to the west by way of Harding Road.

Belle Meade Mansion

By the early part of this century, travel to that direction had become increasingly heavy. This opened West End Avenue to affluent homes and businesses. Broad Street had already become established as the dividing line between North and South Nashville with the housing numbering, the first of which was provided in 1853.

The location of Vanderbilt University, the Cathedral of the Incarnation, Montgomery Bell Academy, Centennial Park, with the Parthenon, the growth of the inner city and the beauty of the countryside had attracted a steady growth for this section of the county.

The first electric streetcar in Nashville made its first trip out West End Avenue to Vanderbilt on April 30, 1889.

By the early part of this century, Broad was busy and West End Avenue was the widest and heaviest travelled of all our streets. It was lined with shade trees and crowded with the homes of prominent Nashville families.

The official residence of the governor was 2118 West End. The old West End Methodist Church was located at 1524. Tony Sudekum's Hippodrome, Wallace University School, the Nashville Conservatory of

Uncle Bob Green—Head groom at Belle Meade Mansion.

Music, the Knights of Columbus Hall, the First Unitarian Church, Moore Memorial and Immanuel Baptist churches—all faced outer Broad Street.

Remember the Jere Baxter monument at 16th and Broad—the beginning of West End Avenue?

Remember the Stone, Roston, Aureole, Avon Lenox, Seminole, Colonial, Donelson, Homestead, Harding Court, Sulgrave—the early apartment houses?

Did you ever go to Chubby's, Nance's Bakery, Anderson's Fish and Oyster Market, Stokes Cagle's, Petrone's Cafe, Weiss and Capley's drugstores, Sidebottom's Ice Cream Store? How about Piggly-Wiggly, Acka-Packa and the H.G. Hill stores?

Remember the *Southern Agriculturist* Publishing Building, Geny's and McIntyre's florists, Finley Dorris the undertaker's, the Eve-Burch Clinic, Blackwood and 638 Tire companies, HOPE and Paris-Burge cleaners, Philly's-Acuff Tire Company?

Remember the old "auto row" and the early automobile people: Cheek, Dorris, Brannan, Reed, Nadron, Platz, Mosley, Caldwell, Miles, Tune, Smith, Stockell, Chapman, Chunn, Dr. Ford, Connors, and others?

Remember the elegant homes that lined West End—those of Hill McAllister, Bishop Dandridge, Jordan Stokes, Nathan Crockett, Judge Guild, W. A. Bryan, Howell Buntin, Tom Hill, Joseph Eskind, Eldon Stevenson, Ed Webb, Percy Maddin, E. A. Price, Alex Hunter, Felix Wilson, G. S. DeLuca, Avery Handly, Houston Dudley, Tillman Cavert, Foskett Brown, Ed Lindsey, Clyde Shropshire, Frank Gillette, William Griswold, Dorris Loventhal, George Killebrew, Charles Cohn, Lou and Sam Shyer, Verner Moore Lewis; the Gilberts, Fensterwalds and further out—H. G. Hill, Charles Trabue, Walter Keith, George Schwab and others.

Remember the fine old homes of the Hardisons, Lipscombs, Hitchcocks and others in old Acklen Park—and how they were all set back from West End Avenue in the beautiful shade of the park?

Can you recall when there was not a sign of any kind on West End? Remember the games and college dances in the old Vanderbilt Gym— the streetcars unloading people going to the football games at old Curry Field—the double rows of streetcar tracks and the trolley lines overhead—the gas lights along the street—the brick sidewalks, the hitching posts, mule-pulled trash carts traveling the alleys—and when each home had a horse barn and carriage house?

Remember seeing the "rich folks" riding out West End in their Winstons, Stutz Bearcats, Stearns-Knights, Packards, Appersons, electric autos, Graham-Paiges, Overlands, Saxons, and Deusen-bergs—when automobiles were first coming on the scene to replace the horse drawn carriages?

Remember the cinders from the old steam locomotives pulling the Tennessee Central trains over the wooden trestle across West End and the L&N passenger trains from Memphis along the highway?

Above all, do you remember the quiet beauty and dignity of the old West End Avenue.

Nothing represents the passing of the old Nashville more than the changes which have taken place from 12th and Broadway to White Bridge Road. The old homes have been torn down or converted into shops and restaurants. Shade trees have been replaced by neon signs and billboards.

Today West End carries the heavy traffic necessary to residents of the western section of the community, the business of the section and the traffic from and to Nashville going to or coming from as far as the West Coast. Approximately ten million vehicles pass any given point each year.

Old Belle Meade Mansion, College Hall on Vanderbilt campus, M.B.A., the Cathedral, the Parthenon, are now almost buried in the jungle of modernity.

They remain to carry the old West End Avenue into the twenty-first century. It is very unlikely that any of us who knew it in its beauty and dignity will be here then.

East Nashville

The first white men to come here to the banks of the Cumberland—the earliest French traders, Charleville about 1710, Thomas Walker about 1750, Skaggs in about 1763, Daniel Boone and Kasper Mansker in 1770—all came to trade with the Indians and all camped on the west side of the river. James Robertson came to establish a settlement on the Cumberland and he, too, selected the west side. When John Donelson led his flotilla of 33 boats up the Cumberland, he selected the west bluff for Nashborough in 1780. They all selected the west side because it afforded protection by its elevation. It was to continue as the main part of the later city. East Nashville, or Edgefield as it came to be known, was to be a lesser part until its union with the city of Nashville in 1880. Before this, it had claimed a separate corporate identity.

One of the earliest settlers, James Shaw, owned most of what is now East Nashville.

By 1869 a great section of the property immediately east of the

Cumberland, which had been owned by John P. Shelby, was subdivided and sold to later residents. Governor Neill S. Brown gave the section its name, "Edgefield." The property to the north was owned by M. W. Wetmore who, likewise, subdivided that section, later known as North Edgefield. On June 2, 1869, the section was incorporated as the City of Edgefield. The section was then drawing tradesmen, grocers, retail dealers, and manufacturers, schools and churches. Many businessmen and well-to-do families began to establish homes in the area. The new city had its own Street Railway Co. by 1872. In 1880 it became annexed to the City of Nashville by the popular vote of 498 for annexation, and 482 against, a majority of only 16 of the voters.

What a difference today. One can't tell where East Nashville ends and Goodlettsville and Hendersonville begin.

Other families came to make their homes on the outskirts of the section. Among these were the Summers, Hays, Craigheads, Loves, Gees, Maxeys, Dismukes, Whites, Stumps, Weakleys, Vaughns, Connels, Hobsons, Shelbys and Strattons. All of these names are still identified with the section.

Until 1822, transportation across the river was by ferry. In that year the first bridge across the Cumberland was built, but it was early found to interfere with the important river traffic and was torn down in 1855. By 1794 there were six ferries operating.

The first road from Nashville was authorized in 1784 by the settlers to lead to Mansker's Station.

The Gallatin Pike was authorized in 1839.

The suspension bridge had been completed by the beginning of the Civil War, but was destroyed by the retreat of the Confederate Army. In fact, the Federal Army was encamped in Edgefield on Feb. 25, 1862, when Nashville was surrendered to General Don Carlos Buell. The suspension bridge was rebuilt and put into operation in 1866. The L&N Railroad, which opened for business in 1859, ran its first train from Nashville, across the river on the old railroad bridge, through Edgefield, and on to Bowling Green. Amqui became a railroad passenger station. The Woodland Street Bridge was built in 1886. By 1890, electric streetcars were connecting the city to East Nashville. This multiple means of access really "opened up" East Nashville as a vigorous part of Nashville.

By 1910 East Nashville was becoming thickly populated, although its municipal area was confined to a small area. It had come to attract many prominent families of Nashville who lived in beautiful homes and on beautiful streets. Remember the homes of the Coopers, Burches, McCarns, Browns, Grays, Chadwells, Dudleys, Creightons,

Sudekums, Watkins, Joys, Herberts, Greens, Fosters, Orrs, Earlys, Forts, Cheeks, Tillmans, Warners—and many others?

Except for the sections along the river and railroad, it remained chiefly a residential section with schools, churches, and neighborhood stores until about 1930, when it began to expand and commercialism made its entry.

Remember the Masonic Home and the T.B. Hospital on Gallatin Road; the Gallatin Interurban; the old Trevecca College; and Woodale Beach? Did you ride the First Street, Main Street, Woodland and Porter Road, Gallatin Road and Inglewood, Fatherland or Shelby Avenue streetcars? Remember the Inglewood Golf Course and when they built the "double boulevard," or Riverside Drive, leading from Shelby Park?

Did you ever get water from Pioneer Springs or Lockland Springs? Did you ever go hunting in Cooper's Bottom? Remember Dotson's Hill, the Dotsons, and later Bishop Adrian? Did you ever take your girl for a boat ride on the lake in Shelby Park; go swimming at Haysboro, or have an ice cream soda at Les Burrus'? Remember Charley Jackson's filling station at 11th and Woodland, one of the first, or Rock City on Cahal Avenue and Dick Bridgewater?

Did you ever go swimming in the "hole" just off of Foster Street by the railroad, or watch the log rafts tie up at the Farris Lumber Co. on the river?

Church Street East from 7th Avenue—ca. 1914.

W. C. Collier Grocery

Remember riding sleds down Shelby Avenue hill during the winter snow season? Remember the fire of 1916 and the two tornadoes that struck East Nashville?

Do you remember Borum's Camp, "Crappy" Shute, and the "Hootennany Patch"? Did you ever attend the political speakings at the Smith's Mill, Warner School, Meridian Park, Phillips' Store, Les Burrus' place, or at the Holly Street Fire Hall? Remember the politicos of the section, Sheffield Gee, Charlie Shaw, Percy Sharpe, John Shea, Charlie Longhurst, Currey Bramlett, Jake Sheridan, Jim Bates, Hugh Freeman, Bob Marshall, "Cockey" Groomes, Jim Dean, Dick Lindsey, Tom Hill, Luther Luton, Howard Wilkinson, John Langham, B. O. Briley, Dick McClure, Romans Hailey and Leon Taylor?

Remember Hull-Dobbs, Dressler-White and the Merchant's Ice Co.? Remember when you had to take the ferry to get to the Old Hickory area—and that road that led down to the ferry before the Old Hickory Bridge was built? Remember the East Side Hospital on Russell Street, and the Belvedere, Woodrow, Altamont, Eastside and Aurelius apartments?

How about Mrs. A. Letty Sweeney and Charlie Crafton, the undertakers, and Mrs. Ramsey's bakery? Remember Uthman's Antiques on Russell Street? Did you know Doctor James Brew, John Cummins, Roger Burrus, Doctor Hyde, Doctor Campbell or Doctor Core? Remember Lewis Tillman—Nashville's first real jogger? Have you forgotten the "Gully Jumpers," or when they built the Sparkman Street Bridge? You oldies, do you remember Dr. Lin Cave?

Did you trade at the Parson, House, Barnes, Stratton, Marshall, Redd, Cox, Robertson, Greene, Phillips, Hewitt, Egan or Young grocery stores? Do you remember the Bradshaw, Knight, Moxley, Greene, Mose Cook, East End, Hooser, Independent, Shelby, McGinnis, Maplewood and Red Cross drugstores? Remember the church "ice cream suppers" on the lawn of Hobson's Chapel, at Meridian Park and at East Side Park, and the picture show at 11th and Woodland? Remember Jim Stewart, the blacksmith, on Gallatin Road? Did you ever ride the Gallatin Interurban? Remember the old Eastland and Lockland schools?

When Edgefield was annexed to the City of Nashville, it had three schools, the high school, located at Main and Fifth streets; Seawright School, located at Joseph and North Seventh streets; and Vandervil School, for the black students, located just north of the railroad junction.

Do you recall the principal and teachers of the East Nashville schools who did so much for the young people: S. H. Binkley, Ms. Mattie Lee Chatham, G. C. Carney, Ms. Lillian Doyle, Cecil Webb, Jr., W.

C. Dodson, Walter Anderson, Noble Cummins, Professor Schumate, A. E. Durah, Ms. Hattie Cotton, W. H. Oliver and many others?

Let's go way back—do you remember Spout Springs School, Ms. Katie Robinson and Ms. Edna Mai Davis?

Remember Carl Cunningham's restaurant, Judge Alf Rutherford, Burton Dornan, Chris Contos, Major Hyde, Ballard and Beaty blacksmiths, Upchurch Mattress Company, Wasserman's Shoe Shop, Pigg's, Lucas', Keel's and Moody's groceries? How about Anderton, the cabinet maker?

Remember the East Nashville colorfuls: Squire Jim Allen, Andrew Vaughan, Ted Vaughan, Dick Taylor, Frank Stull, "Buttermilk" Shelton, "Daddy" Chadwell, and Paul Treanor, Sam Borum, Charlie Smith and D. Canfield?

West Nashville

West Nashville was the last of the four sections of the City to experience real development.

When old Cedar Street was extended into the old road west toward Charlotte, its extremity took the name of the Charlotte Pike, which was authorized in 1842. The old and original landowners of the properties immediately west of the city began to sell off plots and parcels to those who then wished to establish homes in this section of Davidson County. As the city grew, business entered to accommodate the residents.

By the end of the nineteenth century, industry had begun to really open up what became known as West Nashville. The hardwood, chemical and foundry industries had selected the section for their growing enterprises. The railroad expansion began to lend importance to the section. By now, the west was opened up and traffic from that direction came to the city through West Nashville. The State Prison was moved to this section. To serve this expansion, stores, shops, schools, churches and other community necessities had followed fast. It was now a thickly populated and thriving section of Nashville.

Few people know that the Tennessee Fairgrounds were first located two miles west of Nashville, between the Harding and Charlotte pikes. Eighty acres accommodated buildings which surrounded a natural amphitheater capable of seating ten thousand people. It provided a race course with two fifty-foot tracks, with half-mile and mile stretches. These grounds served as the location of the Centennial Military Encampment at the close of the century. The new iron industry took over these properties at the beginning of this century.

Later, when Murphy Road, formerly known as Minnesota Avenue, linked its southern flank with Harding Road, a new section was opened, to be known as Sylvan Park.

Among the early settlers of this section of the county were the Cockrills, Robertsons, Ewings, Howes, DeMosses, Watkins, Drakes, Joslins, Newsoms, and other families whose names are still identified with western Davidson County and Nashville.

Van Blackum Station was an important depot, and the "new shops" was a beehive of activity.

By 1920 West Nashville was an important section of the city of Nashville. It was furnishing some of our leaders in the business, professional, religious and political life of the city.

Then came the Tennessee Highway Department, the broom factory operated by the blind, and the hosiery mill industry. The farming and agricultural activities on its western border were expanding their contribution to city business. Richland Park had come along as well as one of Nashville's first aviation fields. Then came grain elevators, rendering plants, flour mills, appliance manufacturers, fertilizer plants and other industrial concerns.

Remember the C. H. King Transfer Company, Wooden Products Co., Kimmons-Smithson and Higgins grocery stores, Piggly-Wiggly, Green's Barber Shop, Richland Coal Co., Rosenberg's Dry Goods Store, the Elite Theater, Dillday's Billiard Parlor, King's Toy and Candy Shop, Naft's Store, Bernard's Loan Shop, Weise's Hall and Richland Hall, Slaton's, Cox's, Ferguson's stores and Siegrist, the baker?

Remember Gray and Dudley's, Phillips & Buttorff's and Jakes' foundry, the lumber companies and iron works?

Remember the old politicos of the section—Squires Reasonover and Buchanan, Jim Weimer, Warren Sloan, "Tip-Toe" Stevens, J. T. Tipps, Alex Hines, J. D. Ferris, Judge Roscoe Matthew?

Judge Guild Smith, Judge Madison Wells, Bob Mingle, and later, Ralph Worthy?

Do you remember the West Nashville policemen, "Daddy" Coe, Bill Cummings, Foster Briley.

How about Laverte Smith, Ollie Dillingham, Alex Erwin, C. M. Darden, Jim Napier—the Stringfellows, Sullivans, Kennedys, McCoys, Buchanans, Suitors, Mosses, Cullums?

Can you remember "Wes" Ingram during the prohibition days? The old Howse political rallies at the West Nashville Fire Hall and at Sylvan Park? Remember when the streetcar turned right at 50th, and continued on to the prison and came back on 51st?

Remember Mrs. Myrtle Cullum Fly, Miss Susie Finnegan, and

Mrs. Emma Rich, school teachers, and Ms. Elizabeth Sawyers and Ms. Elizabeth E. Williams, who taught music? How about Drake Blacksmith Shop?

Remember when the Tennessee boys returned from World War I, and detrained at the "new shops"?

Remember Mose Levitan who lived in the old Cockrill mansion, which was later torn down for Bass School? How about Dr. Watkins and Professor J. H. Sykes and Mrs. Rebecca Kellerhas and the St. Luke's Settlement House? Did you ever ride the dinkey from Charlotte down 46th Avenue—or pull its trolley at nighttime? Remember the old bandstand in Richland Park? How about McDaniel's store at 50th and Charlotte, and Oehmig's on Murphy Road. Daddy Smith's lunchroom, The Girls' Home for the Blind, Pirtland's drugstore, Piggly-Wiggly stores, Harry Lovelace's barbershop, Coleman's grocery, Abe Arkantz' shoe repair shop, Elmore Wood's restaurant, Kittrell's watch repair shop, Oscar Edmondson's blacksmith shop, Dr. Tom Harris, the dentist, and Griswold's stove works?

The city was to move south, north and east, before expanding to the west. For this reason, there are probably more people living today who experienced this expansion than there are who have any real first-hand knowledge of the early movements in the other three directions. That is why it got its old name of "New Town."

Today, it abounds with beautiful residential sections, tremendous business activity, fine churches and schools, excellent streets and highways, and all the accommodations of modern city life. Its development came late, faster than that of the other communities.

Flat Rock

Old Flat Rock was almost a self-sufficient rural community. Starting at the T. C. Railroad crossing on Nolensville Road, and extending south to Antioch Pike and Radnor College, it extended to the limits of Oriole, Peachtree, Elberta, Lutie, Joyner Avenue and Whitsett Lane on the east, and to the extremities of Caldwell, Kline, Cruzen and Winford, Radnor and Morton avenues on the west.

It was a section of the county which had much rock surface. However, hard-working and independent citizens used the available soil for gardens, feedstuffs, pastures, and orchards for food, fruits, pork, beef, milk and butter. Only a handful worked at jobs "in town," or outside the community.

In the early part of the century it was known as "McLean's Station"—named for the post office located at the corner of the McLean

Estate starting at Thompson Lane and fronting along Nolensville Road to the north. It was in front of the handsome McLean mansion which later burned.

There was no mail delivery then. We picked up the mail at the post office. By 1910 the brothers Jay and Jim Newsom started the subdivision of their properties in the heart of the section and called the area "Grandview Heights." It is said that this was the first real estate development program in the county. It succeeded, but the new name did not.

The older residents were referring to their section as "Flat Rock" for obvious reasons. In the years that followed the more sophisticated tried the use of "Woodbine." They struggled with this name until Metro came along. To us oldsters it has been and still is—Flat Rock.

Originally, it had only Turner School and a school for blacks on Whitsett Lane—later J. K. Rains and Woodbine. Its churches were well supported and attended. It had four stores, R. E. Lee's, Smoot's, Matthewson's, and A. P. May's—later Whitsett's, Norwood's and Matthews'.

It had one Schwartz dry goods store, Mincy's drugstore, and Hosse's ice house and coal yard. It had a number of dairies—Jess Rader's, Woodruff's, Roth's, Harrison's and Neiderhauser's.

We had three doctors—Dr. Caldwell, Dr. Tanksley and Dr. Charles Brower.

Do you remember the two-inch dust on Nolensville Road, before asphalt? The fence that separated boys from girls at Turner School, the stile at the entrance, the stables, the outdoor toilets, and the pot-bellied stoves? Radnor College and the livery stable at the intersection of Antioch Pike and Nolensville Road? Shacklett's and Dodd's blacksmith shops?

Do you recall: Mr. Curtis who repaired clocks and watches, sharpened knives and half-soled shoes? Phil and Walter Langford? The baseball diamond behind the Morehead home on Elberta? The first auto truck in Flat Rock—The Lee delivery truck with solid rubber tires? Mr. Holton's grocery wagon? The convicts and the wagons they lived in while building the streets?

Do you remember watching homes burn down because we had no fire protection? When the Flat Rock boys volunteered for World War I? When horses were afraid of the first automobiles? Rose's spring and the horse water trough at Shacklett's? When Thompson Lane only ran from the Franklin Pike to the Nolensville Road—and Timmon's Lane led only to the Timmon's home? Myer Morris' swimming pool—the first public pool in Nashville?

Or, Mr. Nix's mail wagon? The mansions of the Mortons, Thompsons, Overtons, Shutes, Buells, Roses, Rains, Berrys and Bransfords? Miss Annie at Leo's grocery? Listening to the Randall-Cole School band concerts on Sundays? Randolph's ice cream parlor? Hunting Civil War minie balls in the hills at Glencliff? Closet cleaners, rock wagons, and well-diggers? Good old John Hall, the janitor at Turner School?

Did you ever play marbles beside the drugstore? Steal cantaloupes at night off the farm wagons on their way to the market, or plums from the Morton orchard? Buy watermelons from the wagons of Allen Shacklett or Jim Rader? Fish in Mill Creek or swim in Brown's Creek? Go to the church ice cream festivals at the corner of the pike and Peachtree Street? Remember the Japanese lanterns? Watch Doug Russell kill rabbits with rocks? Crawl through the sewer pipe to slip into the Fair?

Did you ever put an outhouse on Lee's grocery porch at Halloween, soap the streetcar track, or hang a gate on a lightpost? Have you ever had a watermelon rind, corn cob or clay-ball fight? Or walked to town to save the nickel car fare? Been over to see the gypsies camped on Brown's Creek? Gotten a school whipping by Professor Hooper, Wright, Turner or Darrah?

Did you collect colored Sunday School cards? Bust your bottom skating on frozen ice ponds? Have black hands from hulling walnuts? Rock the city boys who came out to see our girls?

It was home to a lot of good people, hardworking and of simple habits. They were law abiding and family loving. They created their own entertainment, enjoyed each other, and knew no different life. They taught their children to work, accept discipline, and inspired them to achievement.

With the war came the railroad—right through the center of the community. With its construction, we lost many homes and much of the productive land. It brought about a new life, the life and work of the railroader, which melded right in with our standards of living.

It brought an expansion that was to change the community characteristics and brought it closer to dependence on the city. This expansion was to continue to its present status of an important part of Nashville.

The section was to furnish leaders from its youth. Two, Ben West and Beverly Briley, were to become mayors of Nashville. It was to produce doctors, pharmacists, nurses, school teachers and professors. There were dentists, engineers, lawyers, ministers, journalists, authors, merchants, business executives, soldiers and sailors, mechanics, artists, and successes in every field of professional, business, political and social life.

We owe a lot to old Flat Rock.

Old Hickory

It is possible that Nashville witnessed and participated in what history will record as having been the greatest single wartime effort of all time. Certainly it was the largest military project undertaken up to its time.

The demands of England, France, Belgium, Italy and Russia for powder and explosives with which to engage in World War from 1914 to 1916, had already overtaxed their sources. The British Munitions Board was already depending upon the American Du Pont productions.

With the entry of the United States into the struggle on April 6, 1917, Du Pont was called on for greater production. Among the five new projects announced for this need was what we were to come to know as the Old Hickory Powder Plant. The location was to be Had-

Aerial view of DuPont Powder Plant at Old Hickory showing Hadley's Bend area.

ley's Bend on the Cumberland River, seven miles from Nashville, as selected by U.S. Army engineers. The rapidity of the progress of the construction was to shake this old comfortable Southern city out of its provincial boots and call upon it for an all-out effort.

Nashville, Davidson County and Middle Tennessee responded in the true character of the Volunteer State, and a construction miracle was the result.

The records of the Du Pont Company reveal the real story of this remarkable undertaking.

It took the labor of 30,000 men and women. They were recruited from almost everywhere. Almost all of them had to be housed. The complete town built by Du Pont included 3,867 buildings, dwellings, apartment houses, hotels, restaurants, schools, churches, theaters, hospitals, a city hall and fire and police stations.

Seven miles of railroad had to be laid to take material to the site. Miles of paved streets, sidewalks, water lines and sewers were laid. All this was in addition to 1,112 buildings comprising the powder plant itself. A 540-foot steel suspension bridge over the Cumberland River was necessary. The seven miles of railroad track had to accommodate 1,100 cars and 31,000 passengers daily. Most of the new and fast re- cruited labor had to be trained to powder making by Du Pont person- nel.

Time was the commanding factor.

Production of sulfuric acid began 67 days after ground-breaking; nitric acid nine days later; guncotton, the raw material of smokeless powder, two weeks after that. The first finished powder was granu- lated 116 days after the breaking of the ground for the plant. This was 121 days ahead of the contract agreement.

Now comes some interesting information, not widely known here, and it represents an example of the loyalty and total response of the American industrial complex in national emergency of another day.

For operating the plant, Du Pont received a fee based on output. After taxes, it amounted to 1 percent of value of product made.

For building this huge project, Du Pont sent the U.S. government an odd bill:

The price, a single dollar.

With the signing of the armistice on November 11, 1918, the gov- ernment ordered the plant shut down, and shortly thereafter it was declared surplus property. In 1923, E. I. du Pont de Nemours and Co. purchased the plant property. The greater part of the city which had been built was later sold to private individuals.

Do you remember the trains, both passenger coaches and flat cars,

DuPont Commissary.

carrying employees out from Nashville each day, and the long freight trains carrying materials over the railroad—one right behind the other, 24 hours each day?

Remember the heavy demand upon our local food supply to feed this influx of hungry working men and women? And the resulting rise in prices—really for the first time in Nashville?

Remember the community fear of the possibility of German spies, and the possibility of sabotage, because of the importance of Old Hickory to the war effort? It is interesting to note that, so far as was known, no significant act of sabotage was committed at the plant. Plant security guards were assisted by the Tennessee State Militia in protecting the employees and the property.

Remember the Old Hickory song, called the "Du Pont Powder Puff," which was sung to the tune of "Coming through the Rye" and went:

> Old Hickory Plant is working nights
>   to make the real stuff,
> To paste upon the Kaiser's nose
>   a Du Pont powder puff.

and the front of the song sheet showed a Du Pont worker hitting the Kaiser in the nose? And there was a poster all around the plant which depicted the helmeted ugly face of the Kaiser, with the words:

> *Push the job*
> *Help fill the empty shell*
> *Give the Kaiser hell.*

Do you recall the horrible winter which brought the influenza epidemic and the deaths of so many Mexican laborers at Old Hickory?

Remember the name of the main construction company—Mason-Hanger?

Remember the Village Commissary Store? Did you wear a "powder ring?" Remember the "jitney buses" that ran from the city to the plant? The Du Pont Hotel.

Did you know Granville Rives and Andy Dorris?

Remember that before the powder plant the area consisted of the farms of the Hadleys, Robertsons, Turners, Dismukes, Livingstons and Tesseys?

Had you forgotten how the neighbors were scared when the blending towers would blow up, which happened often?

Remember John Omohundro's court, Police Chief Will Brown, the Hurts, Wrights, Phillips, Marvin Ball, Bob McGee and "Skinny" Neese?

Remember the old bus station which later became Robertson's store? Remember payday at the plant, when the 13,000 workers would line up for their envelopes?

In the beginning, Hadley's Bend was way out in the country. Now, sixty-five years later, the entire section of the county east of the Cumberland is a vigorous part of Metropolitan Nashville. Like its neighbor, the Hermitage community, Old Hickory claims a great place in Nashville's history and the contribution of Tennessee to defense of our country. Its very name is synonymous with the American Spirit.

CHAPTER 3

How Dear to My Heart
Special Nashville Places

I WATCHED THE MARCH OF TIME pause at a fine old home across the street. I watched as they carried a little old lady's last gift to others. All that was left of her more than 90 years was on its way to medical science. A temporary serenity settled around the stately old mansion she had loved so much, and from which had continuously flowed such concern for others. A silent parade of respect began to come and go in testimony of her simple goodness in life.

Requiem for a Lady

As she had gone, so would go her material possessions. They came in cars and trucks to carry away the material things collected during her long life, to various new locations.

As I saw the larger things placed in cars and trucks, and the smaller articles being brought out by relatives and friends, I wondered how and when she had come to have them. What had each held for her in memory and association? Why did she cling to this or that piece for so long? How many of their memories died with her?

At last, I watched them turn out all the lights, lock the doors, and place a "FOR SALE" sign in the front yard.

Everything had been removed from the old home except the love, the truth, the good and the faith of the old lady.

Neither the trucks, the cars, nor the arms of those she loved could carry these away.

As the night stole the remaining light of the day, I watched the old house in the throes of death. She lay on the ground in an ugly heap. They had knocked her down.

The awesome machines of destruction stood tall, as though they were guarding their kill, and proud of their victory.

Now a jagged timber slipped from its imbalance and sounded as though it was a dying gasp. The dust of her old age curled up from her twisted and broken mass, as though it was her last breath.

A silence then settled over her. Tomorrow the servants of progress and modernity would return to carry away the remains. The old trees which had stood beside her in sunshine and storm seemed to be weeping. A lone pigeon that had roosted in her eaves flew around in quiet frustration.

As I lingered there, alone, I am sure that I heard voices from her past.

I heard the words of pride and admiration of those who had known her when she was new and young. I heard them greeting friends at her front door. I heard laughing children playing in her yard. I heard the pleasantries of her dining room. I even heard the sweet whispers of love from her bedrooms. I heard the expressions of joy over victories, triumphs and good fortune—and I heard the sighs of sorrow, hurt and disappointment. I heard the muffled tread of Death moving through her halls.

It was this last sound that grew stronger in my ears as I turned to walk away.

I looked back—the old house, the old home, was gone.

As its old stones and timbers have gone—so will all memory of her pass, in time.

"Dust to Dust."

Union Station

Again, I paused to look upon another part of the passing of the Nashville which I knew. There she stood, still trying to claim a useful place in our community, but yielding all the while to the passage of time. As I looked at her, my mind closed in to memory.

The beauty and vitality of her young days and the elegance and dignity of her prime had now been worn, battered and bruised by the years of wear, the penalties of age, the summer suns, and the winter snows. She now stands in decay and disintegration, and in the throes of death.

She was once loud and active in her relation and service to Nashville. The sounds of released steam, clanging bells and anxious voices identified her place in the life of our city.

She was a doorway to both happiness and sorrow.

She provided the introduction of visitors and business.

She was the starting point of our ventures into outer worlds and the reception point for our dependence on others.

I could still hear from within, the heavy voice calling the arrival of the Dixie Flyer, or the departure of the Pan-American.

I could still see her benches crowded with those waiting to leave, or for the arrival of friends and relatives.

The noise and confusion of convention visitors making their way from the lower train level and the enthusiasm of boys and girls arriving for schools in the Athens of the South, still echoed from the old station.

I could still see tears of joy from those at the head of the track steps who had experienced long separations, and those of anguish over the departure of loved ones.

I remembered the pain of a few, at late hours of cold nights, upon the return of those who had died in distant places.

I could still hear the greetings for presidents, dignitaries, heroes, and the famous.

I could still hear the martial music, see the flags waving, and feel the heartthrobs of mothers and fathers as they received their sons back safely from foreign battlefields. I could also see flag-draped caskets rolled into the view of those whose hearts were broken forever.

Her door remained ever open to receive and discharge all the componency of life—with its goodness and its bad; its intentions, its emotions, its hopes, its ambitions, and its tragedies, its reverence—and its irreverence.

But now, modernity has subtracted her from the list of useful things.

Her old doors are closed.

Union Station, Summer of 1900.

She now stands only a monument to another day—another life—another Nashville. Abandoned, even by her Mercury, her old clock has long since grown tired of measuring her time.

The only sound she now yields is that of a lonely pigeon claiming a last part of her.

She no longer claims a part in any schedule.

She is removed from all timetables.

The Masonic Hall and Theatre

As I walked along Church Street a few days ago, I stopped to watch the wrecking hammer toiling against the stubborn walls of what was the old Burk & Co. Building to most of us—but which was the Masonic Hall and Theatre to early Nashvillians.

She was the last of two notable structures which had occupied the site for the past 165 years. Nearly every Tennessean and hundreds of thousands of other people have passed her doors. Many of Tennessee's great passed through them. First, there was the Masonic Hall built in 1818, and which was destroyed by fire in 1856. Then there was the second Masonic Hall and Theatre built in 1858. This one was, in later years, to be occupied by Burk & Co. in 1913, and Gus Mayer's department store later. For the last few years she has stood vacant in quiet vigil over memories of her great contribution to the political, religious, civic and social life of the old city. In the early days it was the scene of the greater part of all types of public meetings, as well as lodge meetings.

From the clouds of dust and the moans of her crumbling walls, I seemed to hear the voices of many, prominent in the building of Nashville:

The convincing language of that great intellect, civic leader and Masonic scholar, Wilkins Tannehill, who pioneered its construction; General Andrew Jackson swapping barbs with his old friend Sam Houston to the delight of their Masonic brothers—Ephraim Foster, John Catron, Governor Newt Cannon, Moses Norvell, President James K. Polk, John Overton, Edwin Ewing, and many others.

I thought I heard the spirited sermons of Episcopal, Presbyterian and Baptist ministers to their congregations when they met there before they had built their churches.

I heard the great applause that accompanied Nashville's welcome to General Lafayette at the great gala celebration at the Masonic Hall on May 5, 1824.

The eloquence of Felix Grundy, the great trial lawyer, friend of Jackson and benefactor of the community, seemed to rise above the sound of the cracking timbers.

One could almost hear the arguments and discussions of the members of the state legislative sessions held there before the Capitol was built.

From one quarter one could hear John Overton discussing the building of his Maxwell House Hotel with John Kirkman and William Strickland going over the plans of the new state Capitol with his associates. From another the voice of Ephraim Foster, mayor of Nashville and Grand Master of the Masons of Tennessee, announcing his gift of the ground upon which to build St. Mary's Catholic Church.

This was to be crowded out by the roars of Nashvillians as they welcomed three presidents of the United States in ceremonies held there, and to be followed by the sad lamentations which followed the burning of the first building in 1856.

There followed the enthusiasm of Masons and the city with the building and opening of the second Masonic Hall on the same site in 1858.

As the destruction was halted for the lunch hour, and the noise subsided, I could hear the quiet and serious voices of Mayor Cheatham, John Lea, John Bass, John Brien, R. C. Foster, James Woods, James Whitworth, William Lewis and N. Hobson, discussing the articles of the surrender of Nashville to General Don Carlos Buell and the Federal Army in 1862.

And then the pitiful and anguished voices of the young Union soldiers who were being treated for wounds received in battle, when the Union Army took over the Masonic Hall for use as a military hospital.

These somber reflections were halted by the stentorian voices of the great actors, Joe Jefferson, Fritz Leiber and Robert Mantell, as they rose from the stage of *The Cricket on the Hearth, The American Cousin, Rip Van Winkle, Macbeth, Othello, Two Gentlemen from Verona, The Merchant of Venice,* and other great dramatic productions of the Masonic Theatre. The oratory of Gates Thruston resounded amid the applause of Masonic meetings.

An old friend stopped to speak, and jerked my mind back to my acquaintance with the old building. I remembered going there to buy my Boy Scout uniform and seeing our policemen and firemen buying their uniforms there when Burk was the sole distributor of both. I remembered the Fensterwald family and their contribution to Nashville and what a grand store it seemed to a boy from Flat Rock.

As I looked down toward Fourth Avenue, I got a glimpse of the benevolence of our city, when I saw two prominent citizens of today's Nashville stopped to buy pencils from a crippled unfortunate. As I looked back, I heard citizens meeting in the Old Masonic Hall to raise $1,500 to send to sufferers from a destructive tornado in Natchez in 1840; another meeting there to raise $1,200 for the relief of victims of the great fire in Pittsburgh in 1845, and still another, to raise $3,600 for the relief of the starving people of Ireland in 1847.

I left the scene of destruction with some idea as to how Nashville came to have such a great heart, and thinking about how many great meetings had taken place under the remaining part of the old roof, now sagging in the rear.

One wonders about the artifacts that lay buried in the graves of these two Masonic Halls.

The Ryman Auditorium

The result of the conversion of a rough old riverboat captain, she became an important part of old Nashville and finally rewarded the city's relation with a modern billion-dollar business and many young men and women with fame and fortune.

She was as much a part of old Nashville as the Cumberland River, the Parthenon and Sulphur Dell. She was as local as spiced rounds, chess pie and Jack Daniels.

Nearly one hundred years ago lower Broadway had produced an affront to the moralists of the old city. The wharf, or riverfront, was crowded with saloons. Gambling flourished on the steamboats. Drunks and prostitutes swarmed over the area. This situation attracted the concern of local religious leaders and evangelists of the day. Local preachers were joined by the fiery-tongued Sam Jones in preaching and denouncing the conditions in terms of the "hellfire and damnation."

Tom G. Ryman was converted, stopped all gambling on his boats and as part of his repentance, contributed most of the money and headed the drive to build the Union Gospel Tabernacle on old Summer Street to accommodate, principally, the evangelist. It was completed in 1892. Whey Ryman died in 1904 she became known as Ryman Auditorium.

She gave old Nashville a stage for sermons and evangelism, music, opera, ballet, minstrel shows, big bands, political conventions and oratory, business conventions, graduation, civic meetings, citizen war efforts, and celebration.

Through her doors came Sam Jones, Dwight Moody, Billy Sunday.

Gypsy Smith, Enrico Caruso, Lily Pons, Madame Galli-Curci, John McCormack, Sir Harry Lauder, Pavlova, Sarah Bernhardt, Isadora Duncan, Victor Herbert, Billy Church, Joe Jefferson, Helen Keller, Carrie Nation, Booker T. Washington, John Philip Sousa, Harry Houdini, Sergeant Alvin York, Charlie Chaplin, Bob Hope and many others.

Here we heard United States Senators W. E. Borah, Henry Cabot Lodge, Jim Reed, Robert L. Owen, Carter Glass, Frank O. London and Hiram Johnson debate Woodrow Wilson's proposed League of Nations.

Here we heard the heated arguments over national Prohibition.

Here we heard the emotional and spiritual debates on woman suffrage.

Here we were entertained by the Ziegfeld Follies, the Pavlova Ballet, Fritz Leiber's Shakespearean plays and other Broadway productions.

Ryman Auditorium.

It was here that we heard all the leading chatauqua lectures of the time.

Here we were held spellbound by the oratory of Theodore Roosevelt, Champ Clark, William Jennings Bryan, Edward Carmack, Harvey Hannah, Bob and Alf Taylor, John K. Shields, Nathan Bachman, Cordell Hull, Benton McMillin, Joseph W. Byrns, Albert Roberts, Tom Rye, Ben Hooper, Kenneth McKellar, Wirt Courtney, Gordon Browning, Frank Clement, Jim McCord and many others.

Here we heard Jimmy Melton, Joseph McPherson and Grace Moore on their way to national fame.

From here we sent our delegations to the national Democratic and Republican conventions and our members of the Electoral College to nominate and elect the presidents and vice-presidents of the United States.

In the twenties, she discovered the American appreciation and desire for pure country music when she offered an opportunity to some native Tennesseans, including a country boy from East Tennessee to sing "The Wabash Cannon Ball," to a young country girl from Grinder's Switch to spin some comic tales and to a lover of blue grass music. She took an unknown grease monkey from Huntsville, Alabama, and told Tim Pan Alley to move over and make room on the entertainment scene for simple, honest, cornfield country music.

From then on she provided the graduation stage to national and international fame. Where singers, fiddlers, guitar stringers and comics were once entertaining only at country shindigs for free, and their love for music, they were now singing and playing across the footlights to the entire nation—and the world.

George Hay, "the solemn old judge," named this effort the "Grand Ole Opry" and a new industry was born. WSM leased and operated the old lady from 1941 to 1963 when she became the "Grand Ole Opry House."

By 1974 the enterprise had grown to such proportions that it was moved to the new facility on Briley Parkway as the main part of Opryland.

By this time her child had grown up, won fame, gotten rich and yearned for sophistication. It left home and moved to the boulevard of tinsel, rhinestones and sequins.

Roy Acuff.

Like many old homes of Nashville, she is now mostly a memory, a "thing of the past,"—the "old house."

As we pass her closed doors today we are sure that we can still hear her impresario of the old days, that gracious Mrs. Lula C. Naff, booking her engagements and the ringing applause that came from her old wooden seats for those who strode across her stage.

To some of us, her old red walls call up memories of another age. Some of these are fast vanishing from the memories of the living.

The Old Protestant Hospital

The heavy iron ball of the wrecker is poised ready to tear into the sides of another of Nashville's old landmarks. The last remaining building of the old Protestant Hospital is to be demolished to make way for a new addition to the Baptist Hospital complex. The dream of the late Doctor Evander "Van" Sanders is to fade completely. With it will go many memories—some good, some painful.

By 1918 Nashville had witnessed a phenomenal increase in population during the two or three preceding years. An influx of approximately 50,000 new residents for the city and its immediate area added pressure to the existing public accommodations and was causing concern among the health and medical professionals. The powder plant at

The Nashville Protestant Hospital.

Old Hickory and other war efforts were the main reasons. When the influenza epidemic came, the hospital situation was becoming serious and caused an insistent need for more beds. Local doctors were alarmed.

On Dec. 12, 1918, a group of leading citizens answered by applying for a charter for a corporation to be known as Nashville Protestant Hospital. The initial incorporators were L. A. Bowers, Leslie Cheek, E. B. Craig, R. M. Dudley and John A. Pitts. Mr. Cheek became president and H. H. Campbell became secretary. E. M. Fuqua was the first superintendent.

Since the problem was so acute, it was decided to find property that was suitably located and with buildings readily usable, if possible. To meet the pressing demand it was decided to purchase the Murphy home place and the old site of the Nashville College for Young Women property consisting of two blocks facing Church Street and extending from 20th Avenue to 21st Avenue. The property was purchased for $210,000. It consisted of ten and one half acres with two good buildings. The old home place became the nurses' home. The property was bought through the local Chancery Court. Initial improvements and equipment were purchased for $186,000 which was realized from issuance of six percent bonds.

The need for additional hospital facilities was met as the new hospital opened and she was to flourish and succeed in her early years. During the first year of operation she cared for 2,233 patients. It must be understood that St. Thomas was then a small hospital, Nashville General Hospital was still small and Vanderbilt Hospital was still in South Nashville. Dr. Barr's small infirmary and the Woman's Hospital could care for but a few patients and Hale's Hospital attempted the care of black patients.

By 1920, the "new building" or "addition," which is the building now to be demolished, was already on the drawing board. It was not actually built until 1927 and put in use sometime later. It was to face east on 20th Avenue. The old hospital had faced south on Church Street and was known as 2000 Church Street. The beginning of the new building, of course, was to compete with the depth of the Depression, the growth of St. Thomas and Nashville General and the new Vanderbilt Hospital complex, now in this section of the city. Its financial troubles were to start in the later thirties.

However, in the early years the hospital attracted many fine doctors to her facilities. Dr. Sanders was one of her driving forces. Known as a strong, tough, two-fisted and acid-tongued leader of admired and respected professional ability, he became a dominant force of the institution. He ruled with an iron hand but was loved by his patients and respected by the personnel. His friendship with L. A. Bowers, one of the originators of the hospital, brought him into a prominent place with the institution.

Many prominent doctors of the day attended patients at the Protestant. Tom Pollard, W. A. Bryan, O. N. Bryan, Harrison Shoulders, J. T. Ross, Robert and Tom Grizzard, Charles Brower, Rogers Hubert, Hettie Shoulders, and Dr. Frank Fessey. Doctors Keller, Caldwell, Bunch and many others were to spend much of their professional time on her floors. Many young doctors whose education or early practice had been held up by service in World War I returned to begin in these buildings—George Carpenter, Paul Warner, Sumpter Anderson and many others.

Later, young men like Elkin Rippy, Ray Fessey, Jim Hayes, Jim Kirtley, Cleo Miller, Charles Trabue, who was to later make an effort to save the hospital, and others were to return from World War II to practice there.

Many nurses were to serve in her wards. Ladies like Edith Good, Grace Anderson, Pauline Thompson, Pat Manning, Rose Harris, Nellie Griffen, Emma Parker, Ms. Robertson and Ms. Briscoe, and many others left a good part of their lives in their service to the hospital, the doctors and their patients.

During her thirty years many Nashvillians saw their first light of day from her obstetrics ward. Many entered suffering from pain and left cured. Her halls and waiting rooms have heard the sobs and seen the tears of distressed families.

In the past most hospitals had been operated as charity projects—many by Catholic and Protestant church affiliates or by different levels of government. The big corporate organization for profit was unknown in the hospital field. Every effort was made to keep necessary hospitalization within the reach of all levels of society. Although a corporate organization, Protestant came into existence through the generosity of many and was intended for the same purpose. She was expected to thrive on the postwar booming economy with no idea that the Depression would be waiting around the corner of the following decade.

Of course, there was no such thing as Medicare, Medicaid or government aid of any kind. She was "on her own." It is said that her ultimate troubles were the result of the efforts of her management and doctors to keep her costs to those she served as low as possible. Their intense interest in the public was therefore to contribute to her failure. The financial burden of the new building was to further tax her ability to survive.

As the thirties came to the forties she had fallen on bad times.

Finally she was forced into receivership by her creditors and her assets were acquired by the sponsors of the new Baptist Hospital in 1947 and 1948. The earlier Baptist Hospital located downtown had ceased operation some years earlier. The old Protestant Hospital then became the present Baptist Hospital—one of the leading institutions of its kind in the country.

Do you remember the old red brick building of the original hospital sitting back from Church Street? Do you remember the beautiful marble stairway and floors of the building now to be destroyed? Did you ever lie there in one of the rooms, staring at the walls, searching for something to distract you from your pain or to relieve your worry and apprehension?

Did you ever strain to hear the whispered conversations of doctors and nurses outside your door? Remember the sound of carts moving up and down the corridors? Remember the quiet knock on the door of the nurse as she came with your medicine, a thermometer, or a needle?

Remember the awful silence that settled in after midnight when you could not go to sleep? The early morning hand bath? The scanty food tray? When the doctor finally came in to say that you could go home? Do you remember when "Parson" Preston Pugh would come in quietly, press your hand, say a short prayer and leave—all in about three minutes?

As the last of her walls crumble and her name slips into the past, she will live only in memories. But she will know that she yields her place to the modern effort to continue her mandate of mercy. The crash of the bulldozer will go away—as did the bark of "Doctor Van" and the patient voice of "Doctor Frank," many years ago.

Her path to demise was strewn with never-to-be-redeemed bonds, the broken dreams of her founders and benefactors, the appreciation of thousands of her old patients, and the horrors of the Great Depression.

She served us well during her comparatively short life and with her passes a part of old Nashville.

The Elks' Club

It limped through the years of national Prohibition with protective eyes always cocked on the front door; was never persuaded that slot machines were illegal; and asserted that every Southern gentleman had an inalienable right to bet on a racehorse. But during all of its years, the old building was not big enough to hold its charitable heart.

From 1850, the old residence at 610 High Street (Sixth Avenue, North), had served as a home, until it was purchased in 1904 for a clubhouse by Nashville Elks' Lodge No. 72.

The two iron elks at the steps guarded the entrance to a familiar meeting place for some of the best citizens of old Nashville. They were a liberal bunch who enjoyed the friendship of each other and the opportunity to share some of their good fortune with those who needed help. They were active in the civic affairs of the community. The American flag flew high and proud over the old clubhouse, and the members were intensely patriotic. It was, indeed, a colorful part of the old city. They had a disdain for pretense and a contempt for false sophistication and hypocrisy. Their goodness was sometimes raw, but always genuine.

As one entered the club, one felt the warmness and the relaxed atmosphere of friendship. The good-natured reception and the satisfaction of a true welcome made a good and lasting impression. Men loved the place. It seemed that when they met there it made them happy and free from the heavy cares of the time. It brought out the bright weather of their hearts and caused them to drift into lasting friendships.

Men of all faiths mingled there without controversy. Their religious differences never extended beyond good humor.

They came to know and to admire the sincerity of the members, the club management, the patrons, and the purposes and objectives of the collective effort. They enjoyed being a part of the civic efforts, and especially the Elks-sponsored Flag Day programs. The annual Christmas party for underprivileged children drew their unanimous support. There are grandmothers and grandfathers today who remember the kindness of these men to them as children of poor families.

Many important business deals, political arrangements, civic undertakings and charitable programs came from those big high-backed rocking chairs that lined the front porch.

Remember the big, happy-hearted Harry Connors telling jokes on the porch in the summer evenings? The distinguished Andrew Sona ensconced in the big chair just inside the front door? The always immaculately dressed Hugo Meadows scurrying around in the building management? Charlie Kalomeyes in animated conversation with Hal Mustaine, Dannie Canfield and Harry Hite? Joe Combs and Tom Mooney singing at the piano? Harry Dahlman, the secretary? Have you forgotten the beautiful stained and leaded glass windows? Who could ever forget the excellent food prepared by chef Henry Laux?

One of the great events of every year was the annual Christmas tree cutting party at the clubhouse preceding the later Christmas party for the underprivileged children. On that occasion, the real liberality of the clan was clearly evident. There was food and drink, good humor, high spirits, together with added interest from the services of Doc Mannion, Campbell Hobson, "Big Boy" Leibengute, and Al Alessio. A few days later the children were invited to the clubhouse for their Santa Claus.

Remember how "Jew" Sam would tear his shirt and pull his hair when he discovered that he had failed to "lay-off" bets he had taken on a winner? Remember Dr. Sam Bernow and his young Elks' Club team of boxers?

Among others often seen there were: Vernon Hines, Bill Mallon, J. D. Spain, Jack Price Jones, Albert Gerst, C. H. and Billy Smith, Chris Kreig, Wiley Embry, Jonas Redelsheimer, Campbell Hobson, Dick Lindsey, Louis Kline, Sid Gross, Frank Petway, Dick McClure, Romans Hailey, Walter Johnson, Mack Fuqua, Roscoe Bond, Reeves Handley, Hudson Coombs, "Dutch" Morrisey, "Slick" Welsh, Guild Smith, Al Alessio and John Ambrose.

Remember how they would decorate the outside of the building with flags, festoons, and red, white and blue streamers on the Fourth of July and other occasions? Did you ever attend one of the dances at the old Elks' Club? Don't forget the "brown bag" and "name on your bottle" days.

During both World War I and II, the doors of the club were often opened to service men.

While the Elks were an established and respected fraternity, its membership maintained an excellent rapport with a large public acquaintance at the old club house and enjoyed a close relation with many who were not members. They continue this and its many community services and charities today in their new facility on Old Hickory Boulevard, near Brentwood. They continue as a valuable and pleasant part of Nashville life.

What Used To Be

We older Nashvillians who have seen most of the twentieth century have also known the life and demise of many well-known institutions and places. As the years have passed many have passed into "what used to be."

Buford College, Ward-Belmont, Radnor College, Miss Annie Allison's School, Wallace University School, Duncan School, Tarbox School, Central High School and Bowen School.

Fort's Infirmary, Barr's Infirmary, Woman's Hospital, Protestant

Hospital, Junior League Hospital for Crippled Children, McGannon's Hospital, Masonic Orphan's Home, Protestant Orphanage, the Home for Blind Girls and the Blind School.

Union Station, old Courthouse, old City Hall, Transfer Station, Stockyards, Gas Works, Criminal Court Building, old Market House, the Hay Market, Market House, and Vauxhall Apartments.

Vine Street Temple, Vine Street Christian Church, Gay Street Synagogue, old West End Methodist Church, Maxwell House Hotel, Andrew Jackson Hotel, Noel Hotel, Tulane Hotel, Clarkston Hotel, Utopia Hotel, Bismarck Hotel, Savoy Hotel and Argonne Hotel.

Sulphur Dell Park, Hippodrome, Ryman Auditorium, Princess Theatre, Knickerbocker Theatre, Bijou Theatre, Glendale Park and Orpheum Theatre.

Link's Depot, Van Blackum Station, Amqui Station, Tennessee Central Depot and Cummins Station.

Hermitage Club Building, Elks' Club Building, Inglewood Golf Club, Fairgrounds "Bull Pen" and Fairgrounds Coliseum.

Burk Building, Old Wesley Hall, Baxter Building, Cumberland Lodge Building, McGavock Block, Nichol Building, Vendome Building, Cotton States Building, Memorial Building.

William Gerst Brewery, old River Wharf, steamboats, passenger trains and street cars.

Old Curry Field, the old bell gate of Mt. Olivet Cemetery, the Fairgrounds dirt race track, the old St. Thomas Hospital, the New Shops, Atlantic Ice Company Building, the Davidson County Building at the Fairgrounds, and the old Police Station.

Did you ever go camping at Fernvale Springs or at T. Allison's place on the Harpeth River?

Remember Herman Ball who operated the Nashville Business College, the Nashville Aircraft School, the Nashville Automobile College—and a women's basketball team?

Did you frequent one of the twenty-nine fraternity or sorority houses around Vanderbilt campus? How about the Palace Hatters on Fourth Avenue? Remember the Postal Telegraph Co., the Matthews Travel Co., the first local travel agent, the Travelers Aid Society at the Union Station, Bert Bacherig's beer garden on Church Street, Strobel's music shop in the Arcade, Matt's newsstand on Fourth Avenue, the Markle pawnshop on the Square and the Saratoga diner on North First Street?

Do you remember Hidden Lake? Did you know that it resulted from an old rock quarry from which stone was cut to build the Union Station in 1899 and 1900?

Have you forgotten that the drummer with Dutch Earhardt in the old "Hancock Syncopators" was a young Nashvillian called "Wonder" Harris? He had been a soda jerker at Sixth and Church. He later went to Hollywood and became known as Phil Harris who made a national reputation as a musician with the big bands, married Alice Faye, the movie actress, and later starred on radio and television as a comedian? Do you remember that his boyhood friend, Adrian McDowell, another young Nashville musician, also went to Hollywood and became the music arranger for the big bands and worked with Bing Crosby and Bob Hope? These two and Mickey Kreitner, the popular former baseball player and local restauranteur were protégés of Miss Rhonda Francis.

Do you remember when the salesmen, or "drummers," as we called them then, stayed at the old Savoy Hotel?

Did you ever try your aim at Sam Shea's shooting gallery at 608 Commerce Street?

Remember Nashville native Admiral Albert Gleaves, who convoyed a million American troops to Europe during World War I, without a single loss?

Did you know these leaders: Baxter Cato, Mrs. John McCall, Glenn Bainbridge, William Beard, W. A. Beasley, Norman Binkley, Dan May, Leslie Boxwell, M. P. Brothers Sr., Henry Dickinson, Paul Davis, "Willie" Geny, Bascom Jones, John Meadors, Frank Stahlman, Evelyn Polk Norton, Dr. John Overton, Ernest Parker, Charles Ragland, Dr. Holland Tigert, Mrs. Julius Weil, Rollie Woodall, or Mrs. M. S. Lebeck?

Have you old-timers forgotten how dense the smog could be in Nashville back in the days of uncontrolled smoke from trains, factories, foundries and other coal-burning businesses and homes?

Remember how O. Henry described Nashville smog in the opening paragraph of his "The Municipal Report":

"Take a London Fog, 30 parts; gas leaks, 20 parts; dew drops gathered in a brickyard at sunrise, 25 parts; odor of honeysuckle, 15 parts. Mix. The mixture will give you an approximate conception of a Nashville drizzle. It is not so fragrant as a mothball nor as thick as pea soup; but it's enough—'t'will serve."

Some called Nashville "The Little Pittsburgh."

The Hermitage Hotel

She stands there like a vain old lady with powder and rouge partially hiding her wrinkles and her facelifts. In her high lace collar and wearing her family heirlooms, she still claims the status of a belle and is proud of her name.

The old Hermitage Hotel reaches out from the past to cling on to the present, but she has never lost her dignity and pride.

Her experience records much of the history of Nashville and Tennessee. Her spacious rooms accommodated presidents, generals, heroes, dignitaries and the famous.

The Hermitage Hotel, 6th Avenue North.

Her ballrooms resounded to the music of Francis Craig, other great bands and the gaiety of the community.

Governors, senators, congressmen, mayors and other political leaders have been named in her smoke-filled rooms.

The spacious old lobby has echoed the hearty laughs of Franklin Roosevelt, the quiet language of Cordell Hull, the sharp voice of Ed Crump, the velvet tongue of Joe Byrns, the quiet tones of Hilary Howse, the stentorian voice of Douglas MacArthur, and many other greats.

Her rooms could tell some interesting stories. Once a young baritone singer, anxious to graduate into an operatic career, was staying in one while competing in the regional finals of a nationwide contest in the War Memorial Building sponsored by a radio company to choose operatic candidates. He lost and in disgust decided to study law instead. Thomas E. Dewey became a U.S. district attorney and later the governor of New York and the Republican candidate for the United States presidency.

A great part of the organized charities of Nashville was determined in her meeting rooms.

She was a beautiful garden for the social flowers of yesterday—until they faded. She was a gallery for the gallants of another day.

She closed her doors and went into mourning. But then she arose and refused to surrender to the passage of time.

She refused to give up the throne of a queen.

She went back to the old trunks, dressed up and decided to turn to the cocktail, gourmet and sophisticated new world.

Refusing to admit her age, and with her head high, she welcomed Nashville back to her old-time elegance and ease.

Today, Nashville loves her wrinkles, rouge and gold-headed cane.

We can still hear Howard Baughman making her comfortable and the strains of "Near You" coming up from "downstairs."

The City Hospital

Her doors of mercy opened in 1890 and they have never been closed since. Over the years since she has struggled to exist, despite her noble objectives, she has been praised and maligned, applauded and criticized, loved and cursed.

The City Hospital, as she was first known, later as the Nashville General Hospital and now as Metropolitan General Hospital, has for the ninety-four years of her life experienced some stormy intervals. During all this time she has been engaged in a continual fight for existence. But through it all she has persevered, refusing to surrender her capacity to serve, and resolute in her determination to remain the institution of mercy closest to those who cannot help themselves.

Until she came upon the local scene, hospitals were owned and operated by members of the medical profession and the universities of the day in conjunction with medical study. As early as 1823 the citizens of Nashville were advocating a public hospital. In fact, in that year the state legislature authorized a lottery for the purpose of earning sufficient money to build a city hospital in Nashville. However, the funds raised were insufficient for the purpose and nothing was done.

In 1879 the Nashville city council authorized the construction of the City Hospital. It began its operation in 1890. During the following year, 1891, a school for nursing was established with the hospital. It was the second school of nursing to be established in the United States; the first was in New Orleans.

Remember the two old, redbrick buildings and the adjacent stable for the horses that pulled the horse-drawn ambulance?

During all this time she has had to withstand the variables of local politics, professional and institutional jealousies and fiscal limitations. She has remained undaunted in her purpose despite the fact that she has often been taken for granted and worked unnoticed. Modernity has sometimes neglected her, but she has continued to do her best with what she had.

Metropolitan General Hospital, Hermitage Avenue.

Many Nashvillians saw the first light of day when they left her doors, and many more saw their last daylight when they entered. She has beamed with pride when she saw young mothers look upon their firstborn with adoration, and she has shed years when her doctors and nurses have tried to break the news of death to loved ones. She has seen her young doctors and nurses, unsung heroes, respond, at all hours of night, when life hung in the balance.

Her emergency rooms have heard the agony of pain, the vulgarity of drunks, domestic discord, the frustrations of children, questioning by police, the pronouncement of "dead on arrival," and the prayers of the anxious.

Many doctors and nurses owe their success to her, and many of us our lives to her.

She has never aspired to sophistication—only to serve. She has never expected enrichment—only the necessities to continue her job.

Remember that dynamic Dortch Woods, that sturdy and reliable Dr. Frank Fessey, that lovable Mrs. Tyner and that kind and generous Dr. John Bauman? These and many others have dedicated their talents and loyalties to her.

She continues there, beside the river, quiet and steady, ready by day and night to receive the sick and injured and to do her best to help them.

She could do much more if she could make as much money as do the private hospitals for their corporate owners.

She has been and continues a part of Nashville's heart. As you pass by on old Hermitage Avenue, say a "thank you" to the grand old lady.

Our State Capitol

The old lady on the hill has looked down upon Nashville and its people for one hundred and thirty years. When the State Capitol first raised her nation's flag in 1853, it waved above only about 16,000 residents. The young city was so proud to have been made the permanent state capital that it bought the property for thirty thousand dollars and gave it to the state of Tennessee, some eight years before the completion of the building.

In the years that have followed, she has watched her immediate community grow into a metropolitan center. Once her shadow reached nearly to the city's extremities, now she is almost hidden by modern "skyscrapers." However, she continues proudly enthroned as the centerpiece of the state.

She has stood by as our people have triumphed and as they have failed—as we have known good fortune and when it was bad. She has suffered with us during epidemics, victories and achievements.

She has represented our love for and duty to our country in times of war and in times of peace. She has proudly represented the Volunteer State and our faith in constitutional government. The strength, order, discipline and governmental accommodation of our people have been largely fashioned in her halls. She has provided the heart and mind of our state structure.

She has known depression and panic as well as good times and prosperity. She has frowned upon slavery and enjoyed the moral, social and political relief with the dawn of freedom for her black citizens.

She has looked upon a city under siege, bloody from battle and occupied by military force while her sons wore different uniforms in battle. She has seen her boys returning in victory from foreign battlefields. She has cried with mothers as they left and rejoiced with them when they returned. She, too, has flown gold star flags.

The architect, William Strickland, modeled her tower after the "Lantern of Demosthenes" erected in Athens in 325 B.C. in honor of the great Greek orator, and which is still standing.

He must have known that she would listen to the eloquence of John Bell, Wilkins Tannehill, Gates Thruston, Robert L. Taylor, Malcolm Patterson, Edward Carmack, Albert Roberts, Austin Peay, Joe Byrns, Cordell Hull, John K. Shields, Gordon Browning, Frank Clement, Bishop McTyeire, Billy Sunday, Kenneth McKellar, Estes Kefauver, Howard Baker, and most of the great speakers of the state and nation.

Many presidents have spoken from her rostrums. Nearly every president of the United States since James K. Polk, European royalty, kings, potentates, sheiks, and thousands of distinguished persons have admired her beauty. Generations have paused at her gates to look upon her with veneration and respect. She has smiled down upon hundreds of thousands of school children who came to see her hallowed halls.

She has officially housed every governor of Tennessee since 1853, thirty-three in all. She has heard the discussions, arguments and debates by thousands as they have met as legislators in her House and Senate chambers.

She has known men in political victory and in defeat—in glory and in shame. She has witnessed integrity and hypocrisy, sincerity and shame, intelligence and ignorance. She has seen some graduate to higher callings, and others forgotten. She has been a molding place for individual greatness.

She has been, and continues to be, a hallmark of Nashville.

James Parton, the eminent biographer of Andrew Jackson, while in Nashville in 1857, wrote:

". . . half a mile from the banks of this stream, is a high steep hill, the summit of which, just large enough for the purpose, would have been crowned with a castle if the river had been the Rhine instead of the Cumberland. Upon the hill stands the Capitol of the State of Tennessee, the most elegant, correct, convenient, and genuine public building in the United States, a conspicuous testimonial of the wealth, taste and liberality of the state.

" 'Pleasant Nashville!' It was laid out in the good old English, Southern manner. First a spacious square for courthouse and market, lined now with stores, so solid and elegant that they would not look out of place in the business streets of New York, whose stores are palaces. From the sides and angles of this square, run the principal streets, and there is your town.

" 'Pleasant Nashville' from the cupola of this edifice the stranger, delighted and surprised, looks down upon the city of Nashville, packed between the Capitol-crowned hill and the coiling Cumberland; looks around the panoramic valley, dotted with villas and villages, smiling with fields, and fringed with dark, forest-covered hills."

It may be that this early picture has faded with the modernity that has surrounded and closed in around the old lady. But she still retains her dignity, beauty and history. She still serves and attracts. No other building in the state—and few elsewhere—has caught the eye of so many, has known so many of the great, has witnessed so much history, or has had a greater part in Tennessee and American life.

She continues to be a link with the past, a servant of the present and available for the future. In the quiet of the night, as the city sleeps and with her architect in her arms, I suspect that she joins her old sisters down the hill—old St. Mary's, McKendree, Church of Christ and Downtown Presbyterian—in a prayer for all of us.

As Nashville changes, she remains serene and majestic on her hilltop throne—the old lady on the hill.

Tennessee State Capitol—1955.

Top: Tom Springfield—
Nashville Automobile Club
and popular civic leader.
Bottom: Rev. Prentice
Pugh—Church of Advent.

Holy Trinity Church.

Dr. Roger Noe—Pastor, Vine
Street Christian Church.

CHAPTER 4

Long, Long Ago
Churches and Schools

C ONCEIVED BY A FEW, for the benefit of a few, it has served but a few at a time, but they have always been, and continue to be, a faithful few. This was, has been, and is today the mission of the Church of the Holy Trinity. The "littlest church" still stands proudly beneath the skyline of her older sisters, almost forgotten and unrecognized by modern Nashville. The story of her origin, struggle for existence, tragedies, sufferings and perseverance is too beautiful to be lost in the pride of progress or the indifference of time.

Church of the Holy Trinity

As the early young city started to move south, the rector of Christ Church perceived that, "Numbers of persons residing in and about Nashville, particularly South Nashville, were destitute of those blessings and privileges that were by others enjoyed in the fold of the Church, and determined upon the establishment of a mission in South Nashville in connection with his own parish church."

A house on Summer Street (Fifth Avenue) was rented and St. Paul's Chapel was begun. This was later to become the Church of the Holy Trinity on High Street (Sixth Avenue), in 1852. However, this was only the beginning of the structure. It would be some years before it was to be the completed building as originally designed by the New York architect. That plan called for a tall spire to extend upward from the battlement still located as its topmost part. The fate of the spire is lost in the memory of the living.

In the beginning there were but a few families in the area upon whom the church could really depend. It was never intended to accommodate a large number of communicants. It was often unable to afford a regular rector. Its early years were plagued by the two cholera epidemics which raged particularly in the South Nashville area. Two of its early rectors fell victim, as well as some of its communicants.

It was always a "free church" and its seats were free. It was supported only by its offertory.

It suffered the full force of the Civil War in the weakness of its infancy. In 1862 it was taken over by the Federal Army and became a powder-magazine for about three months to the utter consternation and fear of its small number of members—and the entire South Nashville neighborhood. It was then used by the Union Army teamsters who were quartered there. The old organ was destroyed, the interior almost stripped and the stained-glass windows were all broken out. The altar was used as a meat block upon which to cut meat for the soldiers. Occasionally, the U.S. Army chaplains held services in its humiliated atmosphere. At the end of the war, the government returned some of its damaged furnishings and paid the church $1,600 for "damages and rent."

A few years later, as the still loyal parishioners struggled with its renovation, the Reverend Moses Royce became its rector and threw his entire energy into the restoration. This was to bring the little band of stalwarts renewed suffering, when, in 1873, Reverend Royce fell a victim to the second cholera epidemic to hit Nashville.

The postwar years were difficult. Church money was scarce. Most of the time it could not afford a rector. However, a few volunteered to serve for different periods. The membership varied from a few to a very few—never strong in resources, never self-sufficient, and never secure—but faithful, steadfast and determined.

As the century came to a close, it found the church still engaged in the struggle to survive on the strength of a small membership. But it was active. It kept its head above the water on into the new century, but by this time South Nashville had became populated by citizens of affluence for the time, and such of those as were Episcopalians were attracted back to Christ Church. Growing means of transportation now made the mother church more attractive. Other denominations prevailed in the neighborhood of Old Trinity. It continued to suffer from the lack of regular rectors. Then, too, the growing commercial character of the city was encircling the church, and other new Episcopal churches were servicing other sections.

Was it a decree of Fate, or the conspiracy of circumstance—what was it that denied her progress and subjected her to such repeated misfortune? Maybe it was just the cruelty of modern expansion that spelled her later hardships. But one must remember that she was only conceived as the "Little Church."

Today she is a memorial to the faithful service of those sturdy Anglican churchmen and their loyal followers. In her present atmosphere of isolation, a busy city now only occasionally notices her ageless Gothic beauty. The beauty of the sacrifice that sustained her is unseen except in the few fading pages of her recorded history. She has long since lost the advantage of the memory of her early struggles in the memory of living men and women.

Cornerstone ceremony—First Lutheran Church, 8th and McGavock (note Union Station).

Today she carries on to serve a Black membership, which has inherited her courage and faithfulness. In the light of history it can be understood that it was, somehow, ordained that her present worshipers would follow her torments, humiliations, and sufferings of a Civil War, to make them free citizens and free churchmen, and succeed to the preservation, protection and love of her heritage.

I think that those who had worked so hard to build and save her would be pleased to know this.

A few days ago, I sat before her altar with only her new young rector. It has been nearly seventy years since I had visited there with an aunt. As the conversation ended, I thought I could still hear a small number of voices responding in hymns to her old organ. I heard the exhaltations and pleadings of those brave and inspired rectors of old, from the pulpit. I thought I could hear the whispers of fear before the onslaught of cholera within its ranks—and then the expressions of horror and hurt from the fear of gunpowder stored within her walls. The rays of the morning sun came through her stained-glass windows, and as they reached her altar, I could see the bloody aprons on soldiers cutting meat upon her sacred altar. I heard soldiers barking at contrary mules nearby. Mingled in with these sounds were the voices of Federal Army chaplains striving to soothe the thoughts of young Yankee soldiers, far from their homes in the "North." And then—I thought that I heard the faint whisper of a young love fade into another tragedy.

Looking toward the windows, I saw the mirrored and pitiful faces of the old "regulars" as they looked in upon what was happening to their "Little Church." As I started to leave I heard them, in their anguish, say—"Thy will be done."

As a small child I remember her as she stood serene and majestic, protected from the heat of the sun by the stately trees that surrounded her. Today the broad expanse of Lafayette Street, a monster of modernity, exposes her naked beauty to the hurried, busy and asphalt reality of the present world. Inside, she calls upon her old strength to maintain the sincerity of her faith.

After shaking hands again with the Reverend James Hall, her new rector for the past three months, I left her, confident that his inspiration, ability and plans would add a chapter of credit to this venerable old part of Nashville.

As I passed out of her old iron gate to go to my car, I had to dodge two automobiles passing her old doors at fifty miles per hour.

Tulip Street Methodist Church

Somewhat off the modern beaten paths, her Neo-Romanesque arch, her architectural beauty and dignity are sometimes lost to the sight of most Nashvillians. However, her old chimes still remind old Edgefield of her presence.

Old Tulip Street Methodist Church is still the revered sanctuary of the forbears of many.

First as the Methodist Church of Edgefield, later as the Russell Street Church, and later as Trinity Church, she was to finally take the name of Tulip Street Methodist Church in 1859. Before the first church was built on the east side of Tulip Street (now Fifth Street), the congregation was meeting in a mission house on Fatherland Street during 1859 and 1860.

At the outbreak of the Civil War the church was still under construction and the congregation met in the basement until the Federal Army took it over for billeting and hospital use, as they did in the case of other Nashville churches. It was turned back to the church in 1868. During the war the membership dropped to 37 members. One year after it reopened, it had 265 members. On September 18, 1892 the present building was completed at a cost of $58,220.12.

After the close of the Tennessee Centennial Exposition at the close of the last century, its ten bells, weighing about five tons, were bought from the city and installed in the main tower of the church.

Today the terra cotta figures over her door seem to stand guard over what time and modernity have done to a once-proud collection of opulent Nashville homes. The total existence of the old church is bound up with a great part of the history of the Methodist Church in our community.

The first glance at her reveals her strength. Her stained-glass win-

Tulip Street Methodist Church.

dows, handcarved doors and pews, her ceiling and altar, all bespeak the beauty of her interior. Her unusually large accommodation has provided a comfortable and dignified sanctuary for eight generations of some of the most distinguished families of Middle Tennessee. Her great organ, now ninety years of age, has accompanied hymns down through all her years. The old organ has 1,400 pipes and is one of the few of that vintage left in the country. Tulip Street is the one church in Nashville with chimes.

Strong men of faith have served her pulpit. Beginning with William Burr, the first minister (1859–1860), thirty-four others have followed. Prominent among them were J. H. Gardner (during the Civil War), J. D. Barbee, John P. McFerrin, J. B. West, T. A. Kerley, A. P. McFerrin, W. B. Ricks, W. T. Haggard, T. G. Ragsdale, D. M. Asmus, J. Allison Mulloy, W. Angie Smith, B. B. Pennington, D. E. Hinkle, E. P. Anderson and A. Faxon Small.

Thousands of Nashvillians have knelt at her altar rail. Among the families whose succeeding generations have claimed Tulip Street as their church were: the Horace Smiths, H. W. Grantlands, W. C. Diehls, D. T. Strattons, J. H. Yarbroughs, W. A. Bensons, H. C. Gardners, J. M. Warrens, F. P. McWhirters, Shade Murrays, W. M. Pollards, T. L. Dismukes, Irby Morgans, W. T. Huggins, Paul Riddles, R. T. Morrisons, Byrd Murrays, T. L. Herberts, Will Arringtons, W. S. Riddles.

And then there were E. B. Jones, E. W. Turnley, Volney James, C. H. Rutherford, W. B. Marr, Cecil Woods, A. L. P. Green, Roy Miles, Ernest Chadwell, Lowe Watkins, Robert L. White, White Hall Morrison, Hugh Freeman, Howard Pardue, the Green and Hicks families. Only a few of these are now living, but the new generations travel from all parts of the city to the church of their fathers.

Today, with nearly a century and a half behind her, she continues a strong and vigorous force in the religious life of our city. She has seen the Civil War, two cholera epidemics, two tornadoes and the East Nashville fire rage around her, but she has always stood tall and weathered all storms, to remain the Grand Old Lady of Tulip Street.

St. Patrick's Church

She stands there on old Market Street, a little sad in her old age, but wrapped in the dreams of her importance to South Nashville in the past.

When the young and dynamic priest, Father T. C. Abbott, built her in 1890, she took her place with St. Mary's (1830), and the Church of the Assumption (1858), in the service of the young Catholic population of

St. Patrick's Church.

the city. The new church was to accommodate the growing influence of the South Nashville population which contained about 232 Catholic families. Included among them were: Timothys, Metzs, Breens, Baltzes, Sloweys, Flanigans, Martins, Byrds, Welchs, Burns and Mahoneys. Father Abbott was such a driving force and the citizens so interested that funds were collected and the church was built in about one year. Leading citizens like William Gerst and Charles Nelson, and many Protestant neighbors, were heavy contributors to the necessary costs. It is interesting to note that the famous pugilist and idol of the Irish, John L. Sullivan, made a substantial contribution.

With the church completed, the school began what would prove to be a great service to the community.

A strict administrator of church affairs, Father Abbott was also a firm but fair schoolmaster. He was a continuous help and encouragement to the serious-minded student, tolerant of the ordinary weaknesses of youth, forgiving of minor offenses—but impatient with the indolent and troublemakers. More than one errant young Irishman has had the course of his life corrected by the switch and paddle of Father Abbott.

The success of Father Abbott and the Sisters of Mercy, was to become the later success of their "children" in the religious, professional, business, political and social life of Nashville.

St. Patrick's became the focus of all Irish and Catholic activities and interests in South Nashville. By reason of her name and dedication, she naturally became the center of the annual St. Patrick's Day celebrations in the entire city. The shamrock was never more green, and the head on the beer was never stronger than on Market, College, and Cherry Streets, on each March 17th.

The large St. Patrick representation was the most prominent fixture of the colorful annual parade. The leaders, dressed in their "Sunday best," and wearing big green badges, rode in their "tally-ho" at the head of each parade. They were followed by bands, contingents from other churches, members of the fire and police departments, labor unions, the plumed Knights of Columbus, the Hibernians, and the Irish in general.

After the parade, they would return to the church for further services, and then to their homes for a jolly evening. It was their big day, with feasts—and their beer. The South Nashville saloons of Zuccarello, Hackman and Pomeroy stayed open to a late hour to accommodate those who were "rushing the can" (buying beer by the bucket). The strains of "My Wild Irish Rose" poured from the gatherings. Here and there one could hear toasts like, "Faith and begorrah; he was a fine bloke, he was; Lass, fill up me mug again while I speak a tribute to the temperance of Old Paddy." And: "'Eres to St. Patrick, wish he was here to drive some of the snakes out of Varmint Town."

On this day, South Nashville was truly, "A bit of old Ireland."

The neighbors and Protestants joined in and would say in good humor, "He's as Irish as Pat's pig—he has to go to St. Patrick's today to get his tail painted green," to the delight of the local sons and daughters of Erin.

When one of their number died, there often followed the "Irish Wake." These were stories of their own. It was sometimes difficult to know when the sorrow ended and the pleasure began—or vice-versa.

The ever-moving gypsy population of the country selected St. Patrick's as their church and came at an appointed time each year to have Father Abbott honor their dead. They would come to Nashville in their colorful wagons and camp along Brown's Creek, south of the railroad, and on Franklin Road, to be near the church.

When the church was in need of repairs or painting, Father Abbott would conscript the necessary labor from among his flock with the authority of an army drill sergeant. He took no excuses. He counted the church pennies like a miser.

The South Nashville Irish were a strong, sturdy, honest, hard-working, patriotic, loyal, good-natured and God-fearing people— good, substantial citizens who contributed much to the young city. They loved their heritage, honored their church, and stuck together.

As the city moved west, the sun began to dim on St. Patrick's. Her most generous supporters and influential members began to prosper and seek the more comfortable and affluent accommodations of the more modern western district.

The death of Father Abbott at 77, on May 30, 1932, began the closing years of her prominence in the Nashville Catholic world. As he grew old and infirm, a splendid young priest, Father George Flannigan carried on the duties of the church until the appointment of Father John Murphy as a successor.

The school closed in 1954.

Few, extremely few, of her old communicants and students are still living. Some, like that elegant gentleman, Jack Flannigan, still kneel at her altar. Each time they leave the old edifice, they carry away renewed memories of her old greatness and leave a little part of their hearts.

If one walks around her grounds, one can still hear the laughter and fun of her picnics, school recesses, entertainments, celebrations, and bazaars. When one enters her silent interior, one can still hear the beauty of her mass. When one enters her old school rooms, the voice of Father Abbott still takes command.

As old Nashville passes, old St. Patrick's takes her place in the parade—feeble, but still proud.

The Old Jewish Synagogues

Some of the earliest churches of the Protestant Christians and Catholics of old Nashville still remain, but all vestige of the early meeting places and synagogues of the Jews lie buried beneath the progress of the city.

The old houses of Hebrew worship of Isaac Garriton, Isaac Gershon, K.K. Mogen David, Ohave Shalom, B'nai Yeshurun, Sherith Israel, together with the later Gay Street and Vine Street synagogues gave way to "uptown changes." This was due in part to the fact that from the time the first "wandering Jew," a pack-peddler, is said to have left a steamboat at a landing below Ashiand City and made his way to the young city, to be followed by the "five families and eight young men," they settled "in town." The further facts that they were by nature and history a gregarious people and were attracted to trading brought them to locate in the central part of Nashville. From their earliest arrivals to 1902, Market Street, (Second Avenue) was the residential beginning and community of Jewry.

K. K. Mogen David was the first Jewish synagogue in our city.

As was the case with the first Catholics, in the purchase of the Mt. Calvary burial ground—the earliest Jewish people here bought a burial ground on the old Buena Vista Pike before they built their first synagogue.

Rabbis Iser, Labshiner, Kaleish, Wise, Goldamer, Kantrovich, Welcher, Staltzman and others all worked diligently with the early 320 Jewish men, women and children here by 1861—their number grew to 1800 by 1901—to establish their community and to foster their faith. The entire population of Nashville in 1901 was 80,865. They nurtured the small group, inspired them to characteristic perseverance, and guarded their faith and heritage.

During the nineteenth century the American Christian religions were splintered into many groups, resulting in various denominations and sects, as the result of the new constitutional freedom of religion and in protest to the ecclesiasticism of churches. Early Judaism had the same experience in America—and in Nashville.

Coming with old world differences in language, customs, and liturgy, they found discord and division. It was natural that each strived for a ritual likened to that which he or she had known from birth. By 1901 there were three factions of Judaism—orthodox, reformed and conservative. However, their differences lay in ritualism, not in religious differences. The age-old central doctrine of "Shema Yisrael" (the belief in one God), with emphasis on a way of life instead of strict adherence to a particular dogma, has always persevered. The central theme of Judaism prevailed in the early churches as, indeed, it does today in the local modern and beautiful houses of Hebrew worship.

During this period of local divisiveness Rabbi Isaac Wise came to be the focal force of reconciliation and understanding.

The older Nashvillians of today will remember mostly the Gay Street and Vine Street synagogues. The cornerstone of the latter was laid in August of 1874 and its first service was held on Sept. 29, 1875. The cornerstone of Gay Street Synagogue was laid on Aug. 29, 1901, and its first service was conducted on Sept. 13, 1902.

Vine Street Temple.

During the last fifty years of the nineteenth century and the first fifteen of the twentieth this small number of immigrants from Russia, Poland, Hungary, and Germany, mostly, and their American born descendants had, through hard work, discipline, dedication, perseverance and firm faith, founded and built a strong and influential sector of Nashville. They were now a substantial and solid part of the economic, business, civic and social life of the community. These two new synagogues were the result of this progress and the beginning of the residential change and they were to continue through the first 50 years of the twentieth century.

The Jewish people started to move out of the old sections of Market, College, Cherry and Summer Streets. As the city had grown they

Gay Street Synagogue.

began to operate stores both in the inner and outer city—usually one in each community. They were most often dry goods, notions and clothing stores.

The beautiful and inspiring Byzantine architecture of Vine Street Temple, with its central, massive bulb-like dome, a second lower tier of four smaller ones and the still lower tier of four yet smaller ones, caused it to stand out boldly against the background of surrounding buildings—a bit of old Russia at first glance. On Seventh Avenue between Church and Commerce it ranked with the Hermitage, Capitol, McKendree and First Presbyterian churches and the Parthenon in interest to visitors to the city. Its stained glass windows, beautiful carved oak ark and candelabra and other features of its interior added charm to the structure. It continued to attract learned and energetic rabbis who, in addition to their duties to the synagogue and congregation, became active in the civic and social life of Nashville. Some, like Julius Mark, went on to higher callings in American Judaism. This new synagogue for Jews of the Reformed branch was to have an organ and the seating of men and women together—comparatively new to synagogues.

The Gay Street Synagogue remained with the original situs of the old Jewish community until its demise. The older cantors, readers, schockets (ritual slaughterers), and mohels (those who circumcised) continued in the vicinity. Some old families were loath to leave their old familiar section. The synagogue was more toward orthodoxy. It faced the Capitol from the north side of Gay Street. In Sherith Israel the women and men were divided and separated in seating, as they continue to be today.

As this hard-working and thrifty people began to attain financial independence and a fixed status, and with the steady withdrawal of all uptown residents before the rapid encroachment of growing commercial and business needs for expansion, the Jewish residents started to forsake their old original habitats and join the move westward. So did their synagogues.

Today the three, representing the orthodox, reformed and conservative elements, are located on West End Avenue and Harding Road. So is the greater number of the Jewish population of Nashville now living in the vicinities of their present synagogues.

In the imposing beauty, attractive and comfortable accommodations and services, they all three represent the rewards of the hard work of these good people and their rabbis of the past, as well as the continued proud and dedicated faith of their children and successors.

This story would be incomplete did it not include a tribute to the contributions of Rabbi Isadore Lewenthal—one of the great leaders of our old community. Not only was he held in high esteem by the entire Jewish community, regardless of synagogue affiliation, but by reason of the fact that he lent his talents to every activity which resulted in a better Nashville, he was regarded with great respect by the entire city. He was a Mason, a Shriner, an Elk and an active member of the literary and cultural organizations. He was indefatigable in work for orphans, the handicapped, the poor and the sick of all faiths. A gentle man, with a sweet disposition and personal charm, he was a deep scholar, an avid reader, a strong intellect and a natural leader of men.

As the young Hebrew boys and girls enter their Nashville synagogues today, they can know that they enter a provision that was made for them by the firm resolution of strong and sturdy men and women, small in number but large in dedication to the Jewish faith. In every brick and stone of their comfortable edifices is the "blood, sweat and tears" of the protectors of the faith.

Acklen Hall

Acklen Hall looks down upon the commercialism of Sixteenth Avenue today with her head held as high and as regal as when she looked over the green of the countryside before the Civil War. Her stately structure was the plantation house of Joseph and Adelicia Acklen, built in 1850. Its design was in part the work of the renowned architect William Strickland, the architect of the state capitol and the Downtown Presbyterian Church.

It became Ward-Belmont College for Women in 1913 as the result of the merger of Belmont and Ward's Seminary for Young Ladies. The seminary had been founded by the Presbyterian minister in 1865 and was located on Spruce Street (Eighth Avenue) between Church and Broad streets.

Its forerunner had been Dr. Elliott's Female Academy, founded in 1816 at the corner of Church Street and Ninth Avenue. It was one of the earliest and largest girls colleges of its kind in the country.

For nearly forty years, from 1913 to 1951, when Ward-Belmont succumbed to financial distress, she earned and deserved the reputation of being one of the best known colleges for young women in the nation. This position in the American education world, together with her beautiful campus and buildings, associated her with Vanderbilt, Peabody, Fisk, Meharry, the Parthenon and the Hermitage, in the identification of Nashville as the "Athens of the South."

Throughout her life Ward-Belmont was recognized not only for her

Ward Seminary.

high scholastic requirements but also for her strictly controlled conservative dignity—and her Southern character. Her halls, grounds, activities, regulations and general atmosphere carried the tradition of magnolias and young ladies of the Old South. She held steadfastly to what was required of a lady and one of good mind. She harbored no short cuts or easy paths to education. She placed great value on charm and grace as a correct complement to intelligence. She was strict but pleasant and happy.

To understand the real contribution of the college one needs only to borrow from the memories and loyalties of her former students. They look back upon their association with her with the same satisfaction that they receive from reexamining a valued family heirloom. She placed an enduring name-brand in the character and personality robes of her girls. In homes all across the country mothers and grandmothers turn the pages of their old *Milestones*, the school annual, to proudly tell their children of their school days at Ward-Belmont.

Do you remember the Corinthian Room, the ivy-covered tower, the stables, the statuary and the lawn swings?

Did you ever have your picture taken while sitting in the gazebo or while seated on the iron deer?

Remember the clubhouses and the Triad, Ariston, Eceowasin, Penta Tan, Asiron and other clubs?

Remember the day students' clubhouse with Ro Wyde presiding? Remember the fun of Flag Day?

Can you ever forget Mrs. Ottarson, Miss Morrison, Miss Amalie Throne or Ms. Susan Souby?

Did you dance around the May Pole at the annual May Day celebrations?

Remember the carriage and horses that carried the queen and her maids? Remember Junior-Senior Prep Day? Do you recall the selection of "Miss Belmont"?

And you oldies—do you remember that lovable Dr. Blanton? When you could not go downtown without your hat and long white gloves? Where you could not cross the big rug in Acklen Hall unless you were properly dressed? When you had to conform to the requirements of the chaperone?

Remember when the Belmont streetcar stopped at the entrance? The hockey teams? Jabbering and giggling after "lights out"? Going to Vanderbilt football games on old Curry Field? Class elections? Graduation exercises? The first days of a new term? Getting homesick?

Do you recall when the mother of one of the local girls insisted on her daughter coming to school daily all dressed up in Southern Belle dresses and the school handled the situation by requiring the first uniforms—shirts, middy blouses and black neckerchiefs? Do you remember when a very prominent girl was caught smoking and being threatened with expulsion a number of you protested by transferring to Peabody?

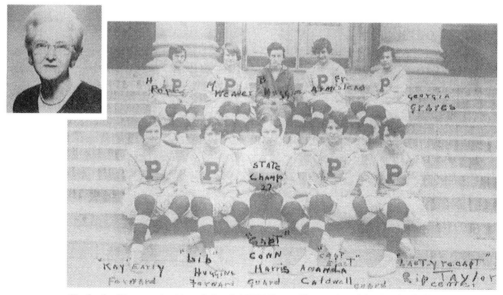

Peabody Demonstration School 1927 State Championship Basketball Team (Inset: Miss Bernice Huggins, coach—also center of back row).

Was anybody ever more devoted to her girls than Miss Annie Allison? Remember when she closed her school and came to Ward-Belmont?

Though formal in many respects, the college recognized the natural instincts, impulses and inclinations. She sought to advance these qualities and mold them with intelligence, charm and unsophisticated beauty in the women. This formality never lost sight of the clever, humorous and good-natured side of life. The little country girl who came to her from Grinder's Switch left as an example of how personality, character, charm and grace were wedded to the capacity for clean humor and the fun of life.

The school closed in 1951 when the properties were acquired by the Tennessee Baptists and started to operate as Belmont College, a coeducational institution.

Acklen Hall has not allowed her beauty to be lost to time or modernity. It has not been less carefully preserved in the memories of her girls. They still see her, in those memories, as the queen of the gardens of their school days.

The day is not too distant when memories of her as "my alma mater" will have faded forever. She will remain only as a part of the history of old Nashville, buried in old archives. But what she instilled in her girls will live in the character of their children. And old Acklen Hall will soon lend her beauty and dignity to a third century of Nashville.

Vanderbilt University

Originating as a Methodist Church school and made possible by the friendship of Commodore Cornelius Vanderbilt and Bishop McTyeire, Vanderbilt University opened on the western limits of Nashville on Oct. 3, 1875. Few of us will remember the university and its campus during any part of its first 50 years. However, there are a few things and persons of the old Vanderbilt that we who were on the campus will never forget.

Who could ever forget Chancellor Kirkland, Dean Tolman, Dr. Steele, Dean Schuerman, Dr. Mayfield, Dean Tillet, Dr. "Eddie" Mimms, Dean Keeble or Mrs. Haggard?

Bishop McTyeire.

They walked the paths of the campus when its original 75 acres was a quiet, dignified and beautiful park-like area. Do you remember when we had only College Hall, Wesley Hall, Furman Hall, the Engineering Hall with the adjoining power house, Kissam Hall, the old gym, "Westside Row," and the chancellor's home?

Do you recall that the entire security force of Vanderbilt University was "Cap" Alley who spent most of his time riding around the campus in his pony buggy and shooting sparrows with his "B.B." gun? Do you remember his "tongue-tied" speech?

Do you remember when the only place to eat was at Kissam or Wesley Hall on the campus, and at Nelson Nellums' pie wagon at the gate, Pat Hager's University Pharmacy soda fountain, or that of Phil Johnson's? When the college dances and proms were held in the old gym building?

Do you remember the Wednesday chapel meeting in College Hall, the attendance at which was required—and Chancellor Kirkland pre-

Kirkland Hall, Vanderbilt University.

siding? The football games on old Curry Field; Bomar, Reese, Wakefield, Sharp, Neil, Ryan, Lawrence, Kuhn, Rives, Kelley, Waller and Cargile? How about McGugin, Hardage and Cody? The track team of Sneed, Stahlman, "Rabbit" Curry, Payne, Casey and Motlow—champions?

Do you remember how Fred Russell, "Hap" Motlow and Red Sanders used to sit on the porch of the ATO House thinking up devilish practical jokes to play on people?

Do you remember when we led that innocent and naive young man from Alabama to believe that we were sincere in electing him the "Freshman B.U. (Bachelor of Ugliness)" at a rally on Church Street? Do you remember how sick our guilt made us when he died a short time later and we learned why he had been so naive?

Did you ever "rush" the Princess Theatre after a Church Street pep rally and try to cheat the curfew getting in or out of Kissam Hall? How about the fight between Tom Ryan and Alf Sharp on Church Street? Do you remember when someone painted the shoes on the Commodore's statue white—and the tongue-lashing all of us got from the chancellor at the next chapel? Have you forgotten the student of one of the professors of religion who bootlegged "White Mule" on the campus and on the train on football trips?

Do you remember the open-sided Hillsboro street cars that stopped at the Phi Delta Theta house? The Glee Club? The Vanderbilt players? Scribblers? Lotus Eaters and the Masquerader?

Do you remember when *The Hustler* got into trouble over some of its jokes—and stories? When the uniform of the band was a pair of white duck pants and a dark coat of your own and you had to furnish your own instrument? When "Blinkey" Horn and Grantland Rice reported on Vanderbilt athletic events?

Remember the lovable Dean Sarratt, the attractive Dr. H. B. Schermerhorn, the gracious and kind Mrs. Ellen Chester and good old Doctor Ott? When the Medical and Dental Schools were located in South Nashville? The chancellor's iris garden? Bob Orr and his long fur coat—about the first student to come to school in an automobile. "Freshman" Cross? Dean Keeble's frock coat?

Do you remember the enforced classes in physical education at the old gym and the bath and dressing rooms in the basement? The old bell sounding the hour at College Hall? The $10 deposit which had to be made when registering for chemistry classes to pay for broken glass tubing, etc? When "student tickets" for all football games sold for $6? When Vanderbilt played Michigan and the Quantico Marines? The "B.U." elections?

Do you remember Thelma Harrell, the first woman admitted to the Law School? When the government first paid the tuition of boys who had missed early college because of their service in World War I? When it cost fifty cents for your picture from A. J. Thuss to go into the *Commodore?* Inspections at Kissam Hall? The water coolers? The benches around the campus? Dr. Tobar, the Spanish teacher, Mr. Van Hook, and Jimmy Melton? The old observatory? Freshman hazing?

How about the annual Vanderbilt-Sewanee football games? The Fugitives? Bachelor Maids? The Arts Club?

Today, after one hundred and eight years, Vanderbilt is one of the great universities of the country with its continued reputation for insistence on high scholastic standards. Its contribution to the professions and the arts and sciences has been felt throughout the world.

The campus, now crowded with buildings and surrounded by the expanding business of the city, is a veritable beehive of activity. Increased enrollment has made necessary high-rise dormitories.

Modern demands on university education have demanded facilities which fill every available space. The hospital and medical school have made the total campus into a city of itself. As in the case of many old institutions, all this has turned the original beautiful acreage into a brick and concrete jungle with slightly more than narrow walkways outside the buildings.

Campus life has changed into a rushing, competing, regimented dash toward modernity. The old sounds of birds singing, the wind blowing through the trees, dogs barking and the clang of street cars have given way to the noise of hustle, speed, motors and machinery.

Nashville Bible College (now David Lipscomb).

The old lazy, quiet, comfortable and dignified campus is now a boiling cauldron of human activity, moving in all directions, with many purposes and objectives and in constant struggle for position and opportunity. Correctly unsatisfied with the present, it is geared to a relentless effort to prepare for an equally different future.

As some of us pass by today, we like to think that we look through all this to our day on the old campus.

Talking about changes with the passing of time, think what: Bishop McTyeire would say if he listened in on some of the discussions of religion on campus today; What Dean John Bell Keeble would say about some of the late decisions of the Supreme Court of the United States; What Dean Schuerman would say about the technology and engineering feats of the present—and computers especially; What Doctor Breckinridge would say about the present wonderful world of chemistry and what it is producing?

What would the graceful Dr. Sanborn say about the philosophy of the present? Can't you hear "Eddie" Mimms exploding over what is selling today as literature? Can't you see the face of "Chance" Kirkland looking upon some of the campus conduct of today?

Can't you see the amazed look on the face of "Cap" Alley if he saw the pistols strapped on the security officers and the elaborate security system necessary to protect the campus? What would Coach McGugin or Grantland Rice say about paying a football player over a million dollars per year?

Montgomery Bell Academy

The history of Montgomery Bell Academy almost parallels the history of Nashville. The alumni of each of the succeeding past one hundred years could refer to "The Old MBA." Although the child was not named, it was really born in 1785. Actually, its great-grandfather was Davidson Academy; its grandfather was Cumberland College; its father was the University of Nashville, with which it spent its first years; its rich uncle was Montgomery Bell, Nashville's "Iron Man," whose name it finally came to have in 1867. It was an established institution of learning before it came to have the name.

It had become an established part of the educational world of Nashville that later attracted Vanderbilt University, Fisk University and Central Tennessee College, the fore-runners of Meharry College and others. Like the other Nashville educational institutions, it was born in South Nashville and later moved west.

Likewise, it was an established private school for boys long before

Wallace, Duncan, Peabody Demonstration School, Bowen and others came and has continued as such as they have left the scene.

It is interesting to note that it came into existence with the following prescribed discipline: "It would be improper to suffer students to attend assemblies, balls, theatrical exhibitions, parties of pleasure and amusement; and more, to frequent gambling tables, taverns and places of dissipation. They should seldom indulge themselves in going into town, except on necessary business, which should be dispatched hastily, that they may return to school without delay."

Now, the space allotted me here will not permit a discussion as to whether John Sloan, Fred Lucas, Tom Sneed, and others I could name, while students at the academy, adhered to this prescription. Seriously, however, the school has maintained through all of its years, an attractive discipline, especially as regards study.

There was a further restriction enacted by the legislature, to the

Montgomery Bell Academy.

effect that: "No ordinance, rule or by-law should ever be entered into so as to give a preference to any denomination of Christians." The school has certainly adhered to this admonition.

Today the $20,000 gift by Montgomery Bell would hardly pay for the new fence around the grounds. The rocks in the old fence are worth more than that amount.

It is continuously appropriate that the old cannon should hold a fixed place on the campus. Montgomery Bell made part of that $20,000 by supplying all the cannon balls which General Andrew Jackson used in 1812, in the Battle of New Orleans.

The standards set by its early administrations have continued to give strength to the purposes and objectives of the school. They gave it an early place in the reputation of the city as the "Athens of the South." They are the real reason for its longevity. They continue to be its attraction.

Its administrators, faculties and institutional conduct have made it one of the most thorough and excellent of American schools. Its contribution to the life of Nashville has been invaluable. But even more than all this, its contribution to individual character, ability, disciplined education and morality of its young men has structured its most enduring gem. It is a remembered, appreciated and honored part of the life of all who have shared its blessings.

With such a great heritage, it bears a great responsibility and challenge today.

Education in these United Stated today, and especially secondary education, is seriously suspect. The American people are justifiably disturbed over the present condition of our schools and their products. I submit to you that the basic education of our young boys and girls, and, for that matter, our young men and women in higher education as a necessary preparation for proper and productive life is being challenged by a misconception of priorities, the temptations of indolence and pleasure, and a down-grading of importance.

The good mind is being allowed to become secondary to the pursuit of entertainment, unrestrained personal and social behavior, and extracurricular activities.

As the young student has seen his parents indulge in license instead of discipline, he or she has claimed the same right. As the supposed image-maker has sloughed off, so has the image-taker.

The difficult and demanding task of study, learning, and the feeding of the computer of our minds is being compromised by the taking of the easy road and trusting to luck or being the beneficiary of a favorable conspiracy of circumstance. There exists an awesome lack of discipline necessary to assure the requirements of academic education. Many are too quick to excuse a total indifference to its importance and necessity.

In short, we face the sad fact that too many young people have lost the will to improve their minds, and, worse than that, our adult society seems too busy in their own distractions to enforce a change of their attitudes.

There is a strong question as to where emphasis is being placed in our school, college and university programs and whether that emphasis is not misplaced.

There is serious question as to whether the emphasis on academic education is not being robbed by a growing interest centered on extra-curricular activities for revenue to satisfy the entertainment-hungry public.

The exploitation of these things is a cruel hoax. It is our young who will ultimately suffer from such diversion of the basic purposes and objectives of educational institutions.

It is not only dangerous, but unfair, to leave young boys and girls to their own electives and their own sense of discipline in matters pertaining to their education. They are not prepared for such, especially in view of the temptations of modern life. In short, they need the guidance of parents, and the schools need the same thing. And the school must stand firm in its requirements and restrictions.

It is here that MBA has earned, and deserves, its name.

It is here that Montgomery Bell Academy, its administration, its teachers, its students, its parents and its alumni, are in a splendid position, by heritage, experience, and past accomplishments, to lead the way back to the main track. The institution can embrace no finer objective for itself and for this community. Let it be set in concrete that the main objective of the school is a sound basic academic education for its students, that it will be satisfied with nothing less, and that all other interests are secondary.

Let it be further set in concrete, that Montgomery Bell Academy decries and denies the present-day view that makes too many of us consider ourselves born geniuses and, therefore, infer that we need not learn more and work hard, that all we will need will come to us by some happy inspiration the moment it is called for.

Let it be further set in concrete that Montgomery Bell Academy stands by its original standards of academic excellence. The insistence on this by the school accounts for its great worth. The early prescription of its administrators has preserved the quality of its standards. This is continually rediscovered and appreciated by succeeding generations. It has introduced thousands to the honor rolls of American universities.

Hume-Fogg High School

She stands on her native ground, dreaming of the past, but still striving to serve the present.

She opened her doors to her first class on February 26, 1855, there on the corner of Broad and Spruce Street (Eighth Avenue).

As she has grown old she has gathered the strength to persevere from her pride in her contribution to Nashville. As she is buffeted by the vicissitudes of time she finds comfort in the appreciation, respect and love of her sons and daughters as they have grown old with her.

But old Hume-Fogg is unwilling to surrender.

She was the first public school in Nashville; until 1917 she was the only public high school in Davidson County. She has gone on to outlive her younger sister, Central High. She has also outlasted her so-

Hume-Fogg High School.

phisticated private contemporaries—Wallace, Duncan, and Peabody Demonstration—all but M.B.A.

Her hold on the hearts and memories of thousands of our citizens is still as strong as her fortress-like structure.

Many can still hear the voices of Professor Kirkpatrick, Ms. Della Dortch, Mrs. Friel, Mrs. Goodwin, Mr. Perry, Mr. Lipscomb, Professor Oliver, and many others.

The old lady still thrills at the victories of Monk Sharp, Jack Diamond, Jonas Coverdale, the Richters, Phil Cohen, and the other "champions of the blue and white."

She remembers the class picnics at Glendale Park and Shelby Park—and the *Echo*.

She remembers the pie-wagon parked out front and the street cars coming and going on Broadway and Spruce Street.

She remembers watching the parades go by—especially those that followed six wars, when many of her sons were returning from battlefields.

She cries when she remembers the gold-star flags she flew in memory of her boys who did not return.

She retains great pride in the success of so many of her children and she weeps from the misfortunes of some.

She remembers the "angel class" of 1916—so named because in that year the second wing was added to the building.

She has watched every building over three stories high, in Nashville rise above her.

She was there to welcome Vanderbilt University into the local field of education, and to later furnish some of her most outstanding graduates.

Her annuals are stored in more Nashville homes than those of any other school or university.

Through her doors have passed the young of many colors, many tongues, and many faiths—and they have all been made better by her guiding hand.

As you pass, tip your hat to the old lady—she has been a solid part of our life.

Central High School

Born in 1917 as the first Davidson County public high school, she was a public orphan until 1921. For the first four years of her life, Central High School had no home but lived first with her little sister, Schwab School, on Dickerson Road and later, for three years, in two exhibit buildings at the State Fairgrounds. She found the home that thousands of us were to love in 1921, on Rains Avenue.

She expired, a victim of the growing Nashville. Her comparatively short life as a public institution was remarkably productive and vigorous and left a deep memory with her sons and daughters. She saw some of them leave her doors as mere lads in the uniform of her country, for service in World War I. She lived to see two of them become mayors of Nashville, and others to become successful doctors, lawyers, judges, ministers, engineers, journalists, authors and businessmen in our community and elsewhere.

She prepared them for the new world of automobiles, electronics, airplanes, radio, television, computers, plastics, aluminum and atomic power.

With no pretense or sophistication she received them from all levels and walks of life. They came to her on foot, on horseback, in buggies and on streetcars, from the four corners of the county.

Men—good men, like professors Carney, Hooper, Caldwell, Smelser, Hutchinson, Moss.

Central High School.

And ladies—queens, like Miss Doyle, Mrs. Fontaine, Mrs. Waller, Miss Sloan, Miss Sneed.

They all received them like a big family and bonded them together in love and appreciation of their opportunities. They took what little they were given to work with in the way of buildings, equipment and facilities, and built it into a great institution, by dedication, hard work and perseverance.

In the early years it was not easy. At the Fairgrounds the buildings were cold and heated only with coal burning stoves, with makeshift classrooms and toilets, no modern school facilities, and no athletic field or equipment, no gymnasium or uniforms. But in her poverty, she held her head high and began to claw her way to recognition.

Do you remember the first uniforms of the football team? Overalls. Do you remember the first practice field? The bullpen.

Have you forgotten the construction of the roller-coaster and how it was first tried out by the students—free?

And do you remember how it was considered patriotic for the boys to wear overalls during the war?

Do you remember Governor Roberts coming out at assembly during the war—the first time any of us ever saw a governor?

You men now, do you remember the annual visit of a speaker to warn us of the danger of sex relations and the possible consequences?

You ladies now, do you remember Mrs. Fontaine's cooking and sewing classes? Some of us still have indigestion from eating your early cooking.

Do you remember catching the dinky or walking over to the Nolensville streetcar line?

Do you remember that pretty and efficient secretary to the principal named Imogene?

The old *Megaphones* will remind you of the athletic exploits of the "blue and gold," and names like Jones, Boone, Paul, Sexton, Knight, Currey, Muse, Sneed, Joslin, Perkerson, Whitsitt, Hagey and others?

Do you recall names like West, Hines, Farrar, Finley, Alexander, Bennett, Torrence, Lester, and many others who were to play such a great part in the later life of the county?

Do you remember that Davidson County Central High School was the first high school in the county to have a system of student government, which was to be later copied all over the nation?

Have you forgotten how proud we were to move into our first real home—the new building?

When she left the scene, she bequeathed to her succeeding family of younger sisters a set of standards, a pride, and a look to the future.

She took her public name with her—but not from the hearts of her boys and girls.

Tarbox School

To many old Nashvillians the mention of the word "school" brings to mind instantly the name "Tarbox." They are carried back to blackboards, pot-bellied heaters, desks, paperwads, slates, recesses and schoolday sweethearts. Nostalgia attempts the return of the irreconcilable pleasantness of their early school days, with sentiment and a bit of yearning. Then follows the parade of familiar faces and youthful experiences.

Tarbox School.

Named for L. T. Tarbox, one of our earliest educators, the first Tarbox School was a frame building on Seventeenth Avenue. The three-story brick building was built in 1876 at the corner of Broad Street and Eighteenth Avenue, South. An addition was added in 1928. From 1856 through 1861 Professor Tarbox had served as the principal of the old high school in Edgefield. Located on the then tree-lined Broad Street it was considered an imposing building of three stories and a bell tower. It was the pride of the growing community and by the early part of this century it was centered in a population density that allowed 98 percent of its pupils to walk to school.

Professor George Elliot was the first principal and some of the early teachers were Mrs. Emma Clemons, Prof. Bailey, Prof. A. M. Cavert, Mrs. Corinne Eastman and Miss Priscilla Polk. The first four were later to have city schools named for them. Mrs. Clemons, later the principal, was the first woman school principal in Nashville.

Among some of the early students were: Albert E. Hill, Dr. John J. Tigert, James G. Stahlman, Kate Zerfoss, Ed Craig, William Waller, Dr. Lucius Burch, Ross Hopkins, Merrill Moore, Charles Rolfe, Buford Wilson, W. B. Marr, Kirk and Dan Rankin, Bailey Roscoe, Mary Stahlman, Wilbur Creighton, George Hearn, Linday Ray, Maurice Weinberger, the seven Adams boys and many others whose names later became prominent in Nashville life.

In those days the boys were separated from the girls in the study hall by an aisle. The rest rooms were on the outside.

Do you remember the "shute"—the metal fire escape built on the side of the building—and the fire drills? They later proved their importance when, on April 1, 1932, fire did great damage to the building. However all of the 1,031 students were orderly evacuated safely by the teachers without injury to any.

Remember Rollow's Funeral Home at 1715 Broad and the fire hall, Engine Co. 7, across the street? It was Arch Rollow who sounded the alarm that the school was on fire. He knocked on the window to notify the teacher who chided him because she thought it was an April Fool's Day trick. A student, Paul Slayden, however, ran over to the fire hall and notified the firemen. Remember the one boy who darted out of the line as they left the burning building and ran back in to get his books? For the rest of the school term some of the students had to attend classes in the nearby churches. By a strange coincidence Wesley Hall on the Vanderbilt campus burned about the same time.

Remember Prof. Webb, the drawing teacher, Prof. Bailey, the singing teacher, the old bell ringing in the tower and jolting the whole building and the beautiful homes along both sides of Broad Street?

Did you know Mrs. Lynn Herndon, Zu Goodloe, Elizabeth O'Bryan, Ms. Ida Cavert and Prof. Wright? Did you ever slip up to the drugstore at Sixteenth and Broad to get a cheri-cola? Remember Robert Neil, the soda jerker? Recall when W. W. Dillon lived where Roesch-Patton is today? A daughter, Ann Dillon, was a student. Was Miss Margaret Rose your study hall teacher. Or was it Miss Carrie Roscoe?

Were you taught by Elizabeth Douglass, Florence Weiland, Alicia Gibson, Elsie Handly, Emma Kirkpatrick, Margaret Rose, Lillian Taylor, Eunice Taylor or the Hollins sisters; Mignon Garfinkle, Sadie Heron, Martha Horton, Catherine Looney, Cornelia Marr?

Old Tarbox served the Nashville school system for ninety years before it was abandoned and the property sold in 1966 for use by the senior citizens. In other words, the building was built to serve children from their birth to the age of sixteen and now serves oldsters of ages between sixty and death.

Cockrill School Baseball Team—1920.

Cockrill School Graduation—June, 1920.

You real oldies, do you remember the horse water trough at the intersection of Sixteenth and Broad before the Jere Baxter monument took its place, and which was to later give way to Goodyear? And now, tell the truth, did you ever spit on your slate to clean it off? And did you ever have to sit on the front bench, or go to the cloakroom, for misbehavior? Were you afraid of Mrs. Louise Gage?

Remember those Tarbox beauties: Christine Tibbett, Margaret Sisk, Mildred Fite, Ruth Baskett, Helen Wilkerson, Grace, Florence and Margaret Cavert, Faith Wade, Mary Evans Tarpley, Elise Chase, Dorothy Hankins, Elizabeth Tate, Eunice Ann and Sara Kincaid, Jane Sutherland, Katherine Bouchard, Blake sisters and the Westernberger girls?

Remember Ms. Irene Ford, the home economics teacher, and the caps and aprons you wore to her class? Did you have a single or double desk?

Remember those Tarbox dandies: L. A. Warner, Will Pope Kirkman, Julian Scruggs, Tillman Cavert Jr., Mike Blake, Henry Lassing, Richard and Howard Douglas, and later Bill and Clark Akers?

Have you forgotten the Aka-Paka grocery, the Daniel and Florence apartments, the Hewett grocery, and Rick's Restaurant—all in the school neighborhood? Have you forgotten that Evelyn Wilson fostered Tom Tichenor's interest in puppets? Mrs. Hudson, Miss Rose and Miss Gibson playing the piano for the students to march to classes and in and out of the building, and when Dr. Milton Cook and Miss Cornelius came periodically to teach art and music? Remember that in the early years the primary grades went to school only a half day and when you thought Prof. Wright carried a paddle up his sleeve?

Remember the one, two, three ceremony in laying your books on the line at the recitation bench?

Today, there remains only a semblance of the old building. But even though the old has been blended with the new and modern, it still exists as old Tarbox—the witness of the struggles of early teachers to train our young, inheritor of memories left by thousands, charged to maintain the school day experiences of many grandparents of today, proud of its contribution to the city.

Even as one passes today, one looks back with an effort to recall his or her days at Tarbox. These memories of youth cannot be uprooted and the very spot signifies this forcibly.

Few things are more pleasant than when one's mind is charged with memories of old school days.

But as we have grown old some of the things, places and people have become lost in the used-to-be—hidden in the yesterdays.

CHAPTER 5

Scenes of My Childhood
The Nashville That Was

A S I HAVE CONTINUED these excursions back into old memories I have been repeatedly reminded of youthful experiences, early acquaintances and the familiar places and things of the yesterdays. The world of the young has continuously pulled me back to its vistas. However, when age reviews them the old eye can't precisely recapture the thrill, the exhilaration and the raw and clear perception which challenged the youthful view.

I have tried to explain with the following lines:

The Wonderful World of Youth

There are many worlds in God's great plan,
A different one for each woman, child and man.
We begin and end in the one that is our own,
And the exactness of another is never known.
It ends with memories, as it began with dreams,
And our knowledge of others is gained in between.

But where is the world that was all mine,
When I was young and cared little for time?
Where are the dreams that carried me on,
And made me impatient for tomorrow's dawn?
Where are the castles which I built in the air,
And the triumphs which I saw there?

Where is the world that kept telling me
That I could be anything that I wanted to be?
Where is the urge of morning and impatience with night?
Where is the confidence that welcomed the fight?
Where is the road which beckoned with each sun,
To the pathway which would lead to victories to be won?

Where are the stars which pointed the way
To capture the prize on the following day?
Where are the keys which would open the door

107

And give to youth a new world to explore?
And where is the world from which all hope sprung?
Where, where is the wonderful world of the young?

Where is the teasing imagination of romance,
And the impulse to leave consequence to chance?
Where is the lure to the free estate,
And the reckless dash to unknown Fate?
Where is the enticing pull of ambition,
And the restless dreams of high position?

It's still here, just as it used to be,
But, still, only for the eyes of the young to see.
It's the same old world of joy and sorrow
That waits each night for the youth of tomorrow.
For the young, in the sunrise—for us, in the sunset.
They will dream dreams, while we will forget.

They will dream of what might be won.
We will dream of what we might have done.
They will dare Fate, and take a chance.
We will remember gains, or losses, from circumstance.
They will face their young world with bated breath,
As we struggle to remember, as we face Death.

Despite what the vain will claim and pretend,
Nothing will prevent the inevitable end.
The candle burns fast in youthful heat,
And it is gone forever when both ends meet.
And so, it is an inexorable truth,
That the world of the young ends, with the end of youth.

The Hay Market

The bartering place of young Nashville was the Hay Market.

It was one city block, bounded by Cherry Street (Fourth Avenue) and College Street (Third Avenue) south of McGavock Street, which had no buildings. Its only structure was a large watering trough for animals.

The farmers from the outskirts of the city drove their horse and mule wagons here laden with farm products to market. It was principally used for the sale and swapping of horses, mules and cows.

It was from the large amounts of hay brought there to feed the animals and for sale that gave the place its name.

It was also the preferred place for carnivals and medicine shows.

It was flanked all along College Street and Franklin Street with animal feed stores and blacksmith shops. The Hay Market mill funneled a large part of the flour and meal for the city. In the spring, summer and fall as one approached the place in the daytime one heard either the medicine show barker, the music of the carnival merry-go-round or the loud voices of the stock traders touting their animals.

At night the country farmer moved in under lantern light to be ready for the early morning sales.

Occasionally a frightened horse or cow broke shackles and had to be taken on the uptown streets.

The only interruption of this uniformity was when the Howse political machine had a political rally there. On such occasions Tony Rose's band would help to attract a crowd to hear the candidates pledge their loyalty to the mayor and promise a greater Nashville when elected.

At midday one heard the streetcars moving along College Street and out Cherry Street, the monotonous sounds of the heavy hammer on the anvil of the blacksmith shop and the anguished complaints of the restrained animals. The flies added some discomfort and the ever present manure demanded careful footwork. Chief Barthell had his blue coats there to guard against the pickpockets and a few drunks went unnoticed.

The farmers were always generous to the poor and often gave their leftovers to the "South Nashville Improvement League." There was no packaging—the customer bought his market basket. Potatoes, apples, beans and tomatoes were sold by the metal peck measures or bushel baskets.

Fishermen from the Cumberland River went through the crowd selling freshly caught fish and sometimes a farm wife who had accompanied her husband offered her homemade quilts for sale. Sometimes a traveling salesman set up his stand to sell collar and cuff buttons, combs, artificial jewelry, etc. Quite often the organ grinder was there with his monkey or a flimflam artist with his card tricks.

But modernity was to replace all this with the supermarket, the auction barn and the rock shows. The peck measure and the hanging scales were to give way to cellophane wrappings. The buggies, surreys and wagons were to be replaced by cars and trucks. The traveling spieler was to be followed by catalog purchase and the cider and "white mule" were to give way to marijuana and cocaine.

The packet steamboat Joe Horton Fall *docked at the Nashville River and Rail Terminal—September, 1927.*

Even the memory of the Hay Market was to fade. It, too, served its purpose and helped to move the young city along the path to a metropolis.

Looking back to its time—it was raw, rough, plain and simple—and a bit uncouth— but it was natural for the life of a time which has passed.

Old Railroads and Railroaders

They were a fraternity, drawn together by daily contact, common interests and mutual concerns. The employers and employees of the Louisville and Nashville Railroad (L&N), Nashville, Chattanooga and St. Louis Railway (NC&St.L) and the Tennessee Central Railway (T.C.) serviced old Nashville and linked her with the outside world.

Engineers, firemen, conductors, brakeman, baggagemen, flagmen, mail clerks, "butch boys," porters, waiters and cooks made the "runs."

Trackmen maintained the tracks along the routes. Switchmen located and assembled the trains in the home yards. Car knockers, car cleaners and oilers, and coal and water attendants serviced the trains at home stations. Station attendants serviced the locomotives with coal and water at route stations. The shopmen handled the repairs. At the stations ticket sellers, train callers, dispatchers, gatemen, porters, clerks and management brought the public to the passenger service and the freight handlers attended shipments.

Along the routes tower operators controlled switching and operated gates to protect the public at crossings. The wrecking crew trains and crews stood ready at pivotal spots along the system to answer emergencies. The duties of all were specific and strict and spelled out in manuals.

All these people were proud to be called "railroaders." They were a hardy bunch, accustomed to hard work, long hours and their responsibility for life and property. They had a deep sense of loyalty to their employment—and to their employers. All this made them somewhat gregarious. This, together with necessity, brought them to live in clusters near railroad activities and their jobs.

The areas around the "new shops"—Union Station, South Nashville and Edgefield junctions—were railroad communities. When occasioned by World War I, the Lewisburg and Northern route was extended through the Nolensville Road section and Radnor yards were built. Flat Rock became another.

Amqui Station (presently owned by Johnny Cash).

To railroaders time was important. The whole system depended upon schedules.

Train operations, both passenger and freight, safety and good business demanded keen observance of timed schedules. For this reason every railroader carried "railroad time." His watch was not only necessary to his job but it was also a prized possession. Railroaders were among the jewelers' best customers. He was embarrassed if his watch was discovered to be "off" three seconds in the habitual comparison of his with that of a fellow worker's. Upon his death his watch always went to his oldest son who would value it very highly.

The engineers, firemen and flagmen who manned the trains could usually be spotted when on their way to their runs by their cleanly washed and pressed overalls and jackets, caps and the red bandana handkerchiefs around their necks. The bandanas kept the soot and cinders from the steam engines out. The conductors on passenger trains wore blue uniforms, with brass buttons, and caps.

All carried their lunch boxes.

Do you remember:

The voices of the train callers at Union Station?

The butch-boys with their baskets of sandwiches, drinks and newspapers?

The call-boys who would come to the homes of employees to summon them for extra or emergency runs?

The spike drivers as they laid or repaired track?

The redcaps?

The crossing watch towers?

The coal and water stations?

The Pullman dining cars and waiters?

The dining room at the Union Station?

The "railroad talk" of railroaders?

The pay car?

Do you recall that they never referred to a train by name or where it was going to or coming from but that they always referred to them by number—"Number 6 will arrive at 6:45" or "No. 9 will leave on track 4 at 1:30," etc.

Many railroad employees and their families got news of the outer world sooner because they would collect and bring home the newspapers and magazines which had been left on incoming trains.

Do you remember the window washers who would go to work washing the windows immediately as the trains stopped in the station?

Do you remember the brass kerosene lamps over the windows by the seats—and the cuspidors? How about the folding chairs on the ob-

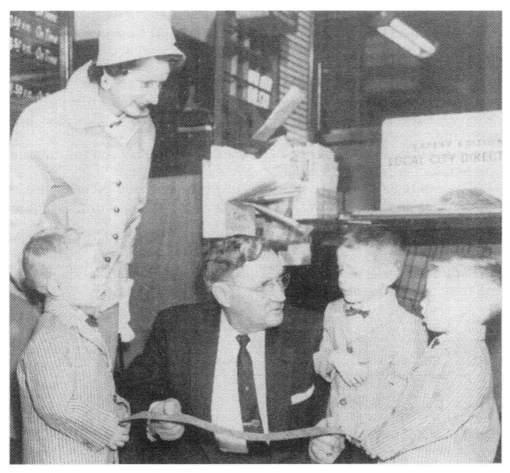

Harry Walker Loftin, Depot Ticket Agent, Union Station.

servation decks of the club cars on the Dixie Flyer, the Pan-American and the Hummingbird? Do you remember how the conductors would call out the approach to stations—and close the windows as the train approached tunnels—and the gas and smoke in the cars as they emerged?

Do you remember waiting at the switch, and slowing down for track repairmen? Can you recall when you first rode the train at the tremendous speed of thirty-five miles per hour on the straight stretches? You will remember the difference between local, expresses and through trains, and excursion trains.

Did you ever get off to watch the engine take on water and coal?

The modern ladies of ERA would have been happy over the fact that all trains were referred to as "she."

How many times have you watched the mail car hook the mail sack from the station post as it passed through without stopping?

Do you remember handcars? And the work crew cars parked on side tracks where they were engaged in grading or repair work? Can you still hear the lonesome whistle of a distant train at night?

Do you remember the dining room steward coming through the cars with his chimes, announcing the first, second or last call for dinner in the "dining car forward"?

Can you recall that before the day of flashlights that the conductors and flagmen would signal to the engineer with lanterns?

The politicians of the day would always have their pictures taken while sitting in the window of the locomotive while wearing the engineer's cap, in courting railroaders' votes.

The railroad families were close neighbors. They enjoyed the company of each other and stood by their neighbors and fellow workers in times of need, grief and tragedy. They were substantial, solid citizens and they made a great contribution to growing Nashville.

The cover picture of the September, 1956 edition of L & N Magazine *showed W. J. "Jim" Fleming, weigh clerk of Radnor Yards, with the following caption:*

"Mr. Fleming is pictured operating the automatic weight-recording device attached to the big (400-ton capacity) track scale, still largest and most modern on the System.".

Do you remember craning your neck to get a peep inside of the elegant private cars of the railroad executives and the wealthy? Do you remember when the Cumberland River would rise and flood the T.C. station?

Do you remember the troop trains of World War I?

The trains and railroaders carried much of the responsibility and burden required for the emergency preparation of the nation for World War I.

As the prospering country later came to demand the luxury and convenience of fast transportation, the railroads of America have been sorely neglected in favor of gasoline and asphalt.

We began to feel the penalty of this neglect during the preparation crises at the beginning of and during World War II.

It is frightening to think of what a terrible price we might have to pay for the continued neglect of this basic type of transportation when and if the country is faced with another like crisis in the future.

Railroads, and railroaders provided a great part of the romance and color of old Nashville life. When the Nashville of the past flows through memory, the noise of the steamer locomotive, the busy Union Station and the railroaders have their place in the passing parade. But we had better take a serious note—"The last train for national emergency danger is leaving on track 13—all aboard please!"

The Transfer Station and Her Streetcars

She belonged to the "nickel age." For five cents she would sell you a sandwich, a bottle of soda water, a box of cakes, a bag of popcorn, a package of chewing gum, a newspaper, or even a cigar. For a nickel you could board a Nolensville Road streetcar at Antioch Pike, ride to the heart of Nashville and into her shed, then transfer to the Glendale line and ride out to the Glendale Park. For just a nickel one could ride from one part of our city to the other when you used her facilities.

Without a doubt, more Nashvillians used the accommodations of the old Transfer Station than any other of her time—or since. She introduced half of Nashville to the other half. She was the most popular meeting place in the old city.

Thousands of our older citizens were the children of marriages which resulted from romances started by her and on the streetcars which she served.

Operated by the Nashville Railway and Light Company in the block bounded by Deaderick, Cedar, Cherry and College Streets, she was busy twenty-four hours each day.

The Fairfield, Nolensville Road, South High Street, Waverly, Kane Avenue, Hillsboro, West End, West Nashville, Cedar Street, Jefferson Street, St. Cecilia and Sulphur Dell Special streetcars entered her southside on College Street (Third Avenue) and exited her Cherry Street (Fourth Avenue) side.

The First Street, Main Street, Gallatin Road, Porter Road, Woodland Street, Fatherland Street and Shelby Park streetcars entered the north side from College and exited from the same side on Cherry Street.

Do you remember:

The turnstiles where you paid your fare when you caught a car in the station?

The long hard benches for waiting passengers on the north side of the food, drink and novelty concessions behind them?

The employees who stood at the entrances and exits to replace the trolleys when they jumped the wires while making the switches?

The odor and graphite of the toilets?

How cold it was during winter time?

The rush of passengers to board in order to get a window seat—or a seat of any kind?

When bold Vanderbilt students drove their rumble-seated Fords through the station—and got arrested?

Have you forgotten:

How, when small, you held on by the brass handle on the back seat of the street cars when you had to stand in the aisles and when as you grew older, you held to the leather straps which hung down from the top?

The advertisements on both sides—over the windows?

The big brass wheel which the motorman cranked to brake the car, or the money changers worn on the belts of the conductors?

The lever which the conductor pulled to register the fare on the big round meter up front and the rope he pulled to sound the bell for the motorman to proceed?

The signs which read, "Five dollar fine for spitting on the floor"?

Do you remember how the horses coming in from the country pulling wagons and buggies would rear up in fright at the approach of the "electric monster"?

The open cars with their long running boards which ran to the Fairgrounds and Glendale Park in the summertime?

Your impatience when the motorman slowed down so he could eat his lunch or supper from a shoe box?

The metal pedal he stomped with his foot to ring the warning bell?

Car Barns, Nashville Railway & Light Company.

When the current went off and the car stalled until it came back on?

And you older men—do you remember when you were one of the little devils who on Halloween "soaped" the tracks with Saxon soap? And you older ladies—do you remember how the "young gallants" jumped up to give you young ladies their seats? I do; that is how I met my Carrie on the Porter Road car sixty-two years ago. Have you forgotten how the conductor would leave the car as it stopped before a railroad crossing, go to the other side of the tracks and then signal the motorman to proceed?

Do you remember how the motorman would change the trolley and the conductor would reverse the seats at the end of the line?

Have you forgotten how the first automobile drivers raced to outdistance the streetcars at the "dangerous" speed of twenty-five miles per hour?

And you old ex-paper boys, do you remember when the four o'clock car would throw off *The Nashville Banner* in the afternoon; and the four o'clock car would throw off *The Tennessean* in the morning?

From all the early outposts of the growing young city the streetcars led to the Transfer Station.

The old girl served us well and after surviving the threat of the "jitney bus," she finally died an "automobile death" and took the streetcars with her—as well as the "nickel age."

The Neighborhood Merchants

As we walk back through time we will always come to the old Nashville neighborhood grocery and drugstores. After we have passed the supermarket, check-out counters and cellophane packaging, we will come to the old grocery building, the counters, clerks' peck measures and sacks of bulk purchasing; and the corner drugstore with its marble soda fountain, its ceiling fans, its prescription counter and big bottles on the glass-doored shelves.

The grocer and the druggist were the best known citizens of the community. The stores were community meeting places. We usually went there to use the only telephone close by. The grocery was the main source of food—supplemented by the "market wagon" and the City Market Place on the Square. The drugstore not only made available the needed medicines but also the advice of the druggist ("doctor") concerning our ailments. These two, together with the butcher shop, the dry goods store, and coal and ice yard, constituted the business of each community. The doctor worked out of his home. Dairy products were brought from the milk wagons. Herbs and spices came from the Atlantic and Pacific and Larkin wagons.

Most groceries provided daily deliveries by horse and wagon. Behind most stores were the stables and sheds for the horses and wagons. Saturday was their big day because that was pay day. In the rear of the stores was stored the horse and cattle feed for sale—and sometimes bales of hay.

Do you remember:

The counters with the roll of wrapping paper and the roll of cord for wrapping the purchases? The scales—the ones on the counter and the large ones on the store porch which provided us with the only way to know our own weight? The coal oil drums and the pump to fill our coal oil cans? The barrel of sour pickles and another of sauerkraut? The potato bins and the peck measure? The coffee grinders the cash drawer and the bell of the early cash register?

How about: Freshly killed rabbits piled up on the porch in wintertime at ten cents each? Country and compound lard paddles to take the lard from the barrel into cardboard trays? Buckets of sorghum and honey? Fresh fruit—apples, plums, peaches, pears, cherries, berries—but no oranges or grapefruit? The candy counter with bowls of chocolate drops, jelly beans, fudge, marble taffy, gumdrops, jawbreakers and string licorice? The cake counter with ginger snaps, lemon snaps and Nabiscos in the tin boxes? The empty wooden boxes that all canned goods came in, piled up behind the stores?

Do you remember: Saxon, Octagon lye and Ivory soap and Dutch Cleanser, about the only cleaner available? Loose eggs in the bushel baskets? Arbuckel's coffee? "Long Johnny," Yucatan and spearmint gum—before Wrigley's came along? R.J.R., Bull Durham, Duke's Mixture and Prince Albert tobaccos, La Edna cigars (two for a nickel), W. W. Ford's Twist, Virginia Cheroots, Bruton's snuff, Favorite cigarettes? The charge tickets or grocery tickets and the spring back or single file where they were kept under each customer's name? Cabbage, turnips,

Newspaper profile of Simon Ghertner—ca. 1922.

greens and onions, etc. in piles on the floors in the corners? The farmers' wagons stopping by to sell the groceries on their way to the City Market? The hoops of "rat cheese" and the cheese cutter?

Can you remember: The ice cream cones, the banana splits, the sodas, the "dopes" (Coca-Cola), Muscadine Punch, Green River, Pepsol, which we bought from the soda fountain in the drugstore from "soda jerks"? The perfume case where you bought perfume poured from large bottles into tiny bottles? When rouge was called "face paint" and that, together with boxed "face powder" and powder puffs, glycerin and rose water and witch hazel, was about all of the cosmetics?

What about: The large glass jars on the shelves containing bulk camphor gum, powdered sulphur, tincture of iodine, cherry syrup for mixing cough medicines, senna leaves, arnica, carbolic acid, and the other medicines? The wood-coated, tin, five-gallon cans of bulk turpentine and linseed oil? Wine of cardui, tanlac, Lydia E. Pinkham's, C. C. Pills, Dr. Caldwell's Syrup of Pepsin, Black Draught, French Calomel, Sloan's Liniment, Grove's Headache Powders, quinine, ipecac, etc.? The salve and patented medicine shelves? The revolving postcard rack? The drunks buying Jamaican ginger during prohibition days? Valentine and candy displays on Valentine's Day, Easter and Christmas? School books and supply counters at school opening days? The cardboard black and white pill boxes? When all medicine bottles had cork stoppers? The secret drawer under the cash register from which clerks discreetly sold and men embarrassingly bought "no-nos" in little aluminum boxes?

Do you remember: The sawdust on the floors of the butcher shops? The meat hooks from which sides of freshly killed beef and pork hung? The old meat block, the saw, the cleaver and the knives? The tubs of freshly ground sausage and the cardboard trays in which sausage, liver and brains were sold? The piles of salted sow belly and the country hams hanging from the ceiling? Hogs heads, pig feet, fresh spare ribs, back strips and pork chops? When you sliced your own bacon? Soup bones and boiling bacon? The bloody aprons of the butchers? The fly papers?

And in the dry goods store—do you remember: The bolts of gingham, calico, percale, muslin, domestic, velvet, bed ticking, etc. and the yardstick tacked on the counter for measuring—or measuring from the nose to the tip of the fingers on the outstretched hand? The house dresses, bonnets, night and dust caps, aprons, blouses, skirts, Sunday dresses, coats, corsets, shimmies, garters, silk, lisle and cotton stockings for the ladies? The dresses, middy blouses, bloomers, hair ribbons, and black and white stocking for "misses"? The high button shoes and slippers for women and girls? The corduroy knickers, macki-naws, waists, heavy ribbed stockings and laced "butcher" shoes or "low cuts" for men and boys, "rubbers" or "overshoes" for winter and canvas (tennis) shoes for summer? The "long johns" for men and boys for winter and "B.V.D.'s" for summer?

When girls were embarrassed to have to pull their cotton stocking over their "long johns"? The wooden display case for Coates threads? Laces, corset strings, shoe strings and drawers? Rubber boots, pon-chos and yellow rain coats?

Do you remember the coal and icehouse? Driving the empty wagon onto the scales for weighing, loading the coal, and then weigh-ing the loaded wagon on the way out to find the costs? The block ice, ice saws and ice tongs—and scooping up the "snow" in the summer time? Lump, nut and slack coal? When you bought cold watermelons from the icehouse in summer time? The coal wagons?

None of the things sold by these merchants carried price tags—you asked the clerk for the price. All the stores were heated with coal stoves. These were the days before H. G. Hill Company introduced their chain stores to outlying neighborhoods.

Hill and Crone-Jackson were the principal grocery stores in the in-ner city. Berry-DeMoville, Warner, Leickhardt's, and Paige and Sims were the main "uptown" drug stores.

The facilities for transportation limited access to the city stores and the people depended upon the neighborhood stores.

They became the victim of the chain store invasion of the suburbs, but they remain fixed in the memory of all of us who saw Nashville grow into a metropolitan center.

These were the days when ordinary survival was more important than style—plain comfort was more important than sophistication.

These were the days when the economy only rewarded those who were willing to work.

These were the days when it was embarrassing to accept a "hand-out" or to expect an agency of the government to support you.

These were the days when you could not expect everything to come free while you sat in your rocking chair.

These were the days when merchants did not spend their time seeking new ways to "stack profits"—they were your neighbors and trusted friends—not corporation executives in distant cities.

These were the days when the grocer would let your bill "run"—would "carry you," when you lost your job or got hurt or became sick, and you would "catch it up" when you got another job or got well—as a matter of honor.

Old Restaurants and Public Dining Rooms

Nothing contributed more to the color of old Nashville than its old restaurants and public dining rooms. They were meeting places. When the public depended upon their newspapers alone for information and news of the world, they served that purpose for local news. Many business deals were negotiated, many lawsuits were settled, many candidates were nominated—and elected—many civic endeavors were born and planned, and many lasting friendships originated over their tables. There were not too many, and they were concentrated in the business district.

Selection of dining rooms and restaurants was made as the result of preference for a certain quality of food, choice of food, the association offered and proximity to one's place of employment. Once established, it became a custom or habit to return regularly.

Many political, professional and business leaders ate lunch at the Maxwell House coffee shop. Familiar faces there were: John J. Vertrees,

City Hall.

Major Vertrees, Hill McAlister, E. J. Smith, Benton McMillin, Lewis Pope, John W. Hilldrop, Judge J. B. D. DeBow, Norman Farrell, Tom Kittrell and occasionally Cordell Hull and J. W. Byrns.

A large number of local political leaders, judges, lawyers and court people frequented one or the other of two restaurants located in the old City Hall Building. Many would be found in the one operated by the popular Frank Underwood. In this plain dining room with good food but no fancy frills, one could usually see: the Wright brothers, Kelly Hill, Henry Lassing, Charles Longhurst, Frank Garard, Frank Langford, J. Washington Moore, Lewis Hurt, Vernon and Reed Sharp, G. B. Kirkpatrick, Bob Briley, Charles Cohn, W. B. Cook, Alec Barthel, Joe McCord, Litton Hickman, Louis Monroe, "Nubby" Johnson, Elkin Garfinkle, sometimes Hilary Howse, and many others.

To be found in the other, operated by the Smith brothers, one would see: Sam Jenkins, Bob Marshall, Hugh Freeman, Bill Jones, Richard Atkinson, Luther Luton, Dr. John Bauman, Guild Smith, Bud Minton, Squires Omohundro, Baker, Allen and Wilkerson, Felix Wilson, Percy Sharp, and others.

The farmers bringing produce to the Market on the old Square would also eat at one of these two.

The Little Gem in Printer's Alley drew many uptown employees who had short lunch periods and were looking for popular prices.

The banking or "Union Street crowd" were to be found at Mrs. Fitzhugh's, Hettie Ray's, and the Satsuma restaurants. Regular patrons of these were: Frank Bass, Frank Berry, Cecil Sims, Ennis Murrey, Buford Wilson, Watkins Crockett, Ed Burr, Mack Fuqua, Roscoe Bond, Ed McNeilly, Jeff McCarn, Oliver Timothy, H. J. Grimes, and many others.

The Utopia Hotel dining room, Conto's "Little Pappas," John and Paul Stumb's attracted many. The Noel Hotel dining room followed these three as the popular place near Fourth and Church.

The Capitol and state employees found their way to the dining rooms of the Hermitage, Andrew Jackson and Clarkston hotels. It was usual to find there: Lonnie Ormes, Porter Dunlap, Jim Bean, Col. Lem Motlow, Gordon·Browning, Jim McCord, Bob Taylor, Andrew Todd, John Hurton, Grafton Green, Dave Lansden, Charlie Cornelius, Henry Horton, Austin Peay, and sometimes Ed Crump, Roxy Rice and others engaged in state government and state politics.

Church Street, Sixth and Seventh Avenue businessmen frequented McFadden's, Shacklett's, and the Manhattan restaurants. In these, one would often encounter Tony Sudekum, Joe Morse, Jim Cayce, Charles Rolfe, L. A. Bauman, Larry Simmons, Jonas Redelshimer, John Bevington, Al Armstrong, Aaron Bergeda, Ed Petway, "Slick" Welsh, Tom Gross, Charles Davitt, Morton Lebeck, Harold Shyer, many doctors and others.

The old Banner Cafe at Third and Commerce accommodated Jim Stahlman, Ralph McGill, Charlie Moss, many Market Street merchants, *Banner* employees, and those of the Third Avenue furniture stores.

Lower Broad Street businessmen and those from lower Second, Third and Fourth Avenues usually gathered at the Wright restaurant.

In one of these you would find William Gupton, Ed Holt, Andrew Clark, Glenn Briley, Lester Liggett, Lillard Foutch, Bob Phillips, E. K. Hardison, the Alloway brothers, A. E. Potter, Bill Carr, Bill Quarles, "Dutch" Morrisey, Lige Munn, Charlie Ragland.

Pete Stumb's restaurant in the Stahlman Building had a loyal following, especially for early breakfast. There you would meet Boyte Howell, Red Bransford, Jet Potter, Tom Shriver, Charles Embry, J. G. Lackey, R. C. Boyce, Giles Evans, John Cates, Lurton Goodpasture, Vernon Hines, Bill Manier, Larkin Crouch, Miller Manier, John Aust, Lee Loventhal and many others from the Stahlman Building.

Union Station personnel, railroaders, Cummins Station employees and other Broad Street people liked the Union Station dining room, the Underwood Hotel, and Charles Kalamaris' restaurant. There you would see Harry Conners, H. A. Blackwood, J. B. Hill, Fitzgerald Hall, W. S. Hackworth, A. P. Ottarson, Harry Loftin, L. G. Durr, Bob Brannan, Jess Talley, "Sally" Walker, John Tune, Burton Wilkerson and many other automobile row people.

Smaller places drew many because of their specialties. Among those were Bruner's and Zager's, both near the Transfer Station, Dave Egan's on Second Avenue, Varallo's and "Tony the Chili King's" for Italian food, George Mooney's, Zanini's, and Charlie Nickens'.

In some cases, the regulars would, over periods of years, eat at the same place, at the same time, at the same table, in the same chair—and usually with the same associates. The waiters and waitresses came to cater to them with their knowledge of their food preferences and personal wants, which added to the pleasantness of the meal.

Preceding most of these, had been Faucon's nationally famous restaurant on Union Street.

In those days the restaurants' daytime patrons were mostly men. Few women would be found at any of them for breakfast or lunch. In the evenings they were escorted mainly to the hotel, the Union Station, McFadden or Manhattan dining rooms. Later they would enjoy Kleeman's, Shacklett's, Hettie Ray's, and Satsuma.

It must be remembered that women were employed mainly as clerks and secretaries. There was only a small number found in professional or business activities. It will be recalled that most Nashvillians of those days ate at the family table and that many working people and students carried their lunch. Eating out was rare. There were no fast food outlets and few private club accommodations. However, the old Elks' Club on Sixth Avenue maintained an inviting dining room for its members and their guests.

Of course, the old pie wagons were the favorites of many, especially that of Hudson and Dan Coombs.

Larger dinner meetings, parties and banquets were held at the hotels.

As time went on and the strictures of Prohibition came to be somewhat ignored, restaurants and night spots sprang up in the outer areas of the city and county: Davenport's Plantation Club, the Ridgetop Inn, the Automobile Club, Five Points, Hettie Ray's on Nine Mile Hill, and others. At about the same time came Mickey Baines and the original Brass Rail in Printer's Alley and Kelly's 216 Club.

Among old restaurant memories is that of H. J. Grimes, a Catholic, Joe Gilbert, a Jew, and R. W. Comer, a Church of Christ Protestant, lunching together at Underwood's restaurant. All three of these gentlemen meant a lot to old Nashville.

Old City Hall and Market House.

Today, there are approximately 1,300 dining rooms, restaurants and food outlets in Nashville.

Today, few people know the waiters or waitresses who serve them in a public dining room, few eat at the same place very often, and few are impressed with the friendships that can result from such associations.

Eating Out

For the first thirty years of this century, most Nashvillians ate three meals each day at the family table—three full meals. Eating out, was only at the occasional invitation of a relative for Sunday dinner, or less occasionally with a neighbor. The workman took his own lunch to the job. The student took his or her lunch to school. The more affluent businessmen ate lunch at one of the few uptown restaurants. It was an unusual and great occasion when those who could afford it had dinner or supper at one of these.

Do you remember: The businessmen's lunch at the Little Gem in Printer's Alley, three vegetables, two meats, bread, coffee or milk, and dessert for fifteen cents? The restaurants of Frank Underwood and the Smith brothers on the ground floor of the old City Hall? Little Pappas, operated by Chris Contos on Fourth Avenue? Paul and John Stumb's on Fourth Avenue? The Bismarck Hotel, and later, the Utopia Hotel dining rooms on Fourth Avenue? Charlie Kalamaris' Royal Cafe on Broad Street? The dining room at Union Station? The Ocean and The Manhattan on Sixth Avenue? Bruner's, just north of the Transfer Station on Fourth Avenue, and Zager's on Third? McFadden's Grotto on Church Street? Warner's drugstore, at the corner of, Cedar Street on the Square; Duncan Hotel, Fourth Avenue; and Peach Restaurant on Broadway? Busy Bee on Broadway? Kleeman's and Zanini's? Mrs. Fitzgerald, upstairs on Union Street? The elegant dining rooms of the Hermitage, Andrew Jackson, and Noel hotels? The Maxwell House coffee shop and The Elks' Club?

Did you ever go to: "Tony the Chili's King's" on Deaderick Street? Have a light lunch at the Mitchell Candy Store and have a piece of free candy from the charming Charlie Mitchell? The pie wagon of Hudson and Dan Combs, the Pimlico, the West End Diner, and the other pie wagons uptown? Charlie Nickens' for barbecue and beans? Jim Douglas' on the Public Square? United Cigar Store's lunch counters? Petrone's on West End Avenue? Candyland?

Do you remember: When the only restaurant in the vicinity of Vanderbilt University was the pie wagon at the Broad Street gate, and later,

Jackson Building—1949.

McFarland's across the street? The pie wagon across from the old Criminal Court Building on Second Avenue?

As the city spread, so did restaurants: Frank Mooney's, Melfi's, Varallo's, the Surf, Clarkston, Brass Rail, and many others. Then came the cafeterias—Shacklett's and others.

Eating out, really started with the general introduction of the automobile.

Can you remember: Hettie Ray's restaurant on Twenty-first Avenue, and then later on Nine Mile Hill? Curb service at Chubby's at West End and Sixteenth Avenue, and at Les Burrus' on Gallatin Road? The Log Cabin, opposite Centennial Park—Josh Ambrose?

Prohibition brought on the era of the speak-easy restaurants and nightclubs, with food and illicit liquor and gambling. The first: the Plantation Club, and then, the Pines, Stanton's, Automobile Club, Ridgetop Club, and others, on the highways. How about lunch at Mickey Baines' at the Allied Club? How about the "brown sack"? Kelly's 216?

The repeal of Prohibition was to bring legal liquor, and later, "liquor-by-the-drink," and introduce many new eating places in and around the city. Eating at the country clubs was to flourish. The hotel dining rooms were to become more popular. Supper clubs and nightclubs were to begin. Gourmet restaurants were to appear.

And then came the chain restaurants, hamburger outlets, and "fast-food" outlets. These were to complete the almost total disappearance of the family table. These were to make eating depend largely upon the amount of gasoline in the tank of the automobile.

The caterer was to come upon the scene.

The affluent began to seek the sophistication of gourmet food, and the choice of French, Spanish, German, Mexican, Italian and Chinese cuisine.

Music and live entertainment were to come along.

Others were to depend on "steaks, potatoes and salad," "hamburgers and French fries," or "fried chicken, mashed potatoes and gravy."

The highway cat-fish houses were to become popular.

School children were to eat at cafeterias.

The carrying of lunch was out for good—for them and workmen.

Regular family meals were practically a thing of the past.

The price of a single dinner was to go up from $2 to $40.

The kitchen stove was to become as cold as the refrigerator and children became unacquainted with vegetables.

School Days

Among the fondest of our memories are those of our school days and school acquaintances. As we grow older and look back, they rush to the front of our recollections. Though we seldom see them now, we retain pleasant memories of our schoolmates, our school associations, and respect and grateful admiration for our teachers. Although we are inclined to stretch the distance we had to walk to school and to point out the lack of facilities of our school days, we enjoyed the experience and knew no better.

Remember walking to and from school—the first day of school, meeting the new teacher and the new classmates, the new room, the new books and your new desk? How about getting the "book list" and going with your parents to the store designated in the community to sell them? Remember the big, thick "Indian Chief" rough paper tablet—and the smooth papered "Blue Horse"? Don't forget the red-backed speller, the book strap, and the satchel. You may have also had a collapsible drinking cup and a pencil box. Remember your parents taking you to the neighborhood dry goods store to buy new school clothes?

Remember the old desks with the place to put your books and the seat on the front side for the pupil in front of you? Did you ever mess up your desk putting the ink bottle in that little hole on the right upper side, or shove your books against your wrapped up lunch which you had already placed in there?

Remember the "recitation benches" up front where your class faced the teacher? Did you ever win the assignment of dusting the erasers or cleaning the blackboard? Remember the weekly tests and term examinations? What color was your report card? Did your school use the grading system of A, A-, B+, B, B-, C+, C, C-, D, D-, or E, E-, S+, S, S-, U, or by the numerals? Remember that your parents had to sign them for the return? Did your teachers ever ask you to "take up" the papers? Did you ever win a certificate for not missing a day during the year, get kept in after school or called down for snapping your fingers when you raised your hand?

Remember the barns where those who came to school in buggies, surreys, or on horseback kept the horses? Remember the dippers on chains around the water coolers and how the boys and girls had separate playgrounds? Did you ever get into your lunch while the teacher was not looking, before recess time? Remember when we had to march out to recess, and back in, and to the front door when school was over?

Did you ever put a rubber band on the red pot-bellied stove and then assume that look of innocence when it was discovered by the smell—or hit the back of the head of someone with a paper wad? Remember the first basketball courts in the schoolyard before the day of the gymnasiums at schools? Remember assembly and the singing in the "big hall"? The hooks on the wall where we hung our coats, cloaks and capes, and leaving our overshoes on the outside? Did you ever have to carry a note to the principal's office for some infraction, and stand there and suffer while he read it—and, sometimes, end up with a switch across the back or a paddle on your open hands?

Remember when the teacher pinned the good compositions on the wall, when we made physical maps out of flour and water on cardboard, and the honor list with stars? Did you ever carve your initials on your desk or the walls of the ten-holer? Remember the good sound of the recess bell or the one that ended the school day? Did the big boys ever make you go through the paddling machine?

Remember the school play and the class picnic? When one raised his hand to get permission to be excused for a call of nature? When the smart students wanted to sit at the head of the recitation bench, and we wanted to get at or toward the end? Did your teacher have a pet? Remember the annual visit of the doctor to talk separately to the boys and girls on sex hygiene and abstinence? Remember the teacher's pointer, the globe map on her desk, the flowers in the window, the picture of George Washington, the coal buckets around the heater, the study periods, and how sleepy you got about 2 P.M. on the spring days? Did you insist on carrying your girl's books, and have a school sweetheart—real or imaginary?

Remember how good a cold biscuit and sausage or peanut butter and crackers tasted at lunch time? Remember taking a fried pie wrapped up in a piece of newspaper for lunch? Did you ever have to go to the foot of the class, or to the dunce stool in the corner? Did you ever get left in a grade, or skip a grade? Remember the thrill of passing and promotion? Remember the mama who came to assembly to play the piano so her darling daughter could sing a song, or how the principal would occasionally come into your room and sit down to observe?

Was your teacher pretty or "ugly as home-made sin"? Remember where the boys left their bicycles? Were you ever assigned to cleaning up the schoolyard? Remember the visit of the school superintendent?

Did you ever play hookey? Remember taking a written excuse to get out, or for absence? Roll calls, vaccinations, going to the library, and fire drills?

Remember the taking of the class pictures, graduation exercises and the day school was out for the summer? How about the specimens in the biology or physiology classrooms, and the map of the U. S. on the wall?

Remember the geography book—the biggest one of all?

Did you ever have to write something one hundred times for punishment? Did you ever take the teacher an apple or some flowers? Remember the penmanship classes with ink staffs, pen points, blotters and pen wipers? Remember your school janitor?

Did you ever help whitewash the school fence, empty the wastebaskets, or water the flowers, or get scolded for talking? Did your room have a pencil sharpener? Did you ever trace a map or get exempted from taking an examination? Did you ever forget and put an indelible pencil in your mouth, or chew on your pencil rubber? Did you have a watercoloring set or did you just break a lot of crayons? Did you make notes in your books, or write notes to other pupils? Did another boy or girl ever tell on you? Did you have a pocket dictionary?

Whatever became of your high school diploma or your graduation presents? Did you ever get your grade lowered for not leaving margins on the pages of your compositions? Did you ever have to go to the foot of the line in a spelling match, as the winners moved up? After you worked an arithmetic problem, did you check the right answer in the back of your book? Remember the debates, declamation contests, and that groove in the old wooden desks to hold your pencil?

Was your school ever closed because of snows or hot weather? Did your school have a cafeteria, gymnasium, inside toilet, water fountain, free books, air conditioning, free food, free transportation, free nurses and doctor's care? Did it have central heating, counselors, calculators, scientific equipment, televisions, sound systems, fire alarms, swimming pools, tennis courts, athletic fields, movie projectors, telephones, security guards, a playroom, lounges, snack bars, vending machines, Xerox machines, typewriters, or computers?

Did you ever know of violence in schools or disrespect for teachers?

Summer Resorts

When summer came to old Nashvillians many could be found at the nearby springs, coves and summer resorts for vacations and weekends. With transportation limited to local trains, early automobiles and poor roads, distance was a problem. There was little travel abroad, few could get to Florida beaches and, of course, no ocean cruises.

We were attracted to Horn Springs, Red Boiling Springs, Castalian Springs, Prim Springs, Fernvale Springs, Diamond Springs, Hygeia Springs, Beaver Dam Springs, Dawson Springs, Ruskin Cave, Dunbar

Cave, Bon Aqua, Craigie Hope, Beersheba, Monteagle and Rock Island.

Nearly all of these were operated by old families and the family atmosphere was found at all of them. They catered to those looking for relaxation during the "lazy, hazy days of summer." There was good Southern cooking, horseback riding, mineral water, swimming, hiking, baseball, horseshoe pitching and dancing. The usual large porches were the gathering places for the ladies with their knitting, crocheting, embroidering, sewing and the accompanying gossip and chitter chatter in the afternoons.

Many men would go back and forth to their work in Nashville on the trains. The ladies and children would all go down to the train stop to see the trains come in, in the late evenings.

The big days of the summer season at these places would be the Fourth of July and Labor Day. The weekends would feature barbecues, games, contests and dances.

There were stables for those who came by buggy or surrey, and someone to care for the horses. A buggy ride through the nearby countryside was another treat.

Nashvillians caught the Tennessee Central at the terminal at the foot of Broad Street and disembarked at the Horn Springs crossing in Wilson County. Joe Horn met the train with a surrey and took passengers and baggage to the big hotel annex. Mrs. Horn could have taught the Kentucky Colonel a lesson about fried chicken. Remember her fried corn, mashed potatoes, hot biscuits, ham and red-eye gravy, fried eggs and fruit? There were always large compotes of blackberry, strawberry, cherry and peach preserves together with honey and sorghum. Remember the big white pitchers of sweet and buttermilk? The children always helped Joe make the large freezers of fresh peach ice cream. Who could ever forget those blackberry, peach and apple cobblers?

The costs of these meals and rooms were only slightly more than what one pays today for just the service charges and taxes for the same. However, there was one extra cost—chiggers, sunburn and increased weight.

Some claimed that they went principally for the mineral waters. Others claimed that the waters were simply spring water with Epsom salts added.

Remember those big comfortable highback rockers that lined the front porches?

Horn Springs was one of the first to have a large public swimming pool. But there were always nearby creeks.

All the resorts offered simple pleasures and plain good food for a society that had not yet become too sophisticated. Long walks in the woods, through covered bridges, across uncontaminated streams, among birds, squirrels, rabbits and other wildlife, past wildflowers, country farm homes and barns and with satisfied friends made relaxation a pleasure and relief.

Since national Prohibition was the law there always seemed to be a nearby bootlegger at all of them with a supply of "white lightning" and "homebrew." Of course, there was always grape and elderberry wine, peach brandy and blackberry cordial for the men who wanted something other than milk and mineral water. And there was usually a Saturday night poker game in one of the rooms.

At these places and in these times the owners and operators did not have to depend upon blaring music, nudity, dirty-mouthed comics, cocktail bars, gyrating vocalists, drugs, pornographic movies, exotic foods, and fancy interiors to attract patrons. They afforded simple pleasures and plain but comfortable accommodations for a clientele that was easily satisfied.

They were the origins of lasting friendships and sources of pleasure to many. Misconduct was not tolerated and rarely occurred. They earned, desired and had the respect of those who sought their accommodations.

In our memories they hold a special place.

The Surrounding Country and the Farmer

Nashvillians younger than fifty years of age cannot know of the great part local farmers played in the early life and in the building of the city. They cannot correctly picture the fact that where a great part of them live today were the farms of yesterday which helped to feed our people.

The asphalt drives and highways, subdivisions, the commercial centers, golf courses, parks, swimming pools, playgrounds, and other components of the metropolitan area of today were then corn fields, wheat fields, truck gardens, pastures and woodlands of "the country" of the past.

The narrow confines of old Nashville were surrounded by farms, even within the immediate areas of Davidson County. After all, the municipal limits extended no further than approximately one mile from the Public Square in any direction. There were no industries located in the rural areas.

Antioch, Bakertown, Wrencro, Brentwood, Vaughn's Gap, Sullivan's Ridge, Bellevue, Bordeaux, Paradise Ridge, Amqui, Donelson,

Hermitage and Una were all "way out in the country." Comparatively few who lived in these sections worked in town. They were sustained largely by their labors with the land. They produced most of their own food and supplied the city with a large part of what it needed.

As it is with the small farmer of today, it was not an easy life. They had to work hard, contend with the elements, live closely and be satisfied with a simple life. Their main contact with the business life was with the local grocer, and their trips to the old City Market to sell their products, and for the dairyman, his "milk wagon route."

Do you remember:

Sweating over a plough behind a mule, hoeing corn, getting in the hay, laying in the wood, preserving and pickling, worming tobacco, herding and milking cows, feeding the chickens, greasing the wagon and buggy, cooling the milk in the spring, the rainwater barrels, hog killing, how long it seemed before the dinner bell when working in the field, going to market with your father, the flies around the outhouse?

And have you forgotten—Trapping rabbits, coon and 'possum hunting, the swimming hole, hunting walnuts, hickory and chestnut hunting, going to Sunday School, the watermelon patch, the grapevine swing, walking to school, womanless weddings at the church and plays at the school? Going to town to spend the weekend with a city cousin, turning the ice cream freezer on Sunday morning, your new pair of overalls, thorns in your bare feet in summertime and getting up before daylight to "feed" or to milk?

Can you remember—the family going into town in the surrey to visit Aunt Ruth and Uncle John—and going to the Fair?

Think back to the first day of school, the new Sears, Roebuck catalogue, and the way the "dumb city dudes" acted.

And you city slickers—do you remember going out in the country in summertime to visit your cousin and passing through the toll gates on the way out?

How about some of the jokes the country boys played on you—did they ever take you into the woods at night "snipe hunting"?

Do you remember the first time that you saw Aunt Polly wring the neck of a chicken, or Uncle John cut the throat of a hog? Did you ever ride the perch pole of a wagon or play in the hayloft? I'll bet you remember that country ham, red-eye gravy, fried eggs, hot buttered biscuits and jam you had for breakfast. But what did you call them when you were back with your city friends, was it "country hicks"?

The farmer, in spite of a hard life, was generally happy and content to stay in the country and come to town usually only when he needed supplies, had to pay his taxes or to serve on the jury, or to bring his produce to the market. The winters were difficult but he steeled himself to what was necessary and took difficulty in stride. He was satisfied to be a good family man.

It was not until World War I that he became attracted to the possibility of making more money for his family at a "job" than he could on the farm. By this time the city was growing out of its narrow limits. Town people were becoming crowded and had started to build further and further out on the highways. Commercial and industrial activity was increasing in the city and there were more jobs with better money. The city began to spill over into the area of the farmlands. The farms close in began to yield to new residential areas. The city's dependency upon local farmers was decreasing. Farm products began to flow into the city by rail and the new motor trucks. The farmer was finding it easier to work at a city job and make more money.

This idea was to spell trouble for Nashville—and the entire country.

However, when we consider those who helped to build Nashville, the early farmers of Davidson County and the nearby areas must be accorded substantial consideration. They were good citizens, as solid as rock, as dependable as an old bridge and as reliable as an old oak, steady in the face of adversity and humble before their good fortune. The farmer asked no quarter but was quick to share what he had with his unfortunate neighbor. He worked hard to maintain his own independence and to help to feed others who were building our city.

He was a man of strong faith—simple, but unfaltering.

Do you ever find yourself thinking about fording the creek, getting a ham from the smokehouse, looking for hen's nests, dropping the bucket into the cistern, stretching barbed wire, sharpening knives on the grindstone, oiling the harness, shelling peas, slopping the pigs, cleaning the lantern globe and trimming the wicks, heating water on the kitchen stove for the Saturday night bath in the wash tub, getting potatoes up from the outdoor cellar, and playing "mumble-peg"?

Did you ever get your lessons by the light of the log fireplace, hold a popcorn popper over the hot coals, or bake a sweet potato in the hot ashes?

And now, do you remember:

The long ride on the wagon to the Market on the Square in the late afternoon and finding a place on the "market line"?

The stern orders of the "market master"?

Unhitching the horses and taking them to the livery stable for the night?

Sleeping in or under the wagon till selling time at 4 A.M.?

Eating breakfast at the Market House or Underwood Restaurant? Selling till 10 A.M.?

The "close-out" at 10:30 A.M. when the sanitation workers moved in to clean up and hose down the market area?

Buying things for the family and the long ride back to the farm?

Memory can provide no more exciting excursion than when addressing the farmer and the country around old Nashville.

CHAPTER 6

Gone Are the Days
A Way of Life

P ERHAPS THE MOST DRASTIC CHANGE in the life-style of
Nashville during the last seventy years has been the evolution of
the modes, facilities and opportunities of our entertainment
habits. In the early years they were confined to a small circle of choice.
There were no neighborhood movies, bowling alleys, public tennis
courts or golf courses. There were no nightclubs, country clubs, supper clubs or fast food outlets. There was no professional football, basketball or hockey. There were no legal beer, cocktails or wine. There
were no public dancing facilities, gin games or game parlors. There
were no slot machines, pinball games or bingo. There was no pop music, stereo, television or radio. There were no neighborhood school sta-
diums, gymnasiums or athletic fields. There were but few restaurants
and they were located "downtown"—mostly serving working people.
There were only a few automobiles and still fewer available for the use
of young people. Until Prohibition, in 1917, young people did not think
of going into a saloon or drinking. From 1917 to 1933 with Prohibition
there were no legal liquor or beer sales or outlets. There were no motels, swimming pools, school cafeterias, or organized country music.

The limited sources of entertainment, the conservative character of
the time, and confinement to home communities allowed only simple
pleasures.

"What Did You Do for Fun, Grandpa?"

Do you remember: Riding the streetcar to Glendale Park and Zoo?
Taking your girl for a boat ride on Shelby Park lake? Making your way
through the hedge puzzle at Centennial Park?

The few times that you were able to see a baseball game at Sulphur
Dell? The Rex, Alhambra, Fifth Avenue, Strand and Elite theaters? The
Princess vaudeville shows and the Haymarket carnivals? Al G. Fields'
and Lasses White's minstrel shows? Fritz Leiber's annual Shakespearean plays at the Vendome? When the circus came to town, and the
State Fair? Gypsy Smith and Billy Sunday revivals at the Ryman? Barbecues, church festivals, womanless weddings, watermelon feasts,
hayrides, school plays, and Halloween parties? Hanging around the
drugstore corner and watching the girls? You and two or three girl

friends walking past the boys at the drugstore corner—and making out like you were not noticing their whistles? The Sunday afternoon date—sitting on the front porch swing? Your date walking you home from church?

Playing "musical chairs," "spinning the plate," and pinning on the donkey tail at parties? The neighborhood baseball game—and "one-eyed cat"? Steamboat rides and railroad excursions? Going to a creek or pond for a swimming party? Your family going to Red Boiling, Horn, Prim, Mint, old Jefferson and the other springs on the weekend? Horseback riding in the country? Picnics, nut hunting, frog hunting, fishing and "snipe hunting"? Trying to escape the attention of the chaperon? Graduation exercises at the local school? Camping out, hiking and taking a buggy ride? Trying to find your girl a four-leaf clover? Going to a Holy-Roller meeting and playing beanball? Inviting your boyfriend to the family Sunday dinner? The Sunday afternoon homemade ice cream? Neighborhood quilting parties, showers, and church suppers?

College and university students had campus activities, fraternity house pleasures, football and baseball—and the opportunities for pleasure not available to the great masses of youth. Do you remember their snake dances down Church Street and their bonfires before games?

These were simple forms of entertainment and pleasure, but this was all we knew and we considered them sufficient.

Church Street—1936.

With the automobiles of the late twenties and the repeal of Prohibition in 1933, life was to change drastically. These changes would start to erode the old conventional and traditional structures of conservative morality and create a thirst for liberal entertainment that was to "go wild." The automobile destroyed community barriers. Repeal furnished temptation to a populace that began to flaunt restriction. Both were to bring on the open revolution against restrictive social standards.

However, the young men who had served in the services overseas and around the world in World War I brought home new ideas. Simultaneously, Prohibition was becoming unpopular. There was a new search for more daring experiences. Youth became anxious to explore what was beyond what had been considered social limits in pleasure and entertainment. Things began to change. All this brought the speakeasy, the night club, public dancing, use of alcohol, and the roadhouse, and more familiarity between the sexes. Old taboos began to fade into license. Respect for law was lessening. The young man put his girl in his roadster, his friends in the rumble seat, turned on the "cut-out," and tore out down the pike.

Do you remember when Kyle Davenport opened Nashville's first night club—the Plantation Club? The Pines, Stanton's place, the Automobile Club, Ridgetop Club, Mickey Baines' place, the gambling bookies, the Allied Club, Frank Petway's casino at the old Mertens Building on Third Avenue? Poker games at the Maxwell House, Elks' Club, and the old Meyers Hotel on the Square? Do you remember home brew, "white mule," the pocket flask and Ridge wine, the Charleston, the bunny hop?

The newfound indulgences brought on unscrupulous bootleggers and others to make money through making these things available.

Then came the repeal of Prohibition which would unleash an avalanche of deeper indulgence.

Automobiles, repeal, and the advent of public eating places were to revolutionize many homes and types of entertainment. Fast food places were to almost end the family table. Eating out was to rob the home of family gatherings and associations. The young were to make the alcohol experiment. The old simple pleasures and entertainments were laughed at in a newfound sophistication, license and determination to "do your thing."

You, of course, know where that all has come to by now.

Without wishing to analyze these changes in profit or loss, one thing can be said for sure: The youthful indulgence in the entertainments and pleasures of those early years did not do the damage to our people, especially the youth, as do the more "sophisticated" availabilities which entice, tempt and engage the young—and old—of today.

Were They Always "The Good Old Days"?

Everything was not always hunky-dory in the yesteryears. We had the usual share of frustrations and distractions in ordinary life.

Did you ever drop your collar button while trying to get it into a stubborn buttonhole? It invariably rolled under the bed or the dresser, and you had to get down on your hands and knees to retrieve it.

Remember that the tire blowout would always happen when you were in a hurry or when it was raining? You had to get out the jack, tire tools, pump, and the can of tire patching and glue and go to work. And have you forgotten when a shower came up that you had to get the isinglass curtains from under the back seat and button them up?

Did you ever get stuck up with that nasty and smelly flypaper?

Remember when the drain pan under the icebox would run over? Did your water bucket ever freeze up in the kitchen during the cold winters? Remember drying your wet stockings on the screen in front of the grate? How about the mosquitoes from the rain barrels in the hot summertime?

Did you ever get kicked by a cow while milking?

It was a maddening job when your wagon or buggy wheels got caught in the streetcar tracks.

You folks in the city used to cuss the horses for their manure on the streets.

Remember when the well rope broke and the sandbucket dropped into the well and you had to fish it out with a hook? Or when the rope froze in the winter? Did your neighbor's chickens ever get into your garden?

It was a catastrophe when you could find no paper in the outhouse, not even a Sears catalog.

Did you have a horse which would not stand while hitched to a wagon, buggy or surrey, and you always had to tie it to a post?

Remember when the wind was blowing you had to keep the doors shut to keep the lamps from being blown out? How about cleaning the lamp globes, polishing the stove and mopping the kitchen?

Please don't mention the chamber and the slop jar, nor the odor of the schoolyard outhouse.

Did you ever get whitewash in your eyes?

Remember cleaning the soot out of the kitchen range? How about the dust on a dirt road when an automobile passed you?

Have you forgotten how cold your feet could get on a streetcar in the winter? Did you ever have a streetcar pass you up because it was already full of passengers?

Remember recess time at school when you had forgotten and left your lunch at home?

Remember when the film burned out just when the hero was to rescue the heroine at the picture show? How about those infected arms after vaccinations?

What fretted you more—broken shoelaces, a lost suspender button, a broken shoulder strap, a slipping petticoat, holes in the heels of stockings, a loose bloomer belt, a broken buckle on your knee pants, or a broken cap visor?

Did you ever have the bottles of milk which the dairyman left on your front porch freeze and break before you got them in on a cold winter morning?

Did you and the other children ever have to wait until the grown folks finished before you had Sunday dinner?

Remember how scared you were when you heard your mother screaming from childbirth pain when your sister or brother was born at home? How about the dread of catching chicken pox, malaria fever, measles, whooping cough, scarlet fever, mumps or meningitis? Remember ear and tooth aches?

Did your well ever go dry in the summertime and you had to get water from a neighbor?

Did a wheel ever come off of your wagon or buggy?

Did your clock ever stop, or you forgot to wind it, and you had to go to your neighbor to see what time it was so you could set it?

Were you ever as hungry, and did cooking hamburgers and onions ever smell as good, as when your money had run out at the State Fair?

Did you ever have to walk home after you had stayed so late at your girl's house that the last streetcar of the night (the "line-up") had gone?

Remember how your winter underwear itched after it started to get warm in the spring but before your mother would let you take it off?

Sometimes the kitchen flue caught fire; we snagged our pants on a barbed wire fence; we gave out of ice and some refrigerator food spoiled; the current went out and the streetcar was stalled; a clothesline broke and the freshly washed clothes fell into the dirt; a finger would get caught in an electric fan or a food chopper; lose the gramophone needle; break an axe handle; have a chicken or animal die up under the house where you could not get to it.

And sometimes the groceries would run out before payday.

Did you girls ever burn your fingers with your curling irons, wrap your hair on a piece of cane to make it curl, or use a "rat"?

Boy, was it bad on the family when an aunt came to stay a week and lived with you for months?

Remember, we would say, "that is the bane of my existence." Yes, we had woes, too—when ants got into the picnic basket; those roaches, before the days of insect sprays; making sure to keep the screen door closed; and when fleas got in the carpets.

Did it "get your goat" when your tablet got wet while you were walking to school in the rain?

Were you "pushed to the limit" when everything was set for your lawn party, but just before the guests arrived, the string of paper Japanese lanterns caught fire?

Did you want to "flip your lid" when you dropped something out of your pants pocket into the two-holer?

Did you "fall into a tizzy" when the horse or cow got into the feed room?

Some of these things would "drive you to the jumping off place," or "turn you upside down," or "drive you up the wall."

And remember back then you did not always have the right to "do your thing." You rather did the family thing, or the community thing. This was, of course, before the day of so-called personal independence and license to serve only your own purposes—regardless.

Were you "fit to be tied" when someone "told on you" and "got your dander up" to the point where you "blowed your top"? Did you ever exclaim that something "beat the band"; "the jig's up"; "fly the coop"; "that takes the cake"; or "that's the fly in the ointment"?

The sweet old ladies simply said, "Well, I declare."

Home, Sweet Home

Some called it their residence, some called it their house, most called it their home; a few called it by name.

To older Nashvillians it was where the family lived. It was the center of their lives. It was the birthplace of their children. It was where dreams were dreamed, plans were made and life was sustained.

It housed the family table and provided rest and relaxation. It maintained the family altar, the family discipline and the blood relation. It was the family love, pride and sanctuary. It was the supreme contribution to society.

Like many other standards of life, it has seen many changes—

physically, socially and morally. The ever-increasing search for a "better quality of life" has left its mark.

The continuous thirst for ease, comfort, entertainment and excitement has changed its character. Pretense and sophistication have chilled its warmness.

But to many it is still home—with all its satisfactions, promise, love and beauty.

A home was not available to all young people in other days. Often the young married couple started out in the home of the parents or by renting rooms. Many struggled and built their own homes in time. It was their ambition and goal—to have their own home. This came before anything else of a material desire.

Do you remember the "shotgun" houses and the bungalows? Dormer and bay windows? Back porches, attics, and cellars? Mantles, horse barns and buggy houses? Weather boarding, tin roofs, underpinning and wooden shingles? Transoms, portieres and window seats?

Do you remember the kerosene lamps and later the green cord that hung from the ceiling with the new electric light? The well or pump near or on the back porch or the water hydrant outside the kitchen? The outdoor toilet with the lattice in front? The coal house, the scuttle, the wood box?

In the kitchen, do you remember the wood or coal range, the warmer oven, the hot water reservoir, the stove caps, the cap lifter, the soot rake? The safe, coffee grinder, flour sifter, the water cooler or water bucket and dipper, the cabinet, the ashes? The stove pipes, the damper and the flue?

Did you have to polish the stove and mop the linoleum, wash, dry and put the dishes away, and clear the table, so you could get your lessons on it? How about the dishpan, the iron pot, food grinder, the big granite tea kettle, the iron skillets and stew pots?

Do you remember the parlor—the front room where the shades were always kept lowered and it was not used except for company?

How about the long lace curtains and the artificial flowers under the glass cylinder on the parlor center table? Its old family furniture and the big framed picture of Grandma and Grandpa, the velvet covered rocker and that uncomfortable settee?

What about the bedrooms—the wardrobe, chifforobe, the dressers, the brass bed, the rocker, the wash stand with its big china bowl and pitcher, the grate, the poker, the fire screen and fender?

Did you ever roast sweet potatoes in the hot ashes or pop popcorn on the dying hot coals?

Do you remember feather beds, folding beds, cots and heating flat-irons to warm your feet at the foot of the bed? Setting the crock jar of milk near the fireplace to keep it from freezing in the wintertime? When all the family ate a hot breakfast together and gathered for the family supper? The Sunday dinner?

And the dining room, do your remember: the long rectangular tables before the round oak pedestaled tables, or when dining room suites came along? The china cabinet, the punch bowl and the cups that hung from its sides—tureens, the glass butter dish, the preserve or jam dish, vinegar cruet, meat dishes, the sideboard, and the white milk pitcher?

Do you remember using matting for floor covering, oil cloth for table covering and "druggets"? Straight razors, shaving mugs and shave brushes? Curling irons, player pianos, and phonographs with horns and cylinder records? Cedar chests, trunks, footlockers and valises? When the house keys were all lost—but you didn't have to bother with having one?

Remember when you planted morning glories around the back porch and let them grow to the roof on strings to provide shade? When you had grape arbors in the back yard? The iron nutcracker that sat by the fireplace? The iron frog doorstops, and boudoir lamps?

These were all simple things for simple living but quite adequate. Few afforded automatic results and comfort. All required work, care and attention, but they were improvements on what our grandparents had in their day.

Today the "quality of life" is the result of automobiles, electricity, the telephone, radio, television, plastics, home appliances, fast food outlets, professional entertainment, frozen and modern food preparation and packaging, refrigeration and all the other inventions and innovations of this century.

A different life has made a different home: modern indoor plumbing, gas and electric heat, refrigeration, lighting, furnishings, construction materials, fabrics, furniture, water, bedding, foods, decor—all have made the present-day homes into palaces as compared to most of those of old Nashville.

However, all these have made many homes different in other and important ways.

The family hearth and dining table have been deserted by many. Seldom is the entire family present in the house at the same time.

Eating out is "the thing." Entertainment entices the young and old. The automobile is on the constant go to pacify the restless. There is no such thing as home chores.

Family discussions are rare. The world "out there" beckons. Community visiting is a thing of the past. Pride in the home is scarce.

You say these conclusions are too strong—then I suggest that you stop and consider how many nonsleeping hours teenagers are at home. When was the last time that your entire family had as many as three straight meals together?

Playthings and Other Diversions

The great-grandchildren ask what kind of toys we had when we were children and what did we play with. I try to explain that bought toys were few and far between. There were the iron trains and fire engines and papercap pistols, BB guns, tin horses and red wagons for little boys, and dolls, doll buggies, doll furniture, and jumping ropes for girls. However, we made most of the things we played with.

Do you remember getting a wooden Octagon soap box from behind the grocery, two wheels and an axle from an old baby buggy and making a wagon with a tongue on it, or using four wheels to make a coaster wagon which was guided by a rope attached to each side of the front axle? Since every family had a baby buggy in those days, one could always find some wheels.

Do you remember cutting a fork from a tree and using two wide rubber bands, some string and a leather shoe tongue to make a flipper? How about the pop gun made from a small section of cane and a whittled ramrod to shoot hackberries with? Remember when we all made our stilts, slingshots and kites from sweet Annie weeds, newspapers, flour paste, a rag tail—and how we would wind the cord on a stick?

Did you ever make a tent out of bran sacks? Did you ever throw clay balls from the end of a stick? Do you remember taking a large Karo syrup can, mounting a little wooden paddle above a hole in it and with the can filled with water sitting over a fire, the steam would turn the paddle?

Did you ever build a fort or a tree house? Remember trapping for animals? Remember catching moles and skinning them to make powder puffs? How about skating on ponds frozen over in the wintertime? Did you ever roll a hoop or throw rocks at a tin can on a post?

Remember walking the rails of train and streetcar tracks? Did you ever make a miniature pair of scissors by having the streetcar run over crossed pins? I wonder if you ever took two tin cans and after attaching two wires to them talked on them. Remember how proud we were to own a Barlow or H. Boker pocket knife? How about those wooden sleds we made—some with steel runners?

Have you forgotten your marble box or sack? Don't forget one-eyed cat, mumblety-peg, hopscotch, leapfrog, granny, knucks, Boston ring, and whittling on cedar. Did you ever race on ponies, bicycles, or coaster wagons? How about following the trail of a leader through the woods? Remember digging worms or catching minnows for fishing bait? Do you remember when parents built playhouses in yards for children?

Did you ever collect rags, bottles, bones, iron and copper to sell to the ragman? Did you ever try to make music through a comb with paper over it? How about a flute made of a piece of cane with a peg in one end and four small holes on the side? Did you ever make a balloon out of newspaper which, when lighted, the ash would rise intact? Did you ever make a boat from a wooden shingle with a paddle wound up on a rubber band that would move across a pond?

Remember the lucky boy who had a goat, wagon and harness? Did you ever tie your coaster wagon to the back of a wagon pulled by a horse to pull you up a hill or hold onto the back of a wagon while riding your bicycle to help you up the hill? Remember when we would steal a ride on the back of an ice wagon? Did you ever make an ink pen out of the tail feather of a turkey?

Remember making your own valentines? Remember the game we played when making a trip through the country by counting horses and if you came to a white mule, your score was nullified and you had to start over? Can you remember when those little aluminum match boxes first came out? Did you ever dam up a branch or dig out a spring? How many times did you catch lightning bugs and put them in a glass jar? Remember skipping rocks across a pond, or blowing up cans with wet carbide?

I wonder why we liked to climb trees, walk rock fences and hunt for caves. Who came up with the idea of boys wearing swimsuits, shoes in the summertime and neckties anytime? How difficult was it for you to learn to whistle through your teeth or two hands? Remember "teeto-taler" and jacks? How good were you at pitching horseshoes or at potato sack racing? Did you ever win a watermelon-eating contest?

Did you ever make ragdolls or doll clothes? What was the name of your dog? Did you ever hitch him to your wagon? Did you ever spit into a grubworm hole and then stick a straw down in the hole and jerk it out quickly to get the worm? Did you ever get gum off a gum tree? Or the honey from honeysuckle? Did you ever help quilt a quilt? Remember shelling corn? And churning butter? How about wiener and marshmallow roasting? Or frog hunting? Remember the first automobile or plane or movie you ever saw? Could you hear what was said over the first crystal set radios?

Remember your disbelief at the first announcement of television? Remember your first date? Remember three-legged racing? Did you ever play follow-the-leader or bandy? Did you ever make dippers out of gourds? Remember when we made little wooden cars with spool wheels, pinwheels and clay dishes? Did you ever play in a hayloft or on a haystack, or make mudpies? Did you ever blow up a paper sack and tie it to a cat's tail? Do you remember cleaning the cake bowl or the ice cream dasher? How about chewing sugarcane?

Did you ever play tag or drop the ball in the hat? Girls, did you ever go wading, make pin cushions or pen wipers? Remember side saddles and girls' tricycles? How about the little box in which you kept your collapsible drinking cup? Your pencil box, and your hair ribbon box? Remember those leather hair curlers and head bands? Do you recall when you would put a new pen point in your mouth and wet it, stick it in the pen staff so the ink would hold to it?

Remember the cork-tipped pen staffs and the ink bottle wells in the school desks? Did you ever cut notches in a swing seat so the seat would not slip off the rope? Remember chinning bars and hammocks made out of old barrel staves and wire? How many tops and spinning cords did you have? Could you make a strong bow for your cedar arrows? How many *Rover Boys* books did you have? Remember masquerade parties, painting hen eggs for Easter and the Christmas tree cuttings? How about those wooden swords you made? And tying thread to the legs of a June bug? Did you ever keep white rabbits, guinea pigs, white mice or pigeons? How about one of those iron horse banks?

Boy! We were a bunch of squares, weren't we? But we had fun and caused no trouble. We didn't know much that was different from this—and we were satisfied with what we had. What a difference time makes.

Fashions—A Passing Parade

In Nashville, as elsewhere, clothing, or articles of dress, have been suited to different occupations, sports, climates and seasons and costuming and times. This century has witnessed an enormous increase in the number and variety of garments worn. It has seen a remarkable development of clothing manufacturing, fashion, art and patterns. We have seen the transition from the handmade and the home sewing machine to machine-made ready-to-wear clothes, stock sizes and mass production.

The invasion of the idea of style and comfort was to further revolutionize the concepts of clothing. Later the synthetics were to take over.

But back to the clothing of old Nashville. There were no shorts, bras, panty hose, tennis or golf outfits, jogging suits, jockey shorts, windbreakers, sweat shirts, colored trousers or coats, zippers, loafers, colored footwear, and little costume jewelry.

There was only face powder and paint for cosmetics, no beauty parlors, fashion shows. Neither men nor women showed any skin below their Adam's apple and no women wore trousers.

We had two wardrobes, if they could be called that—summer and winter clothes. As the season ended the clothes of that season went into the trunk or rear of the wardrobe or closet and those for the new season came out of the moth balls (which smelled for two days).

If they had to be replenished, and if one was able, they might have come from: Lebeck's or Loveman's for women's and girls' dresses, coats, hats and gloves; Hirschberger or Chas. P. Ellis for men's wear; Gilbert's for the boys; H. J. Grimes' and Timothy's for dress goods and notions; Hopkins' and Meadows' for shoes. Or they may have come from the neighborhood dry goods store.

Passing Parade—Downtown Nashville.

Winter imposed the heaviest need for clothing. For the first twenty years of the century women's dresses and skirts went nearly to their shoe tops—whether they were low cuts or slippers, or high button or lace shoes. Those for girls or missess went almost that low. They were gradually to creep up and ease the strain of the male gaze.

Ladies, do you remember the long silk or voile skirts with white waists, high lace collars supported with whalebone stays, corsets and corset covers and cotton stockings? Heavy cloth coats, capes, fur neck-pieces and muffs? Those wide-brim hats with their decoration and ostrich feathers held on with hat pins? Petite coats with lace around the bottom and those elbow length white and black gloves?

Do you remember house dresses, kitchen aprons, flannel gowns, camisoles and knee length heavy underwear, drawers with lace? Large combs worn in their hair and Mother Hubbards? Dust caps, sleeping caps and bonnets? And the folding fan?

You who remember being girls, do you remember the bloomers and middy blouses, hair ribbons, everyday clothes, Sunday and party dresses, ribbed stockings, heavy coats, heavy sweaters, leggings, leather sandals and the first tennis shoes?

How about the elastic bands in the bloomers? Your first lipstick and rouge? Having holes punched in your ears for earrings? Plaited hair, bangs, buns, chemises, your first silk underwear and compact? When a parasol became an umbrella? When a lady carried her handkerchief in her bosom (and the way the young things lifted their eyelids when they took it out!)? Little black dots worn on the cheek? Your first daring black slip—and ankle bracelet? Girls and women washing, drying and combing their long hair? Wrestling with the seams in stockings?

Fellers, do you remember the Sunday suit, the everyday suit, overalls, work pants, work shoes, worsted and blue serge suits, galluses to hold up pants, the buttoned flaps, mackinaw coats, rubber overshoes, mufflers, mittens, stickpins, earmuffs, colored collars, attachable white collars, collar buttons and colored silk handkerchiefs for the upper coat pocket, and the dusters and goggles of the first automobile drivers?

Boys of yesterday, do you remember the knee pants, garters, buckles on knee pants, waists, homemade pants, caps, straw hats, soda-water caps, button shoes, corduroy pants, suspenders (store bought or handmade), Norfork coats, going barefooted in summer, shaved heads, pompadour haircuts, your first razor and shave, your first long pants, or your first B.V.D.'s?

Do you remember your mother fitting her tissue paper patterns, sewing dresses and waists on the foot-propelled Singer, threading the bobbin and the needle, putting the scraps into a basket for quilt making and her button, needle, thimble and thread basket?

Can you remember pulling the corset strings tight, union suits, shirts and drawers, broken shoestrings, trying to get a lace which had lost its metal tip through an eye in the shoe, looking for the shoe buttoner, the shine box with the shoe brush, dauber, and the Two-in-One and Shinola shoe polishes, perfumed sachets, the family clothes brush, boys' underpants made out of flour sacks (I once had a pair that still had "Self-Rising" on the seat).

As time went on women were to dress more comfortably. Hemlines went up and necklines came down. Heavy clothing gave way to lighter garments and bright colors replaced the darker tones. Clothes fit closer to the natural form. Silk stockings, high heels, cosmetics, shorter hair, costume jewelry, bras, shorts, pants, suits, light underthings, gowns, synthetic materials, and feminine dress freedom were to present the modern woman.

The wide-legged pants were too narrow for men, coats were to become longer, ties were to be narrow in width, no more detachable collars, belts came in, shoes were replaced with oxfords, zippers came along, seersucker suits were to appear, varied colors were to become accepted, synthetic materials and style were to bring the male into the fashion and comfort race. Half of his new wardrobe was to be for golf, fishing, tennis, jogging, swimming and sports clothes—and his tuxedo! He was to outdo the female sex in loud colors.

Laced shoes and buttoned shoes were to vanish, the ankle was to become unprotected and comforted with loafers and comforts and the foot doctors were to come on the scene to treat the results. The drive to expose feminity and masculinity goes on unabated, and nothing is left to discover. As the length of dresses went higher, so have their prices. As the neckline has lowered, so has the male curiosity. As the male has increased his attraction to fashion—so has he increased his vanity.

But time brings changes.

If Sir Walter Raleigh were living today and met the queen, he would probably expect her to take off her T-shirt and spread it over the mudpuddle so he could keep his feet clean. If Henry VIII were living he would be bankrupt from alimony—and wearing a barrel; If Prince Albert were living he would wear nothing but shorts, and Cleopatra would be wearing a pair of blue jeans.

The Animal Kingdom

We did not realize at the time the contribution to our general education and the extension of the limits of our imagination which we were gaining from our relation to the barnyard family.

Few children of today have these opportunities. We who lived on the outer limits of the city enjoyed the pleasure of this relation with the fowl and animal life. From them we learned more of the demands of survival, our obligation to and dependence upon them, and the wonders of nature. Moreover, they added to our sense of tolerance and loyalty.

Their loyalty inspired us to a softer reception of the rigors of life—to a sense of closeness, affection, and even love.

Remember? There was old Charlie, the horse; old Bossy, the cow; Shep, the dog; and old Beck the mule? Old Big Red, the rooster, strutted his authority over the chicken yard. Most of us had our favorite hens. And don't forget Tabby, the cat.

There was no greater American picture than that of the boy and his dog. Can you forget old Bugler, Rastus, Spot, Shag or Rover, your pup? Remember that look in his eyes when he craved your attention and love? Remember that he was your sentinel at night, ready to warn you of the approach of anyone with his bark? The first thing we boys learned to build was a doghouse.

Our pup, like us, was more satisfied with what he was able to have in the old days. He didn't get forty-five-cent cans of dog food twice a day; he got the table scraps and what he could hunt.

He was our friend, our companion, and our slave. Sometimes when things were going wrong, we would just go out and let his love quiet things down for us. When you felt deserted by the world, old Rover would crawl up to your feet and lick your hand. Somehow, you thought that he knew and cared.

However, he could upset us at times—when he chased the cow or the chickens, barked at the horse, brought a dead rabbit onto the porch, or wallowed in the new flowerbed.

Remember how old Charlie would come up behind you and push you with his nose, begging for attention or an apple or to get you to brush him? How he liked the currycomb? Can't you see him now, fighting a persistent horsefly?

Have you forgotten old Bossy and the other cows under a shade tree during the heat of a summer day, chewing her cud and switching the flies with her tail? How mad we would get when she got into the garden, when you tried to drive her to the bull, or when we stepped in a cow pile?

Do you remember the chickens roosting in trees, dogs barking at night, roosters crowing in the early morning, chicken-eating dogs, the cat up a tree and afraid to come down, the sound of cowbells, the dog trying to get to a rabbit in a rock fence, the "gee" and "haw" directions to old Beck, the mule, while she pulled the bull-tongued plow in the garden?

Aren't you glad that your experience as a youth gave you the opportunity to see a mare with her colt, a cat with her kittens, a dog with her puppies, a newborn calf learning to stand on its legs—and to watch the young grow? Remember the wonder of seeing the newborn go immediately to its food source, and baby chicks breaking from their shell to start immediately to scratch for food, and the old mother hen clucking as she led her brood? Remember how they all protected their young?

Do you recall how frustrated you became when, after working hard to build nests for the hens and to make them comfortable with straw, they would ignore them and lay their eggs in the bushes or under the house at the hardest place to reach? How the ducks would lay their eggs wherever they happened to be? Were you ever awakened in the early morning by disturbed guineas—or by the noise from the chicken house when it was invaded by a weasel?

The old concern for our barnyard inhabitants ran deep. Did you ever get up during a cold winter night to let old Shep in to get warm by the fireplace, get out of the loaded wagon and walk to lighten the load as old Charlie struggled to pull it up a steep hill, mix some hot water with the bran or corn-hearts into a hot mash for old Bossy when you went out to milk her on a cold morning, ask the neighborhood butcher for meat scraps for your pup, make sure there was fresh straw in the barn stalls, provide all of them with cool water in the summertime, give the horses and cows rock salt, or clean the hooves of the horse?

Remember when you refused to eat fried chicken, even though you were hungry, because it was from one you had known ever since it was hatched?

Remember the chickens dusting in the sun, roosters fighting, colts frolicking, bantam roosters strutting, horses neighing, ducklings marching in precision behind their mothers, and the cat moving her young kittens from place to place? How about the odor of wild onions from the milk in the early spring, and cows getting too much clover?

We oldsters are better men and women for having had our barnyard friends.

Crossed Fingers and Other Superstitions

Modern education and sophistication has steadily buried a part of the color of the life of sixty years ago.

Remember the old omens—signs of augury believed to foreshadow the future? Remember the superstitions concerning unlucky days, lucky numbers, chance encounters and warning dreams? Remember the old signs of good or bad luck—that unknown force that brought good fortune or adversity? Remember the places, situations, discoveries and chance events that would portend good or bad results? Do you recall how strongly people believed in them and adhered to their supposed warning or really looked forward to the promise of some?

It was bad luck to break a mirror, have a picture fall, walk under a ladder, accept a saltcellar from the hands of another, have a black cat pass in the front of your path, give another a pocket knife without having that person give you a coin, lay your hat on the bed, count the hacks in a funeral procession, walk with one shoe on and one off, for the bride to see the groom before the wedding ceremony, raise an umbrella in the house, the number 13, Friday the 13th, and many others in different locations.

It was a sign of good luck if one found a four-leaf clover, nailed a horseshoe on the house or barn, carried a rabbit's foot, found a penny, wished upon a star, threw salt over your right shoulder, knocked on wood, carried a buckeye, caught the bride's bouquet, wore certain things with her wedding dress, kept your fingers crossed, etc.

One that I could never understand was the two-dollar bill—some claimed it was bad luck, and some said it was good luck.

Remember the one about two people walking around opposite sides of a post, or the one which claimed that if a girl could kiss her elbow she would find the right husband?

Have you oldies ever stopped to think that the grand and great grandchildren never heard of most of them, or noticed the look of disbelief, if not disgust, when you indicate a remaining adherence to any of them?

Have you been able to completely get them out of your mind when confronted with a situation which brings them back to your attention? Tell the truth—did you ever go to a gypsy fortune teller, fancy your own set of good or bad luck circumstances—ascribe the bad luck of another to some act or event—expect a dream to come true—claim that someone jinxed you—claim that someone put the bad eye on you—play your lucky number—or have your own set of good signs?

Did you ever carry a luck piece—wear certain garments for good luck—dare to venture and trust to luck?

Some claim that all of us have some relation to omens, openly or secretly. We were closer related to the age of these notions, beliefs or legendary practices. There were many or different kinds. Some related to natural phenomena, especially those with relation to farm planting, animal behavior, bird flights and migrations, movements of the sea, insect invasions, and other things and actions of nature.

Of course, there were many related to different religions, worships, incantations, figures, animals, and spiritual beliefs and manifestations. Some approached witchcraft, sorcery, magic and voodooism.

This carried over, strangely enough, into the old ideas of cures, remedies and panaceas for all types of illnesses and mental depressions.

Remember about wearing a copper bracelet as a cure for rheumatism—the promise of the asafetida ring around the neck, and the drinking of black sulphur water for almost everything? Remember the use of leeches for blood letting, cupping for the relief of muscular pain, the promise of sex stimulation from ginseng? Remember the mad stone, the piece of rock which, when dropped into hot milk, was thought to provide a liquid which would draw out the poison from a wound made by the bite of a rabid animal and thus prevent rabies? Of course, there were many others.

The passing of the years of discovery, education, examination, chemical analysis, scientific exploration, together with the sophistication of the modern world, has erased most of this from the minds of modern society. However, people still conjure up different things to try to win the conspiracy of circumstances in life.

Looking back with the experience of long life, more study and reflection, and deeper faith, we conclude that these old customs, beliefs and practices evolved from the misguided concept that fortune is a blind and fickle goddess who dispenses at random her acts of good or ill to the human race, that fate is a wheel which is turned by chance and lifts man up to the stars or casts him down into the depths, that these omens responded to fortune's folly or fate's indifference.

It may be that their abandonment by the younger generations represents a more intelligent understanding of the inner workings and patterns of nature and a closer acceptance of and dependence on the hand of God in all our actions and their results.

With them we meant no offense to our spiritual dependence; we inherited them, like many other things which time has overruled and corrected.

Me, I still won't walk under a ladder or take the saltcellar from your hand, even if the great-grandchildren do laugh at the old crony. And you know, I think God may laugh at me, but I don't think He marks it up against me.

We've Come a Long Way

If we accept all of the advice being continuously offered by the press, radio and television, there is nothing that we eat, drink, breathe, smell or feel today that will not make us sick or give us a disease.

Any intake will result in something from acne to cancer and from indigestion to heart failure. However, we hear daily of the doctor-proclaimed discoveries and inventions which will cure all of these health threats, later—just around the corner. In the resulting confusion, we older confused people wonder how we ever reached our present ages.

With all the claimed discoveries, cures and inventions of the last fifty years, we wonder how we ever survived—and how our parents did before. But we have come a long way.

Do you remember when in Nashville and Davidson County: There was no indoor plumbing? There was little or no refrigeration? There was no air purification or conditioning? There was no garbage collection or disposal? There was no rodent control? There was no mosquito control? We had open, unprotected trash dumps? We had open sewage in some parts of the city? There was no ragweed or pollen control? There were no pest and insect repellents? Many homes had no screens? We drank rainwater from cisterns? There were no dishwashers or water heaters?

Our children and grandchildren will think that we are talking about things and health conditions of the last century, and before, but do you still remember: The open toilet pits and toilet cleaners? The long rod with the attached slips of paper which the housewife waved over the dinner table to keep the flies away? Those nasty sheets of smelly flypaper? The backyard alley rats? The kitchen roaches before pest control? The smell of the city dumps, especially when they were burning? The rats around the river wharf? The dust from the city streets before the time of asphalt? Horse manure on the streets before automobiles came along?

Do you recall: Spittoons in public places—and in homes? Slop jars and chambers? The outside school toilets? Horse barns and pig pens in the rural home enclosures? Fresh meats hanging in butcher shops before refrigeration? Reusable milk bottles and the way milk was dispensed from the milkwagon? Reusable soft drink bottles piled behind the stores? Rat and mice traps? Unpackaged foods? The odor of discarded food cans? The stench and danger of public toilets? The water dippers on chains at public and school water coolers? The family wash pan? Heating water on the kitchen stove for the Saturday night bath in the wash tub? The flu epidemic of the winter of 1918?

Do you recall that, as late as 1928, the entire County Health Department consisted of Dr. John Lentz, his secretary, two nurses, a milk inspector and two other people—seven people? When the department was quartered in two small rooms under the stairway of the old Criminal Court Building? When the whole County Health Department budget was less than the salary of the present director? When the likewise small health department of the city and the dispensary were situated in the rear of the old Market House?

Do you remember the twenty-four hour work day of Dr. John Lentz, his dedication to his work and his continuous, unsuccessful pleas for more funds and increased attention to public health? Can you remember the quarantine signs which were posted on homes to warn of contagious diseases—the different colored signs for chicken pox, measles, whooping cough, mumps, scarlet fever, malaria, diphtheria, etc.? Do you recall sore arms from vaccinations; the "no-spitting" signs on streetcars, on sidewalks and in public places; the annual talk of the visiting doctor in school on the danger of venereal disease transmission through sex; when electric fans first came along; when those who could afford it used Howe's distilled water, or that from Pioneer Springs; and the inverted bottles in the coolers?

Back then, mothers were both doctors and pharmacists, and the neighborhood druggist served between her and the only doctor in the neighborhood. It was sulphur and molasses and sassafras in the spring, and coal oil and sugar in the winter for cough and croup, and worm medicine in between. It was turpentine for cuts; mustard plasters for chest congestion; camphor for fainting; salts, c.c. pills, castor oil and senna leaf tea for you know what; fat meat to draw out splinters and thorns; Gray's ointment for boils; soot from the kitchen stove to stop bad cuts from bleeding; copper bracelets for rhematism; and Morgan Springs sulphur water for everything. The older women in each neighborhood had other suggestions.

But then it was a different day—only ten percent of the people used alcohol. Today, probably not much more than ten percent don't. Then, you would only occasionally find an unfortunate "dope-addict," who had become addicted to morphine or laudanum. Think of the situation today. Then the youth was almost totally apart from the use of alcohol—and certainly from drugs. How different today. Then heart attacks were somewhat unusual—the real dread was "consumption."

Cancer has always been with us, but the pollution of the air, ground and water is the new threat—born of progress and potentially as dangerous.

And so as medical science and knowledge increase, disease prevention improves, health care progresses, sanitary precautions develop, and treatment becomes more available, we remain confused, uncertain and scared. As we have defeated some, new threats have come along.

Our city has built an enviable reputation for progress in these respects through our medical profession and hospitals. Our people have made great progress in public sanitation and attention to public health, but we, like those of the rest of the country, are seriously confronted by and concerned with the new problems and controversies.

Looking back, if we and our forebears survived the older conditions, surely our young people will survive those of today. I remember my grandfather, who was the sexton of the old City Cemetery, telling me about the horrors of the cholera epidemic which hit Nashville in 1872 and saying how much better off we were then than the people of his youth.

"Sound As a Dollar"

Like all old-timers, I miss the old-fashioned American dollar and what it represented.

The dollar that was twenty pounds of sugar.

It was ten pounds of round steak.

When ten of them were a suit of clothes at Kibler & Long's ($9.99) with one cent change in a small celluloid horseshoe. Remember the clock in front of the store on the sidewalk on Fourth Avenue? Remember when a dollar bought twenty loaves of bread or two bushels of potatoes, or ten dozen ears of corn or ten pounds of lard? Remember when it was pay for a day's work for many, for a half-day for others and for three hours for some?

When it bought twenty fares on a streetcar to any place in the city? When for three you could have a round trip on the excursion trains to Chattanooga, Atlanta, Louisville, Memphis or Birmingham? When it bought a pair of pants and a waist for a boy, or a dress for a girl? When one dollar would carry four children through the gates of the State Fair? When it would buy ten hamburgers or twenty bottles of soda water? When it bought twenty school tablets or one hundred penny-pencils? When it bought enough to feed a family of six a good supper? When one bought a box of Belle Camp chocolates?

When it paid for lunch for four at the Little Gem Restaurant in Printer's Alley? When it bought a gallon and a half of Sidebottom's ice cream? When it would take you into ten picture shows on Fifth Avenue? When it would buy twenty boxes of cakes or four pounds of fudge at S. K. Kresge? When it would buy ten cans of sardines, or twenty ice cream cones? When it would buy an Ingersoll pocket watch? When two hundred of them would buy a building lot 75 feet by 200 feet in the suburbs? When three thousand of them would build a comfortable house? When twenty would buy a good milk cow? When 381 of them would buy a 1915 Ford?

When one bought five gallons of gasoline? When it bought either daily newspaper for a month? When a hundred dollar bill was a rarity? When two brought the doctor on a house call? When three paid the home electric light bill for a month? When one bought two pairs of children's tennis shoes? When one bought a gallon and a half of sweet milk? When one bought ten watermelons? One bought two neckties? Two bought a good pair of shoes?

When you did not have to pay any of them as income tax? When one would open a bank account? When two bought a box of 50 cigars? When one bought 500 pounds of ice and two bought a ton of coal (delivered)? When three paid for a hotel room for a day? When one bought ten dozen eggs? When one paid for fifty letter-carrying postage stamps or for one hundred postcards?

Beginning with the postdepression era, the old dollar began to shrink, not only in value but in size. Remember the old bills? When one bought 20 sacks of Bull Durham cigarette tobacco with free cigarette papers to roll your own? When it bought 20 large boxes of Searchlight matches? When it bought 100 pounds of horse feed? When it would buy you six pounds of bacon, or two dressed hens, or a Christmas turkey, or a 24-pound sack of flour?

Do you remember when a family thought it was doing well to save one each week? When not more than one teenager out of fifty had as much as one in a month? When the first cash register registered up to only ten dollars? When one bought 20 cups of coffee, with refills, at a restaurant? When it would buy 20 soup lunches with a soup bone thrown in for each? When a man could get a shave and haircut four times for a dollar?

Those were real "dollar days." The old American dollar, twenty "gitneys," eight "bits," one "simoleon," one hundred "coppers." The old-fashioned dollar was, indeed, a "buck," the "iron man" of all money.

Some Random Thoughts

Have you ever been able to understand why advertising companies think that the public is going to listen to a football player's recommendation on iced tea; a guitar picker's choice of buttermilk; a movie actress' choice of detergents; an astronaut's selection of headache remedies; a comedian's preference for Jello; a pop musician's advice about automobiles; a baseball player's choice of encyclopedia; a hymn singer's suggestion about flour and meal? Why should we make our choices of almost everything on the paid suggestions, the tastes and the preferences of athletes, movie stars, rock singers, actors, comedians, dancers or singers?

Have we arrived at the point where our choices of food, drink, clothes, medicines, appliances, automobiles—and even lawn care, carpet cleaning, dishwashing, window cleaners—can be decided by listening to some idiots singing us jingles.

Does the extent to which a woman is willing to expose her body on television enable her to tell me what is the best soft drink?

Is Bob Hope really an expert on gasoline?

Do you remember when merchants and advertisers tried to sell the true value and quality of their products instead of criticizing, debasing and condemning those of their competitors? When they respected the intelligence of the public and did not make false and ridiculous claims for their products—and did not insult the intelligence of prospective buyers?

Do you remember when we did not have silly kooks attending football and basketball games in idiotic get-ups and acting like lunatics to gain attention—especially of the television cameras?

And do you remember when it was the fashion for athletes to be humble in their successes instead of doing temporary victory dances, throwing the ball against the ground or into the seats, waving to the crowd, joining hands in disgusting rituals, applauding themselves and jumping all over each other?

You old sports lovers—do you remember wrestling at the old Page garage and at the old Hippodrome—and Henry Graham, "War Horse" Rogers and Jack Price Jones? Do you recall watching Zybysko "Strangler" Lewis, Joe Stecher, and Jim Londos—and the feuds between Jim McMillen, Paul Jones, Red O'Shocker and "Gorgeous" George?

Remember Bobby Green?

Can you remember when the Cumberland froze over so hard on January 26, 1940, that people walked across the river? It is now claimed that this will never occur again because of the changed chemical condition of the water.

The Cumberland River (at 1st and Broad) frozen over—January 27, 1940.

Have you forgotten that little kiosk on the corner of Eighth Avenue and Broad Street where the weather bulletins, service recruiting posters and pictures of wanted criminals were posted?

Remember police officers "Jelly" Drennon, Dick Swint, "Blue" Green, Jack Dowd, Chester Borum and Pat Mulverhill—John and Steve Hood, the photographers—Ray Cooley, the book seller—Ruby English and her shop for ladies—Sidebottom's ice cream—John Roesch, the undertaker—Frank Welch, the real estate broker—Norman McEwen, the laundry owner—Dick Norvell, the lumberman—Glen Briley, the hardware dealer?

Don't ever forget that dapper Cliff Hancock and the "Hancock Syncopators."

Have you forgotten that it was once safe to stop and let someone ride to town with you in your car—and to leave things in your car while parked on the side of the street?

Remember when there were no one-way streets in Nashville—or parking meters? That was as far back as ten-cent-per-gallon gasoline and seven-hundred-dollar automobiles.

Remember when a broom cost a quarter?

Did you ever have to patch a tar paper roof—or fish a sand-bucket out of the well when the well rope broke?

A Question of Morality

Whether the general morality of a place or particular time is best judged by introspection at that time or later, by retrospection, is subject to controversy.

It is, however, human nature, after a degree of failure at introspection, to award ourselves higher marks through retrospection. It becomes easy, if not habitual, to conclude that the morality of our youth was much better than that of the present.

With this explanation, we ask the question: What was the morality of our older Nashville?

Certainly, there was a deeper relation to religion.

Certainly, there was more respect for the rule of law, the courts, and law enforcement agencies.

We know there was no threat of drugs.

To be sure, women and youth were not associated with alcohol.

There was, of course, more dedication to the home.

Without a doubt, we had greater respect for parents.

There were, indeed, better community relationships.

Certainly, there was a greater will to work and earn one's way.

And, yet, to tell the truth: Were we not still holding to old prejudices, narrow concepts and unfair attitudes?

Were we not still holding on to our inherited subjection of black people?

Were we not still prejudiced against foreigners and Yankees?

Was there not still a tendency to look down upon and neglect our poor?

Were not our political processes too controlled against the real public will? Were not our higher educational facilities out of the reach of many? Was not the rescue from the demands of old age, poverty and disease more difficult? Was there not still a prejudice against Jews and Catholics? Did we not still have lynchings?

But do you remember when: There were no race riots or organized and professionally led protests? The only pornography was the annual opportunity for the male to review the female long underwear section of a Sears, Roebuck catalog or take a secret look at a revealing French postcard? Bathing suits covered femininity as well as masculinity? Children did not curse or hear, much less repeat, filthy stories? You only occasionally saw a drunk?

Do you remember when: Vagrants and loiterers were arrested? A "dope addict" was an infrequent curiosity? Churches and ministers did not advertise or compete? Police officers earned, deserved and received the respect of their communities? The discussion of sex was left to the home? Doctors would come to homes? Debts were obligations of honor? Virginity was an honorable estate?

Do you recall the time when: An oath was sacred, and perjury was dangerous? It was not necessary to lock the doors to the house and it was safe to walk the streets at night? A male gave his seat to, tipped his hat to, and assisted a female? Women did not smoke or drink—especially in public? It was natural to say, "thank you?"

Do you remember when: There was a fear of the consequences of law violations? There was a greater respect for leadership? There was a natural impulse to be courteous and respectful to those who were entitled to such? The home was the center of thought and action? Public schools were quietly apart from social and political controversies? The schoolteacher was an assistant to parents, and vice-versa? We knew that we could not have everything we wanted unless we worked and earned it? We were afraid of indebtedness?

Population increase has imposed severe new demands on public morality. Invention, industry, innovation and education have striven to overcome them. A continuous and restless effort to create a new quality of life has created new impatience and dissatisfaction with even the best we have accomplished.

Our appetites for more have only increased. However, we are learning that the quality of life is one thing, and public morality is another. They are not necessarily interrelated.

As we have conquered some of our old social habits and faults, we have created more, of a complex nature. We now find that the rush, demands, complaints, rebellions, dissatisfactions and desires continue their contributions to a new social immorality.

As we have changed from the family table to fast food counters, we have created new problems.

As we have left rook, flinch, Chinese checkers, Parcheesi, and lemonade for cocktails, beer joints, gin games, slot machines, video games, nightclubs and peep shows, we face new dangers.

As we have left the church and Sunday school for rock shows and television, we have created new threats.

In short, when we abandoned standard social limitations and restrictions for total license to "do our thing," we have asked for trouble and we have it.

But, do you remember that our parents and grandparents said the same thing to us in their day?

You find your own answer to the original questions.

Then and Now: A Comparison

The other morning when I went out to get my paper, it was foggy, cold and damp at 27 degrees.

Automobile traffic was lined up en route to town, bumper to bumper. In the line was a double city bus, carrying eight passengers. As I picked up the paper, about fifteen men and women in short shorts were jogging along the sidewalk.

A well-dressed man, stopped in the traffic line, threw a large plastic coffee cup out his window into the street, and two workmen in a truck threw out their paper breakfast plates onto the sidewalks.

Then came a school bus loaded with school children, none of whom would probably walk more than a quarter of a mile all day long.

About the same time, I noticed a Cadillac drive up to let out a neighbor's maid.

I went in the house and my cat was begging for a forty-one-cent can of cat food—and I had little enough sense to give it to her. That's about what supper would cost our family in the old days.

I turned on the television for the morning news and heard the important fact that they were investigating a policeman for DUI, and about a murder trial, before the news concerning the President's State of the Union message and the situation in Lebanon. After that, I listened to a doctor, who had been on the program two or three times every day for the past two years, prescribing for every ill that any person could ever have. I wondered when he had ever had time to practice his profession and if he ever had a special field. He advised that we send for his booklet.

Then came the sporting news and I heard that a football player had just signed a contract to play professional football for three years for five million dollars. Just a few days earlier I had heard the president of the United States call the coach of a football team to congratulate him.

I came to town and parked my car in a garage—$3.75 for three hours. Remember when it cost a nickel to come to town on the streetcar and there were stores and residences where the parking lots and garages are today?

I read in the paper that Harveys' downtown store was closing Saturday and I remembered the dynamic Fred Harvey's statement on the store's opening—"The store that will never know completion."

As I drove on West End Avenue and Broad Street, I remembered the trees that lined the streets and shaded the beautiful houses, now replaced by commercial buildings, neon signs, and billboards.

But then I started to thinking:

Instead of having to get up and make a fire in the grate and kitchen stove, I had only to turn up the gas and turn on the electric stove. Instead of lighting a lamp, I turned on a switch. Instead of going out to an outhroom, I went to a warm bathroom. Instead of heating water in a washpan, I had instant hot water. Instead of going out for fresh water from a well or hydrant, I had only to turn the tap.

The news of the world was before me at the flip of another switch. The electric refrigerator made it unnecessary to carry out the drip pan. I did not have to worry about the milk left at the front door being frozen—it was safe in the refrigerator. Instead of walking to the streetcar line and waiting in the cold, I got into my car, turned on the heater and drove to town in comfort. Instead of searching through a Sears, Roebuck or Bellas-Hess catalogue, I could buy anything right here in any number of modern stores.

Tonight I would not have to get in wood, coal or kindling or water for the night. I would not have to bank the fire in the fireplace. On a cold night there would be no chambers or slop jars. There would be no frozen hydrants to thaw out in the morning.

There would be no necessity to put heated bricks at the foot of the bed. There would be no need to worry about children having to walk to school in the snow and ice. There would be no ashes to take up. It would not be necessary to heat water to wash the dishes—there was the

Harveys Department Store and Church Street—1956.

dishwasher. It was no longer necessary to put the wash-boiler on the stove to heat water to wash clothes—there was the electric washer and dryer. No more flat irons heating on the stove—there was the electric iron.

No more going down to the store to use the telephone—there was one in every room in the house. No more summer heat and fans—there was the air-conditioning. No more flies and mosquitoes—there was the insect spray. No more scarlet fever, smallpox, measles, whooping cough or diphtheria warning signs on the houses—there are the preventive serums.

These and a thousand other things separated me from the Nashville I once knew.

We oldies have lived in two different worlds. Then we worried about it being too hard. Now we worry about it being too easy.

Now we just flow with the stream, remembering, wondering—and waiting.

Shriners entertain on 4th Avenue—1923.

Jack Keefe (former WSM star, lawyer, city attorney and candidate for mayor) entertaining orphanage children.

CHAPTER 7

Dear Hearts and Gentle People
And Other Interesting Folk

OUR CONTEMPORARIES will remember some of the colorful and unforgettable people who were familiar to the streets of the old Nashville which we knew. Some were recognized because of their successes, some because of their outstanding service to others, some for their friendliness, and some for their individual characteristics.

Remember Bob Skinner with his frock coat, top hat, white vest, walking cane, and the big bouquet of flowers attached to his lapel? He was only about five feet tall, but all of this gave him a place in our memory. Remember when those local devils wrote him forged letters from Theda Bara and the poor old man took them seriously?

Unforgettable Characters

How about old Ike Hirsch, the newspaper seller who sometimes sold newspapers that were two or three days old? You might see him on our streets one day and the next day, on the streets of Chicago or Louisville.

Remember "Pluto" Jones yelling at the umpires at Sulphur Dell?

Who could forget Dr. Gus Dyer, the brilliant professor, who claimed the title of being the ugliest man in Nashville but who was loved and respected by everyone?

No one ever walked our streets with more of the love of our people than that tender, understanding and sweet personality, Dr. George Stoves. Remember his brogue, his nervous activity, and his warm greetings?

And Frank Underwood, the genial owner of the famous old restaurant in the old City Hall Building on the Public Square, the friend of the prominent, the farmers, and everybody, who never let one who came there hungry, but without money, leave without a full meal.

Can you recall the dignified Judge John A. Pitts with his black frock coat and winged collar, and his flowing white hair, one of the great lawyers of the city and county?

Remember the rotund and jovial John Hilldrop, his carefree dress, his Virginia brogue, his old-time oratory? He was an extremely successful trial lawyer and a great conversationalist.

Did you ever know "Jew" Sam, a professional gambler who dressed impeccably and who would go into tantrums when he lost bets? Sometimes he would butt his head against the wall, wail and weep, and even tear off his collar and shirt when his horse lost the race? But he was absolutely honest, and successful.

Can you ever forget Mayor Hilary Howse? A self-made man of little formal education, he worked hard and was successful in business and in local politics. His engaging personality, his impressive physical stature, his uncanny judgment of men and public sentiment led to a political leadership that was almost invincible. This man restrained his associations with his political lieutenants so that when he did come among them it was like the appearance of a king before his court.

Hilary Ewing Howse.

Intelligence, dignity, business acumen and the desire to serve his community were the attributes of that distinguished gentleman, Mayor William Gupton. He served us as mayor and postmaster. A quiet and unostentatious man, he was gentle, friendly, and a fixture in our memory.

No more venerable status could be claimed by any of our old citizens than that which belonged to Moses McKissack. He participated in the early twentieth century progress of Nashville and founded a family of excellent and successful architects. When he walked our streets, he enjoyed the pleasant greetings of our people.

How could you describe the beauty of the personality and work of Rabbi Isadore Leventhal? A man of great intellect, patience, benevolence, he went about his endeavors on behalf of his faith and that of others with sincerity and love. An untiring civic servant, he deserved and had the respect of all who knew him, which was most of Nashville.

No more colorful personality ever walked our streets than General Jeff McCarn. An energetic, shrewd and forceful man, he was known as one of our best trial lawyers. His beautiful tributes, acid denunciations and his mastery of facts in summations were as well known as his frock coat and winged collar.

Remember that handsome, intelligent and friendly Dr. John L. Hill, and his widely known Sunday School class?

Did you know the remarkable Jack Keefe? A Bostonian, he married one of the Litterer girls and brought an amazing ability as a medical scientist, lawyer, musician, entertainer, churchman and leader to Nashville. He organized the first Pendleton Roundup, traveled on the old Keith vaudeville circuit before coming to Nashville, where as an early entertainer and radio announcer on radio station WSM, he invented the reporting of simulated sports events from the telegraph wire. He was later an unsuccessful candidate for mayor. Remember why he left the station as an announcer?

Can you ever forget the happy Mickey Baine and his restaurant in Printer's Alley? A big, good natured Irishman who loved his friends, he thrived on his pleasantness. Too bad he would never let some who knew tell of his generosity to the poor. The writer had instructions from him to send coal during the wintertime to any family that needed it—with one provision: that they would never know who sent it.

Do you remember the imposing appearance of Joel Cheek and the news of the sale of his Maxwell House coffee?

Can't you still see the handsome, able and well-liked Doctor Haggard walking down Church Street?

Go a little farther back. Do you remember the dapper, but tough, Alec Barthell, an early chief of the Nashville Police Department?

Remember the colorful John Omohundro, Gus Kiger, Leo Flair and the Redmond brothers? Uncle Bud, the friend and benefactor of all the newsboys, who sold newspapers on Fifth Avenue for many years? Few knew that he took orphaned and neglected boys into his home and raised some to be useful citizens, or of his kindness to those in need. He borrowed from himself and spent it on others. Few knew how many boys he counseled and taught to work for a living. He was one of the great men this writer has met in his life.

Jim Washer, the professional gambler, who spent thousands of dollars on those who needed help? He paid hospitals, doctors, and undertakers vast sums for those who were stricken with illness, or were injured, or died without means, without ever letting it be known except by those who attended to it for him.

There were many others. I am sure as you oldies read the following names, the pleasant memories will be revived:

Bob McKinstry, one of the first traffic officers, stationed at Third and Union; Sheriff Laurence Bauman; Luther Luton; Paul Treanor; Pete Stumb; Dick Swint; Judge Charles Gilbert; Chris Kreig; Wiley Embry; Father Abbott; Ewing and Lawrence Wright; General John P. Hickman; "Parson" Prentice Pugh; Dr. Noe; Dr. Gernert; Lee Loventhal; Harry Sudekum; Sol Cohen; "Titsy" Carter; "Polly" Woodfin; Dr. Billy Taylor; "Blinkey" Horn; Ralph McGill; Jim Stahlman; Silliman Evans, Sr.; Fred Harvey; Colonel Luke Lea; Squire Jim Allen; Mrs. Lizzie Uhlian; Mrs. Dempsey Weaver; coaches Dan McGugin and Bill Anderson; Dr. Keim; Rogers Caldwell and his father, James E. Caldwell; Dick

McClure; Jack Price Jones; Judge Lytton Hickman; Elkin Garfinkle; Mrs. A. Letty Sweeney; Hettie Ray; Dr. Powell; George Armistead; Charlie Rolfe; "Pink" Lawrence; Hugh Smith; Jim Cayce; Joe Wallace; squires Ira Parker and Ed Holt; Douglas Binns; John Early; Bush Sneed; T. L. Herbert; Tom Joy; Charlie Mitchell; Julian Underwood; Bill Jones; Harry Connors; H. O. Blackwood; Dr. Walker; Alexander Looby; Richard H. Boyd; Bishop Adrian; Governor Hill McAllister; and Ed Sulzbacker.

An interesting book could be written about the life, personality, character, service, success and characteristics of each of these men. They were colorful and are all unforgettable. Two of the most well known are still with us. Willie Wilkie, the "Mayor of Fourth and Church," a simple, good man who is a friend to everybody—and the pigeons—still holds his position on "the corner" greeting his friends. Few people know of the many things he has done for others, especially the unfortunate.

The other is Billy Pappas, the immigrant from Greece who, after coming to Nashville, came to know as many people here as any person. He has worked hard all of his life but always kept a warm greeting for all. From the old cigar store at Fourth and Union to Candyland, he has greeted Nashvillians by the thousands, with his still broken English, and good humor, and honest service.

There were, of course, many others, but we have been fortunate, and the number is too great to list here.

Five Men Who Made a Difference

Sincerity has kept much of the golden heart of old Nashville hidden in secrecy. Much of it throbbed with compassion in unsuspected places. Cameras and reporters were never allowed to look upon it.

Men who were considered by their contemporaries as hard, two-fisted, tough and distant in business and in their everyday appearance have been among our most charitable and beneficent benefactors.

Some, who have even lived on the outer limits of the law, responded to a beautiful impulse to help those who could not help themselves. These did not wish the recipients of their generosity and kindness to be embarrassed by its origin, and they sought no credit for their actions. They found that from within.

In some instances, while some were being critized, castigated and condemned for their actions, sharp personalities, hard-boiled business activities, lack of social proprieties, and other alleged faults, many of our unfortunate were being relieved and comforted by their unknown tenderness. At the same time the public heard only of those having their pictures made holding a crippled child, or taking a food basket to the door of the poor while engaged in a charity project, usually with corporate funds, or for tax deductions.

I know this to be true from actual facts.

One of my proudest experiences was the honor and respect which some of them paid me by asking me to act for them in some of these beneficences. They trusted me not to reveal their names in these charitable undertakings. I have honored that request as long as they lived.

However, it should not be as Shakespeare said: "The evil that men do lives after them,/The good is oft interred with their bones."

These friends are entitled to more than this. The ones I shall mention belonged to vastly different facets of Nashville life.

Jim Washer was admittedly a bootlegger and a professional gambler. These faults were well known to this community. By and large he was considered a negative in local society. However he was solid proof that one never knows what goes on in the mind and heart of men— their inner feelings, their natural impulses. We are too slow to learn that a tough skin can cover a tender heart.

Over a long period of years Washer commissioned his friend Harry Chitwood and me to execute many charities for him, in secrecy and confidence. We each paid out thousands upon thousands of dollars of his money to help the unfortunate. Just to mention a few, a young woman was painfully and seriously injured as the result of a bomb explosion sent to her in hatred. Washer authorized the payment of nearly $20,000 in hospital and medical treatment for her. He had never heard of her before her injury.

Another young woman was drowned in a fishing accident in another city. He authorized the payments of all the expenses of a proper funeral. He had never known her before. The two of us have paid hospital bills, doctors' bills and funeral expenses for a number of other unfortunates, both known and unknown by him, at his request and from his funds.

There are ministers still living who know of his generosity to local churches.

Hardly a beggar was ever turned from his door or business. A list of his total beneficences in dollars would stagger the imagination. He literally "clothed the naked and fed the hungry" in his own quiet way.

On the other end of the local social and business spectrum was Ralph Nichols. He was a very successful member of our business community, a gentleman, and a prominent Nashvillian. However, Ralph was a tough, two-fisted, rugged and tight businessman who found great delight in ardent transactions and stubborn trading. His frankness could be sharp, and he approached every proposition or confrontation with an awesome zeal. A good many misjudged the inner man. Beneath his roughness was a heart as big and as mellow as that of any man.

Many years before his untimely death he approached me with the revelation of a grateful heart for his financial success in the world and with a desire to express his appreciation for the good fortune he had experienced and which had enabled him to serve his family. However, he desired complete anonymity in his charity.

As a result, for many years after that, he forwarded to me thousands of dollars to be donated to the Shriners' Crippled Children's Hospital in the names of others as the donors of record. He bound me to secrecy with regard to the origin of the money. No one ever knew that while Ralph was perhaps sometimes cold in financial transactions he was helping to heal little crippled legs and arms with this money.

That big Irishman Mickey Baine did not altogether agree with the strictures of Prohibition in the conduct of his excellent restaurant in Printer's Alley. He assumed a strong-armed tough attitude, but in his heart he was impelled by a natural sense of quiet benevolence. For many years I had carte blanche permission to order coal from any dealer in Nashville to be sent to anyone who needed protection from the rigors of Nashville winters. He gave this same permission to others. No one ever left his restaurant hungry when they could not pay for their food. All of us were forbidden to reveal the source of the charity.

And from an entirely different facet of Nashville life was Uncle Bud Underwood of West Nashville.

For many years Uncle Bud could be seen on the uptown streets of Nashville selling newspapers. He was there from early morning until late at night, in sunshine and in rain and snow. Always friendly and good natured, struggling to earn an honest living, he never overlooked the opportunity to help the aged, the infirm, or the blind across the street, to give directions to a stranger, or to have a happy "hello" for everybody. The young newsboys looked up to him as though he was a father. He advised them, he helped them, he encouraged them, he arbitrated their differences and he kept them out of trouble.

Little did the public know as they passed Uncle Bud on the street that during all these years he was taking orphaned and homeless boys into his home and devoting his hard-earned money to help them go to school and teach them to make something of themselves.

You could not get Uncle Bud to talk about it; he just kept on doing it until he died.

Now I will mention one who is still living. As a police officer for many years he was considered a hard, ruthless, persistent and stubborn policeman. People did not know of his great heart.

He was for years, in fact, a "Robin Hood" in East Nashville. Hundreds of the poor have shared in his beneficence. I happen to know that for years he helped to clothe and feed many who could not help themselves. It is true that he might have used his badge at times to increase donations of food and clothing for these people, but nevertheless he put his heart and soul in his charitable endeavors and spent his own money in these causes. He was the real Santa Claus to the unfortunate children of the neighborhood at Christmas time.

I have been with him on some of these occasions and witnessed the tender look of self-satisfaction on his hard face for having helped them. This was the only reward that Morgan Smith ever got for his charitable heart, but it was sufficient for him. He wore his police badge with a hard sense of responsibility, but he wore an inner badge of tender concern for those who needed his help.

These are but a few of those who could not close their hearts against the suffering and needs of our unfortunate. We have had many here who never considered their own good fortune as obligations paid, but as obligations made. They all really believed that "charity ever finds in the act reward, and needs no trumpet in the receiver."

Many others, in all our neighborhoods, responded like these. You know something? I have seen all five of these men cry.

Politics and Politicians

Looking back, it is difficult to understand how a proud and independent young southern city like Nashville succumbed to and tolerated such a tightly controlled, uncompromising and sometimes vicious political machine as that which directed its political fortunes during the greater part of the first three decades of the twentieth century.

The Howse machine was in almost continual total control in Nashville and Davidson County until the last of the twenties.

Hilary E. Howse, a former furniture dealer, came upon the scene in the early years of the century. He was an uneducated man, but of strong will, a genial personality, and great energy. He was an organizational genius, and a strict political disciplinarian. He built a machine that allowed no weakness in its personnel. He demanded obedience to the machine judgments—and got it.

He became associated with the Ed Crump Memphis machine in

state politics, and the two dictated many of the occupants of the governor's office, the legislature, and the U.S. Senate and the Congress. Certainly, there were no officials in the two county courthouses who owed their allegiance to other political leaders.

The old city of Nashville was less than half of Davidson County. The city and county governments were entirely separate and held different elections. However, the county officials were all part of the Howse machine and owed their election and tenure to the Howse organization.

The mayor drew around him a small number of close, intelligent, able and loyal friends as advisors, and he would listen to them. Among those who served in this inner political circle for years were:

Reed Sharp, Vernon Sharp, Hill McAllister, K. T. McConnico, Charles Cohen, Ed Smith, Kelly Hill, Bill Jones, Charles Longhurst, Elkin Garfinkle, Dr. Bauman, Luther Luton, Frank Garard, L. G. Durr, and Laurence Wright.

However, the continued success of the machine depended upon the ward and district leaders. There were twenty-five city wards and fourteen county civil districts. Each ward elected one member of the City Council and each district elected two magistrates, squires, or members of the County Court. Generally, the leaders were the councilmen, magistrates or city employees—and all "Howse men."

The wards, vicinity, and leaders for years were:

First and Second Wards—North Nashville: Gus Blodau, Bill Jones, Mrs. Lizzie Uhlian, Frank Swint, and Sam Smith.

Third Ward—Jo Johnston Avenue, "new shops" vicinity: "Dingham" Bell.

Fourth Ward—Capitol area: Mike Reardon.

Fifth Ward—Uptown: Harry Hite.

Sixth Ward—Uptown hotel area: Harry Cohen.

Seventh Ward—South of Broadway: Elkin Garfinkle.

Eighth Ward—11th Avenue area: Seth Mayes.

Ninth Ward—Church Street: Dr. Billy Taylor.

Tenth Ward—Broad Street and Vanderbilt area: Henry Lassing.

Eleventh Ward—Alec Hines.

Twelfth Ward—West Nashville: Jim Weimer and Squire Reasonover.

Thirteenth Ward—Broad Street to Oak Street: W. C. "Titsy" Carter.

Fourteenth Ward—Wharf Avenue area—George "Hoots" Lowery.

Fifteenth Ward—South Nashville: Branch McConnell.

Sixteen Ward: Sam Stanley.

Seventeenth Ward: B. O. Briley.

Eighteenth Ward: Charles Longhurst.

Nineteenth Ward: Jake Sheridan.

Twentieth Ward—East Nashville—Treutland Street area: Sam Borum, Charles Shaw.

Twenty-First Ward—West End and 31st Avenue area: Charles Cohen.

Twenty-Second Ward—Charles Willard.

Twenty-Third Ward—Woodland Street, 17th Avenue area: "Cocky" Groomes.

Twenty-Fourth Ward: John Lechleiter.

Twenty-Fifth Ward: Charles Buchanan.

The County districts, areas, and longtime political leaders:

First—City of Nashville.

Second—Una area: Pete Carter.

Third—Donelson: John Omohundro.

Fourth—Old Hickory: the Hurts, Phillipses and Robinsons.

Fifth—Antioch area: Brileys, Bakers, Kelly Hill.

Sixth—Flat Rock: Jim Wilson, Ed Hosse, Mr. Mason, and Squire Whitley.

Seventh—Belle Meade: L. G. Durr.

Eigth—Charlotte Road area: "Tip" Stevens, Squire Reasonover.

Ninth—Bellevue and Pegram: Huttons, Tom Morgan, Squire Howe, Squire Joslin.

Tenth—Goodlettsville: Bill Connell, Everett Cunningham.

Eleventh—Inglewood area: Frank Stull, "Daddy" Chadwell and Jim Dean.

Twelfth—White's Creek Pike: Dick Taylor, Jim Allen and Charlie Smith.

Thirteenth—Bordeaux: Dr. John Lentz, Squire Hyde and E. Jordan.

Fourteenth—Joelton: Howard Wilkerson, Joe Toso, H. Hackerbiel, Casper Aita.

All of these men were extremely active in maintaining the machine political fences. They, the "city fathers," got jobs for their constituencies on the police, fire, sanitation, and other city and county departments. They saw that the poor and their neighborhoods were cared for. They got their streets fixed, lights put up, and other services for their wards and districts. They made their recommendations to the "inner circle" and to the mayor.

During this era, a citizen had to pay an annual tax to vote, the "poll tax." The political leaders would see that those who were able had a poll tax receipt so they could vote. Some of them would buy poll tax receipts for the poor so as to increase the vote in their areas. In fact, some of them would hold the tax receipts and distribute them on elec-

Governor Jim Nance McCord speaking to the Tennessee Association of Broadcasters—1949.

tion day and then re-collect them for safekeeping and to keep them in line.

The average total vote in the city elections was approximately ten thousand—sometimes less. The average total vote in county-wide elections was about fifteen thousand. Neither varied much from election to election.

It was a fact that this inner circle of the administration could, after receiving reports from the ward and district leader, tell within three hundred of the number of votes a candidate would receive.

The machine reins were so complete and tight that in a number of wards and districts, the leaders could tell within ten to twenty the number of votes a candidate would receive in their precincts. For instance, in the fourth ward, the Howse candidate would receive approximately 250 votes and the opposition would get not over ten. The twelfth district ran the same ratio, as did the fourteenth district, the thirteenth district, the fifth ward, and some others.

Of course, there was no radio or television, and campaigning was done by public speakings. Preceded by a big, expensive rally at the Maxwell House, where the mayor made his only political appearance, there would be a series of campaign speakings. They were usually held at locations around the city and county, such as: Meridian Park, Burris Filling Station, Porter Road, Woodland Street Fire Hall, Warner School, Chestnut Street, Eighth Avenue Fire Hall, West Nashville Fire Hall, The Hippodrome, Flat Rock, Wharf Avenue Fire Hall, Buchanan Street, Bordeaux, Una, Antioch, Lebanon Road, Old Hickory, and other places. The campaigns usually ended with a final rally between the old City Hall Building and the old Courthouse. Of course, all the election officials were appointed by the Howse election commissions.

To drum up crowds for these political rallies, Tony Rose's band, in a two-horse wagon with signs, would play up and down the streets of the speaking area in the afternoon before each engagement.

In 1910, Howse was ousted as mayor by the courts for misfeasance in office, for failure to control vice, and liquor violations.

Three other mayors served during part of the time before Howse returned as mayor: Gupton, Sharp and Wilson. However, they too, ruled through pretty much the same political organization.

Strangely enough, Nashville and Davidson County enjoyed fair to good government under these administrations and prospered.

The hold of the machine was broken in the late twenties by Gus Kiger, Richard Atkinson, and Charles Blanchard, who bucked the administration candidates and won in popular elections. The electorate slowly became independent, repudiated many of the old leaders, and the elections became less controlled and more open to outsiders.

A strong crusade and a series of prosecutions and convictions against poll tax violations and other election abuses by the then district attorney general, Carlton Loser, was to sound the death knell to the old system.

During all this era, both of the big city political machines were intensely Democratic, and only Democrats were elected in the two counties and for the state offices. There was practically no Republican opposition.

The only media exposure the candidates received was a few paid advertisements and the endorsements of leading citizens. The *Banner* was always with the Howse-Crump candidates, and the *Tennessean* maintained a weak opposition but always encouraged independent opposition.

During part of the era, the city had a semicommission form of government. Among the prominent Nashvillians who served as commissioners were: Bob Elliott, George Thompkins, Paul Treanor, J. O. Tankard, Dr. J. W. Bauman, and Luther Luton.

Good Neighbors

There is a tendency to retain the names of some professional, business, religious and political leaders who have gained prominence in the past and to ignore and forget the contributions of thousands of good men and women who have gone about their various works, services and enterprises quietly, sincerely and unselfishly. They never sought nor received much public notice, but they were constant in their duties and responsibilities. They really formed the bedrock of the community foundation.

Remember the neighborhood music teachers: Miss Gussie Gatlinger, Mrs. Blodner, Professor Schmitz, Professor Simmons, Professor Gebhart, Miss Rose McGregor, Milton Cook, Kenneth Rose, Mr. French, G. S. DeLuca, Mrs. W. C. Brown, Mrs. Hankins, Mrs. Van Valkenberg, Mrs. Throne, Marguerite Shannon, Mrs. Elizabeth Sawyers, Mrs. Mary Smith? All of these, and others, labored to teach children who wanted to learn, and toiled with those who weren't interested but were taking lessons only because their parents demanded it.

Remember the old neighborhood seamstresses and garment makers who toiled over their old Singers with the foot pedal, to make a few dollars to augment the wages of their husbands?

You must enjoy the fond memory of the old blacksmiths and their colorful old shops, where men would come for business and for neighborhood conversations and news. Remember the sound of that heavy hammer against the red-hot shoe on the anvil—and the flying sparks? Remember the bellows, dipping the hot shoe into the water, and the leather apron of the smithy?

Do you recall the neighborhood carpenters, knife sharpeners, chimney cleaners, well diggers and cleaners, "horse and cow doctors," piano tuners, gardeners—and the family undertaker?

Some of us will never forget the loyal, honest and trustworthy cooks and helpers who came to be considered members of the family and who helped raise the "chillern," who loved them.

Remember the milk wagon man, the market wagon man, the old tailor shops, the old shoe cobbler who half-soled our shoes, the watch and clock repairman, the umbrella shop, the coal and kindling yards, the ice houses and the harness makers?

The old family doctor who came through rain and snow, regardless of the hour, to relieve the injured and the sick was a loved and respected citizen of the community? For little pay he came to us with the fidelity of a shepherd to his flock. Remember doctors Lucien Caldwell, W. H. Tanksley, John Bauman, Charles Black, Charles Griffin, John Lentz, and doctors Reiger, Dozier, Cummings, Tucker and Altman?

Remember the black bag containing the medicines which they mixed right on the spot?

And there was not a rich one in the bunch.

How can one forget those little-heralded grand ladies of the neighborhoods who came into the homes of their neighbors at all hours of the day and night, to assist at childbirths, in times of sickness, tragedy, emergency and death, to lend a hand and to stay away from their own household duties for as long as necessary to assist the unfortunate, the sick or the aggrieved. They expected no reward except the satisfaction of love and the status of a true friend.

Remember those gracious and patient ladies who worked at Thompson's, Loveman's, Grimes', Timothy's, Lebeck's, and other old stores, standing on their feet long workdays six days a week and then taking the streetcars and walking home where they had to do their household work at late hours?

Don't forget the community helpers at hog-killing time, canning season—and who helped at making lard, hominy, kraut, pickles, preserves, sausage and getting in the hay.

Remember when a house caught fire in the suburbs or in the city, where there were no fire hydrants, how the neighbors would rush in to help save people, their furniture and properties; the "water-bucket brigade," and how the neighbors would take those who were burned out into their homes until they could adjust? Remember when there were

John J. Lentz, M.D.
Director of Health,
Davidson County Health Department.

but few telephones and how your neighbor who was fortunate enough to have one would let another use it?

We couldn't list all those good ladies who assisted the Protestant Orphanage, the Fannie Battle Home, the Florence Crittenton Home, the Martha O'Bryan House and their like institutions, quietly and sincerely, over all the years; the long list of women who volunteered for hospital work, and their efforts on behalf of the Red Cross is a credit to our community.

Remember Mr. Thuss and Mr. Calvert, the early photographers, with their black boxes on tripods, their black cloths, and when they would squeeze the rubber bulb while you "watched for the birdie" before the days of cameras?

Do you recall the old livery stable keeper and the care he gave your horse or pony; the old "corn doctor"; the neighborhood paper hanger, painter and paper boy? How about the Larkin and Atlantic & Pacific Tea and Coffee men, and their wagons—the walking back-peddler who came by once a year with his laces and ribbons?

The grocery man, the druggist and the dry goods and clothing man of the neighborhood, who extended credit where necessary and was a friend to all? The school teacher, the preacher, the Sunday school teacher were all members of the neighborhood family.

They all worked hard, lived simply, and enjoyed being good, substantial citizens and good neighbors. We knew them personally; they lived next door or down the street. Their children played with and went to school with us; they were all our friends. They were dependable, satisfied with their lot in life, lived within their means, and accepted the title of "good neighbor" with pride.

They earned and kept the respect of their neighbors. They had a sense of what was due others, and their good conscience prompted the payment of that debt in sincere service.

They were the cement of the communities of old Nashville. They helped to build the city.

A Service Rendered

Even having been struck by an automobile has not deterred him from continuing in a civic effort which most people would not deign to undertake.

Most every day one will find Jim, as he takes his daily exercise walk, picking up litter from the sidewalks, yards and vacant spaces in the West End Avenue, Elmington Park and Whitland Avenue residential sections.

Because of his physical limitations, it is not easy for him to gather the beer cans, bottles, plastic cups, paper and other refuse which slobs of good health pitch there from their cars and trucks. Some are sticky, smelly, and nasty, but Jim gathers these by the armfuls and takes them to a trash receptacle. It is Jim who gathers the signs and placards which have fallen down from the utility poles where they have been unlawfully placed and left to litter the ground. He receives nothing from his effort to relieve the community of this trash. Those who provide the litter don't care—Jim does.

Watching Jim in his effort to do something worthwhile for others is like finding a flower in a patch of weeds. He goes about his chosen task quietly, unobtrusively, and alone. He seeks no notice or reward. He gets his satisfaction from performing a service and contributing to a more orderly, clean neighborhood. Even some of the neighbors, seeing him with armfuls of cans and litter, do not offer him the use of their receptacles to keep him from having to carry it a longer distance. But Jim does not complain, even when the dirt of the litter is rubbing off on his body and clothes.

Jim represents the good of Nashville. He represents many who are willing to mess-up their hands, to render a service, to help, to assist, and to contribute. He represents many who do not serve through dollars, but by work which would be unacceptable to most. He has found his work for others as the result of the indifference of others.

His motives toward this service are not enforced by economic limitations. He enjoys a freedom from want that exceeds that of most litter tossers. This election on his part comes from an impulse which they could not possibly understand.

There is nothing more inspiring than a man who is limited in helping himself, helping others. Maybe God has given us the Jims to compensate for dirty and indifferent slobs. His type of civility consists in borrowing something from himself and turning it to the advantage of others. It excludes formality and is satisfied to be addressed to a menial task.

I am a little better by having known Jim.

A Toast to the Ladies

Nashville today finds many women active and prominent in the professions, business, civic and charitable affairs, and in government.

However, their recognition and reception into these areas of public life came slowly. It really remained the task and determination of the women of this century to train and fight for this advancement. With the effective date of the nineteenth amendment to the Constitution of the United States on August 26, 1920, they had their real start.

In the earlier years they had earned and received some recognition as the result of their labors for charity, public and private education, nursing and civic activities. But the job markets had restricted them mainly to work as clerks and secretaries. It was the common and expected fact that they would remain with the duties of mothers and home attendants.

The local progress of women parallels the successive lives of many of the prominent names of the last eighty years.

Great ladies like Ms. Fannie Battle, Ms. Edna Clemons, Ms. Will Allen Dromgoole, Ms. Stella Vaughn, Mrs. Luke Lea, Ms. Julia Green, Ms. Annie Allison, Mrs. John Trotwood Moore, Miss Lillian Doyle, Mrs. George Mayfield, Mrs. Elsie Sharp, Mrs. Walter Stokes, Mrs. Weaver Harris, Mrs. Pauline Duncan, Mrs. Graham Hall, Ms. Mille Hale and many others—all had won the hearts of Nashville for their contributions to the unfortunate and to education of our young people.

We Nashvillians continue to live in the shadows of the charity and benevolence and their dedication to our early community welfare. Their hearts glowed with generous sentiments. They were lovingly liberal with their time and material possessions.

Little did these ladies know that many would follow to go further and to make their names in what was then considered the exclusive fields of the male.

Mrs. Guilford Dudley, Sr., would be one of the early leaders of the emancipation of women with her work on behalf of the Woman Suffrage Movement in 1920. She had already established her name as a leader with her work with the Red Cross during World War I. In this latter activity she was ably assisted by Mrs. Will Cheek.

Who could ever forget Mrs. L. C. Naff, the impressario of the Ryman Auditorium for fifty years? She was responsible for a great part of the early public entertainment afforded this city.

Mrs. Lyon Childress and Mrs. Albert Hill were among the first ladies of Nashville to exert political influence.

Cornelia Fort and Mary Stahlman Douglas were the first Nashville women to find interest in aviation.

Fannie Walton was to lead a corps of 12 nurses to serve in Europe in World War II.

Mrs. Louise Lindsley and others were to direct the activities of the Ladies Hermitage Association.

Mrs. W. E. Norvell was to take a leading role in the repeal of Prohibition in Tennessee.

Mrs. Fitzhugh and Miss Hettie Ray were early into the restaurant business.

Mrs. Laura Brahnan was to become a leader in the world of publishing and business.

They helped Nashville to respond to every demand of our tragedies, war efforts, charitable needs and civic enterprises.

Do you remember: Mrs. Louella Bellah, the grand old lady of the Protestant Orphanage? The Sisters of Charity who have played such a great part in the history of St. Thomas Hospital? Mrs. Helen Wair, the "second mother" of the children of the Junior League Home for Crippled Children? The ladies who took such a lead in the work of the Nashville YWCA? Mrs. Rogers Herbert for her leadership in various activities for women and in civic affairs?

How about Ms. Lutie at Phillips-Buttorff; Miss Lottie Hatfield, one of the first ladies at the Courthouse; Mrs. Haggard at Vanderbilt; and Mrs. John Akin; Mrs. D. F. C. Reeves; Mrs. Blanche Fensterwald? Mrs. Humphrey Hardison, Mrs. Sara Jeter, Mrs. Robert Cheek and others who served so wonderfully? Some of them are still with us.

Think of the good works of that bundle of female energy, Miss Mildred Stoves, a lady whose face has always beamed with benevolence, whose hands have always sought the opportunity to assist the unfortunate and whose intentions have always been those of the Good Samaritan—a fine daughter of one of Nashville's most lovable characters, Dr. George Stoves.

And we still have Dr. Kate Zerfoss, one of the first woman doctors, if not the first. Bernice Huggins, who did so much for girls in athletics; Mrs. Cecil Sims who, with Miss Mary Ryan, was among the first woman lawyers. Miss Ryan was active in the courts until her death.

Today, Nashville women occupy responsible positions, not only in the professions but in all types of business. The flourishing music business has graduated women artists and executives into wide prominence. Some are now leaders in the financial structure of Nashville. They are now identified with the leadership of our civic efforts. They occupy a high position in our religious endeavors.

In the changing roles of women in social life, professions, business, politics and religion, Nashville women are performing in these new adventures with ability, energy and intelligence and without compromising their grace, charm, and dignity as ladies.

In a way, the progress of women in Nashville has been timed to the general progress of the community and they have responded to the new life and its requirements in admirable fashion. They are worthy successors of their older sisters in service to our community.

Passing the Torch

As the years have passed, many Nashville mothers and fathers, who by reason of their integrity, industry and civic contributions have left their family names prominent in our history, have had their children and grandchildren carry on their splendid reputations.

These later generations have not been content to rest upon the accomplishments and security left by their forbears. They have taken their inheritance as a challenge to build an even greater community respect for the family name. They have taken the torch of business, professional and civic successes, carried them high and added luster to old reputations. As parents and grandparents have faded into the sunsets of yesterdays, the young have sought new horizons, new challenges and dared to push forward.

Our city's history is resplendent with these names. Among others are:

The Forts, Creightons, Herberts, Omans, Werthans, Hills, Sloans, Cains, Napiers, Dudleys, Burchs, Huttons, Stumbs, Baltzes, Redmonds, Evers, Trabues, Gilberts, Noels, Craigs, Streets, Lansdens, Holts, Harrisons, Joys, Varallos, Curreys, Armisteads, Hardisons, Benedicts, Sudekums, Dyers, Harwells, Berrys, Sharps, Cheeks, Caldwells, Potters, Lipscombs, Jarmans, Clements, Davises, Schwabs, Keebles, Basses, McKissacks and many others.

While they were making their continued contributions, many new faces and names were earning their way into the ever-growing list of prominent Nashvillians. There has been a constant parade of their efforts and successes across our local scene.

Our years have produced many young men and women of humble backgrounds who are fired with the determination to succeed. These determinations have introduced new family names to community distinction and respect. They have proven that honest industry is always rewarded, that no young man need complain of being kept poor if he rolls up his sleeves and goes cheerfully to work. Hard work, diligence and honorable endurance have lifted them above the follies and inequities of the world. And this, together with integrity, self-respect and community interest, have made them outstanding Nashvillians. They, in turn, will bequeath a rich heritage to their sons and daughters of tomorrow.

Many years back, a popular national magazine carried a widely-read article calling Nashville a "son-in-law southern town." The article provoked gossip resulting in much unfair embarrassment to several fine young men on the local scene. However, in most cases, the young

Horace G. Hill, Sr.

Tony Sudekum.

victims of this injustice were to later prove their mettle. These young husbands of the daughters of proud local families were to devote themselves to the protection and promotion of the estates and the good standards of citizenship to which they had been introduced by marriage. They refused to take the easy way out, but in the end proved that they were worthy of their advantage, and they have added honor to the ancestral names of their children.

As the years pass the curtain of time constantly reveals the new accomplishments, new endeavors and new successes of younger men who are earning roles on the present stage.

Among these are such names as: Beaman, Matthews, Currey, Neal, Simpkins, Akers, Eskind, Seigenthaler, Roberts, Harbison, Andrews, Hooker, Cook, Ingram, Houghland, Raskin, Byrd, Massey, Johnson, Danner, Fleming, Freeman, Rogers, Haury, Gibbs, Banker, Dozier, Nichols, Gamble, Cummings, Rebrovick, and many others.

The local public would be surprised to know how many young millionaires we have in our city. The children of many are ready and able to carry on their work and public service.

There was a time when it was difficult for outsiders to penetrate the shield of provincialism which seemed to protect the native sons of Nashville. This obstruction to free progress toward success here has been cast away. Our doors are now open to the ability and industry of all who wish to join our march toward a better and more successful community. New ideas and new dreams are welcomed. Our potentials are at the disposal of any who can "make a better mousetrap."

All the while we have had thousands of others who have quietly, and almost unnoticed, gone about their chosen objectives with such diligence and dedication as to be successful in a material way and rich in entitlement to the appreciation of the city. In every walk of life, these steady workers and planners have helped to shape a better way of life for themselves, their families and the community. Their names are known to but a few, but they have been the backbone of our society. Their reward was not in a name, but in a consciousness that they had been good citizens.

From all of these viewpoints, Nashville has been and continues to be fortunate.

Names to Remember

In other years the men of Nashville had their favorite stores and shops, like their favored eating places. They came to know the owners, salesmen and employees personally and to enjoy seeing them.

In turn, these people came to know their customers, what they preferred, and they strove to please them. This was especially true with clothing stores. Remember Jack Minton, Ed Petway, Charlie Davitt, Tom and Sid Gross, Larry Semmons, Tom Crouch, James "Slick" Welsh, Lewie Monroe, Jake and Chick Gilbert, Lawrence Bauman, Joe Morse, Charles Hirschberg, Dave Lowenstein, Charles Ellis, Joe Frank, R. Z. Levy, Allen Pomeroy, and John Henry Newsom?

Buying jewelry was also personal. Remember these dependables: E. J. Sain, Charles Rolfe, Jim Cayce, Aaron Bergida, Sam Small, Phil Brodnax, Fred Goldner, McGee Brothers, John Guinner? And a little further back, Huelebrands, and Calhouns?

When one thought of a need, one almost instantly thought of a name, a local friend. Coffee meant Cheek; groceries meant Hill; drugs meant Berry, Spurlock, Neal, Demoville, Warner, or Jennings; flowers meant Joy, Geny, Haury, Tritchler, Harrison, or McIntyre.

One traded with friends and acquaintances and seldom dealt with strangers. Most of the stores were Nashville-owned.

Remember: Tinsley's, Green Vale Milk Company, R. W. Bratton Company, W. W. Dillon Company, B. W. Graves Company, Fuller-Cunningham Company, George R. Gillespie Company, W. A. Roarke Company, Troy Laundry, McEwen's Laundry, Uncle Hiram Roofing Company, Fred B. Cassetty Company, Olshine Company, Zophi Construction Company, and Williams Safe and Lock Company?

It was the same with barbershops: The old barbershops were the headquarters for male gossips, chauvinistic protestation, good humor, and "earbending." Here one could receive more advice, hear more bragging, listen to more stale jokes and find the origin of more rumors, than any other place in town. Here one was with friends. Remember any of these names: Ladd, Schlosser, Heinie, Jones, Timberlake, Breedlove, Oakley, Troutman, Baird, Greer, Washer, Cone, Caudle? Remember their hot towels and fifteen cent shaves?

Can you imagine what T. Ladd would have said or done, had one of our modern "long-hairs" addressed him as a "hairdresser" and proceeded to tell him how he wanted his hair done? He might have done more damage to him than he did to lawyer Lawrence.

Have you forgotten the uptown traffic officers at the corners before the days of electric traffic signals: Bob McKinstry, Mr. Hosrich, Enoch Shelton, Dick Swint, Bob Leonard, Emmet Franklin, Charlie Holt, Dick Norris, John Leathers, Frank Graves, John Steinhauer and Charles Sanders? How about Nashville's first three motorcycle officers—Chester Borum, John Burgess and Jack Boyd? There were no such things as squad cars. I'll bet you remember "Butch" Plique who drove the "Black Maria," and Inspector Ed "Big Tap" Wright.

Did you ever get lime whitewash in your eyes while whitewashing a fence, or wrap a piece of fat meat on your foot to draw out a thorn which you picked up while going barefooted in the summertime? Remember boils and Gray's ointment? Did you have a popcorn popper to use over the fire in the grate? Remember the smell of jimsonweed? Did you ever make a cane whistle or flute? Could you pull the lever of those penny electric machines located in the drug stores? Remember punch boards?

Have you forgotten the Oriental Golf Club, with Shriners Carlton Loser, Syd Haley, "Nig" Allen, Leon Gilbert, Nolen Wright, Pete Gunn, Ivo Burton and Jed Apperson?

I'll bet you don't remember when letter carriers carried whistles which they blew when they left the mail.

Remember Buster Brown's dog Tige, and what Bo McMillin of little Centre College did to Harvard's football team? Did your boyfriend ever bring you a box of Belle-Camp chocolates, and did you ever find the dime in the black-eyed peas on New Year's Day?

Remember "Open the Door Richard"; the Mecca restaurant on Church Street, and Porges; The Kit-Kat club on Hermitage Avenue; and McIntyre's beauty shop?

Remember the army maneuvers around Nashville in the World War II days; Silliman Evans' party for "Big Jim" Farley; Jim Stahlman's "From the Shoulder" column in the *Banner* and T. H. Alexander's column in the *Tennessean*?

Have you forgotten those round wooden containers that powdered blueing came in?

Some sparkling personalities of an older uptown Nashville: Sam Bittner, Lewis Cline, Harold Shyer, Tommy Little, Jerry Atkinson, Lynn Meek, Dick McClure, Luther Luton, Ike Wright, Dan Phillips, "Dog" Ward, Mickey Baine, Frank Mocker, "Skinny" Stumb, Jack

Price Jones, Jack Keefe, Joe Coombs, "Dutch" Morrisey, Phelps Smith, Tom Mooney, Francis Craig, Beasley Smith, Martin Hayes, Harry Sudekum, Jonas Redelsheimer, Charles Warwick, and Jimmie Sanders.

Today I bought an ordinary pair of suspenders. They cost $14.95. Seventy years ago I could have bought a suit of clothes (Kibler & Long) for $10, a pair of shoes for 75 cents, a shirt for $1, and a pair of suspenders for what I paid for the suspenders today.

I think I'll just drink a glass of dandelion wine with some tea cakes and forget those days.

People, Places, Things: A Kaleidoscope of Thoughts

Did you ever make a corncob pipe, skip rocks—sailers—across the top of a pond, or swing on a grape vine? Remember the pain of a stubbed toe suffered while going barefooted in the summertime? Have you forgotten horse flies, lady bugs and wiggletails? Could you shimmy?

I never figured out why school slates had that red cotton cord laced around the four sides.

Some other sparkling personalities of old uptown Nashville: Red Bransford, Jet Potter, Judge Boyte Howell, Leon Womble, Howard Baughman, "Gorky" Nichol, Hugh Smith, Tom Joy, Harry Connors, "Slim" Embry, Buford Wilson, Harry Grimes, Doctor Keim, Jonas Coverdale, Harold Shyer, Maurice Weinberger, Ed Holt, Judge Gardenhire, Manus Bracey, Dr. "Big Six" Hamilton, "Pappy" Joe Wallace, Allen Dobson, John Early, Billy Smith, "Tot" Potter, Harry Stone, Jimmy Melton and Jimmy Gallagher.

How about Sara Jeter, Margaret Shannon, "Flo" Redelsheimer, Dollie Dearman, Mary Lyle Wilson, Hettie Ray and "Hank" Fort?

Remember when Bob Hope appeared with Doris Day at the old Colemere Club when he first started out? And when Ralph Bellamy starred in stage plays at the old Orpheum when he was young? And Nick Lucas singing "Tip-toe Through the Tulips" on the stage of the old Princess Theater? And when the Ziegfeld Follies used to play at the Ryman Auditorium?

Were you one of the young things who wore the "new bob" and the thin, short-sleeved flapper dresses of the twenties?

You footballers: Do you remember when "the Kingfish," Governor Huey Long, brought his LSU team to Nashville to play Dan McGugin's Commodores in 1934—the same year that Franklin Roosevelt paid us a visit?

Do you recall who was the first Nashville woman to enlist in the

U.S. armed forces? Miss Will Allen Dromgoole, a well-known poet and journalist, (for the *Banner*), enlisted in the U.S. Navy on May 1, 1917, and was assigned to the recruiting service.

Did you ever wear a striped silk or crepe de chine shirt when they were the style? Remember the Sam Browne belts and swagger sticks that army officers wore and carried during and after World War I? Did you have a scarecrow in your garden? Did you ever jump off the lowered end of a seesaw when your playmate was on the upper end?

Do you remember what was meant by sorrels, chestnuts, bays, blacks, whites, iron grays, grays, and dappled grays? How about Rhode Island Reds, Brown Leghorns, White Leghorns, Plymouth Rocks, Wyandottes, Bantams, and Dominicas, and Topknots?

Remember sitting in the shoe shop watching the cobbler half-sole your shoes? There were nearly 100 shoe repair shops in Nashville as late as 1930. Remember splicing rawhide to make a whip—and that old expression, "let her rip"?

Were you a member of the cast of the 1927 Junior League musical, *Bonnie Bell*, at the Orpheum?

Did you know that Union soldiers brought baseball to Nashville in 1862, and that the first professional game of baseball was played in Sulphur Dell in 1885? The last game played there was in 1963.

Do you remember the sickening odor of iodoform and chloroform in the old hospitals?

Did you chew California Fruit gum?

I wonder what Carrie Wilson would say today if she could hear her business debated by Congress and the President of the U.S.?

Remember when you could be fined up to $500 and sentenced to serve up to 11 months, 29 days for possessing a drink of whiskey; the Sunday blue laws that made it unlawful for any store except drugstores to be open on Sunday and forbade picture shows on Sunday?

Remember Zeh's Bakery, the Cupboard, the Main Street Bakery, and the Dainty Maid? How about Uneeda biscuits? Do you recall the old ads: "See Winning and You'll See," "His Master's Voice," "Service with a Smile," "I'd Walk a Mile for a Camel," "Say It with Flowers," "Fit for A King," "The Best in Dixie," and what they advertised?

Remember "Dutch" Earhart, Milo Collins, Charles Howell, John Jolley, Henry Heins, and the Hurd brothers—house painters?

Did you trade with J. D. Allen, Alloway Brothers, Lon Capley Coles, Corlew-Smith, Frank DeMatteo, Graves, Ezell, Holbrook, Keef, Jackson, Shepherd, Tollar, Morton, Moskovitz, Munn, Overton, Reeves, Wade or Wilkerson stalls in the old Market House?

Remember the old real estate agents of Nashville: Biscoe Griffith,

George Gillespie, G. W. Allen, W. W. Dillon, R. W. Bratton, Dorris Loventhal, Arthur Campbell, William Coleman, Charles Coggin, Bill Criswell, Theo Eckhardt, Ike Gibson, C. B. Kelly, Ivo McAllister, Rucker & Pearson, Pritchett-Thomas, Henry Vance, Eugene Hollins, the Armisteads, Friersons, Bransfords and Martins?

Victoria Carter

Victoria came to us on the occasion of the birth of our first child in 1927. She was a young country girl from Hartsville when she entered our home. She was to continue through the years which saw the birth of four more children—and as they grew up to marriage and the birth of their children, she then changed over to one of their homes to remain until their children became grown and married, and then she was to nurse some of the great-grandchildren.

Pia Norman Hardin with Victoria Carter.

For more than a half century, Toto, as all the children knew her, has hovered over her "chillun," as she called them, like an old hen over her chicks.

They never saw the color of her skin.

There was never a better, kinder or more loyal person than Victoria Carter. She earned, and has had, the status of a member of our family. She shared the joy of all as the babies went on to teen-age, then to young ladies and young men—and later, as they became parents and grandparents. She laughed with us—and she cried with us. She stood by us at births, marriages—and deaths. The children went to her with their hurts, as they did to their mother. She soothed their pains and tended them in sickness. She glowed with pride in their accomplishments, and she corrected them when they were wrong, but always with love and care.

All the time she was attending to household duties with fidelity and excellence. She went about her work with enthusiasm and discipline—never complaining and often to the point where she had to be stopped.

She brought to our home a pleasantness, an industry, a loyalty, and more than all this, a love.

The "little rascals," as she called the children, came to love her, to confide in her and to respect her for her simple goodness.

As the years have passed and carried her into a much-deserved retirement, she continues to be an important member of our family circle. The children visit her in her home where she personally prepares her "cookin" for them, and they proudly take her out to restaurants with them. She is always present at any special function of the family. Her needs are attended to, and every effort is made to see that she is comfortable.

I am sure that all of us have profited, to some extent, from her goodness.

We are all proud to say that we love her.

In paying this tribute to our Toto, I am quite sure that I speak for many older Nashvillians who have shared similar relations. She represents a type of love and devotion which society needs. She represents a loyalty to duty and obligation to proper understanding. She represents pride in endeavor and the rewards of loyalty. She represents the victories that can be won with love.

I am confident that these lines will bring back some wonderful memories to many of you and that you will agree that these relations have helped us to a better understanding of many of the problems of the present. Our community is better with people like Toto.

There have been many of them in our community, and they have left us better for having been close to them.

They earned, deserve, and have a special place in the hearts of old Nashville. They represent an institution that has survived, as love and devotion have overcome bitter and ugly prejudices.

They represent a love which is plain and natural, a loyalty that knows no limits.

CHAPTER 8

Fond Recollections
Memorable Events

IT WAS A SATURDAY MORNING in July of 1915 when my grandfather awakened me to begin the day. I had come in to his home on the corner of Cherry and Oak streets the afternoon before when I was able to catch a ride from Flat Rock in a wagon coming into the Market. Grandma had made us a good breakfast and we started out. He was the sexton of the City Cemetery across the street. I helped him open the big iron gates of the main entrance at eight o'clock. Since there was to be a funeral that afternoon we walked south to the circle and then through the grounds to open the east gate, which opened on Cherry Street just south of Mallory. The funeral procession would enter from the front and leave by the back gate. On the way we passed through the middle of this twenty-seven acres where approximately twenty-three thousand had been buried since 1822.

A Day at the City Cemetery, July 1915

Among those buried were James Robertson, the founder of Nashville, Felix Grundy, Felix Zollicoffer, William Driver, who named the flag "Old Glory," Felix Robertson, the first white child born in Nashville, Governor William Carroll, Judge John McNairy, George W. Campbell, who had lived on what is now the site of the State Capitol, and many others whose names were prominent in the early history of our city. As the streets of South Nashville had been named for trees, so were the avenues of the cemetery.

I have helped to cut the grass from every lot out there and I think I came to know the names of the avenues in the cemetery before I learned those of many streets in the city.

We then made our way across the south section through the avenues and, sometimes cutting through the lots and around monuments, to the place where the burial was to take place at 2 P.M. Ben, the old black grave digger, and his two helpers had opened the grave late in the afternoon before. It was neatly dug with even edges and the dirt carefully piled to the side and covered with a green tarpaulin. In those days there were no grave-digging machines. The graves were dug with picks and shovels.

The south section bordered by the railroad tracks always interested me because this was where nearly 12,000 Yankee soldiers had been buried. Years later they were removed to the National Cemetery. It was in this section also that many victims of the cholera epidemic of 1873 had been buried. The citizens of the city, however, fearful that the cemetery would become a health hazard, stopped burials there and in 1878 closed the cemetery to all except owners of unfilled lots. This policy still continues.

Grandpa had told me how much the cemetery was damaged during the Civil War because of its proximity to the Fort Negley bombardments.

We spent the rest of the morning cutting the grass on different lots. We used the old-fashioned push lawnmowers but we had to trim around the stones with hand sickles. Naturally my attention would turn to the names, dates of birth and death, inscriptions and peculiar forms of the tombstones. I remember the grave of one girl who, after a quarrel with her lover, had committed suicide. He later had a large unhewn rock placed over her grave. It had a lantern suspended from an iron support which he would come and light every night because she had always been afraid of the dark.

There was another of a little girl where her grieving parents had placed her doll in a glass case which was embedded in the stone monument. And there was the grave of Mabel Imes, a black woman who was one of the original Fisk Jubilee Singers. Once while Ben was digging a grave in this back section, he had dug into a then-unmarked grave which was over 65 years old. The coffin was made of cast iron and had a glass window over the face of the body of a young woman which seemed to still be in perfect condition. Many people were buried in this type of casket during those years.

At about 11:45 we quit because we had to go up to the storeroom adjacent to the office to let Ben load some chairs. The office was on Oak Street and faced the mouth of Summer Street. After the chairs were loaded onto Ben's wagon, he drove them down to the funeral site and we went to the house for dinner. Some good cold ice water from the cooler sure tasted good.

After dinner Pa filled his pipe and sat out on the side porch until it was time for us to go back across the street to the graveyard. We walked back down to the grave site and Ben had already set out the chairs, put the slabs around the edges of the grave and laid the lowering straps across the opening. Of course, there were no tents in those days but the grounds abounded with large beautiful trees which provided shade almost everywhere.

We then walked back up to the main gate. Some few people were coming in on foot or in buggies and surreys and we would tell them how to get to the grave site. The undertaker's flower wagon came by next.

At about one forty-five the procession came into view as it approached from the north on Cherry Street. It was led by a horse and surrey driven by a black man and carrying Mr. Billy Witherson, the undertaker, and the preacher. They were followed by the hearse drawn by two beautiful black horses. It was long and jet black, with hand-carved sides and long glass windows through which the coffin was plainly visible. There followed about eight black hacks, carrying relatives. Each accommodated four persons and each was drawn by a pair of horses. Other vehicles followed with friends of the deceased. The traffic going north and south on Cherry, including the streetcar, came to a respectful halt to allow the procession to enter the big stone gateway.

It was somewhat of an eerie sound to hear the shoes of the horses clicking against the cobblestones of the street but every other ordinary

Grave of Captain William Driver of "Old Glory" fame—Nashville City Cemetery.

noise was hushed. Pa got in Mr. Wilkerson's lead surrey to show him how to get to the burial plot and the procession followed.

The hearse drew up along the lot where the deceased was to be buried and stopped. The horses, long accustomed to their job, caused no trouble. One by one the hacks drove up and let the occupants out and then moved down to line up on Pine Avenue headed toward the rear gate from which they would leave after the funeral. In the meantime, some of those who had arrived early and had been visiting the graves of relatives and friends were gathering as the family was seated around the freshly opened grave. Ben and his two helpers stood by in the shade of a tree. All the ladies attending funerals were dressed in black and wore heavy black veils suspended from their hats.

In those days no one left until the grave was filled. The hacks would carry the relatives back to their homes and then return to Vincent's livery stable where they were kept.

After the funeral was over the people went back to the hacks, buggies and surreys and left through the east gate. Ben gathered up the grave boards and shovels and loaded them on the graveyard wagon, which had been left nearby. He would close the back gates as he went out. I then went up to the office with Pa and waited while he entered the facts of the funeral in the cemetery records. By then it was about four o'clock and the Saturday afternoon *Banner* with the weekly funny papers had come and I was anxious to see Timekiller, Buster Brown and Tige, Slim Jim and the Katzenjammer Kids. We walked on down Oak Street, closed the front gates and went home. I would take a bath and eat supper early so I could go down to Mr. Gobel's picture show on the corner of Cherry and Ash. I had earned a dime—a nickel for the show and one for popcorn.

As time went on, these visits continued. I came to know some of the history of Nashville there and many of the names who helped to build our city. When I go back now to visit the gravesites of my grandparents and my brother, I relive a good part of my youth. I found that you could learn a good deal from a cemetery.

Our old cemetery is one of the few places where Old Glory is authorized to fly twenty-four hours a day, because the man who gave it this name is buried there.

A modern and busy Nashville now hurries by this old city of our dead.

The State Fair, September 16, 1915 (From Memory)

I went to the State Fair yesterday. It was children's day and we were out of school.

My father, mother, brother and sisters were going, but I went early. Papa had given me fifty cents. They were going around noon, but I wanted to go early so I could "slip in" and save a quarter of my half-dollar. I walked from Flat Rock and got in easy.

First, I went down to the bull pen, which was a circular one-quarter-mile covered track which housed the cattle, sheep and hog exhibits at fair time and was used as a horse training track in the winter. I saw the ones which had won the blue ribbons, and then I went up to the poultry building and saw the prize-winning chickens, ducks and rabbits. By this time, they were parading the blue ribbon cattle and mules and having the mule-pulling contest in front of the grandstand.

I left there and after looking at the new farm machinery exhibits on the hill, I went into the Davidson County or "Woman's Building." I had bought myself some of that new cotton candy for a nickel. They had music and there was a big water fountain in the middle with pretty flowers and plants around it. I saw the prize-winning quilts, embroidery, lace, ladies' and children's clothes, and other pretty things, and then went over to the agricultural building. Farmers from many counties of the state had exhibits of fruit, vegetables, grains, smoked meats,

Tennessee State Fairgrounds.

and all kinds of canned food and preserves. They were giving away free apples.

I then went to the industrial and business building. The National Casket Company had a lot of coffins on exhibit. Products were shown by Phillips-Buttorff, Cheek-Neal, Berry-Demoville, Crone-Jackson, Lebanon Woolen Mills, E. and N. Manufacturing Company, Tiller Piano Company, Early-Cain Company, and many others were giving away souvenirs. I got a free yardstick, a ruler, some needles and pins, a paint stirrer and other things. I got a soda water cap from Diehl and Lord's. Another exhibit was giving away apple cider, and H. G. Hill grocery company was giving free candy to the children and hot coffee to the grown-ups.

My father worked for Gerst brewery, so I got soda water free at the Gerst stand.

Next, I bought a hot dog and a bag of popcorn and headed for the midway. I rode the merry-go-round for another nickel. The carnival barkers were touting the sideshows and I paid another nickel to see Jo-Jo the Dog-faced boy, Tom Thumb and the Midgets, the Fat Man, and others.

They had a place where, if you pitched a little ring around a pocket knife, you would win the knife. I paid fifteen cents for nine tries and got nothing. I hated to lose my money and went over to watch a man with some scales trying to guess how much people weighed. When he failed he had to give the ladies some candy and the men a cigar.

The whole place was now getting crowded and it was hard to walk. It was time for me to meet my family who had come in the surrey and had hitched the horse down by the Vine Hill (Gerst) stables. While they visited the exhibits, I went back to the midway. I paid a dime to go into the motordrome to watch a lady ride a motorcycle around the top black line.

At 2:15 P.M., I met my folks at the water cooler, and we went to find seats in the grandstand to watch the free acts. Tony Rose's band was giving a concert, and they had started the harness racing. I got real excited trying to pick the winning trotters and pacers. Mr. John Early was the racing judge in the little tower on the side of the track.

Next came the parade of the Confederate and Spanish-American war veterans. When General John P. Hickman raised his sword to salute the grandstand the band struck up "Dixie" and the crowd broke out in the rebel yell.

Now—the big show. There was "auto-polo" on the track and on the big stage were the Flying Cadonas trapeze act, jugglers, acrobats, dog and pony acts, seals, bears and monkeys, and other performers.

Clowns were going through the grandstand entertaining children and the aisles were full of men selling cold drinks out of buckets and others selling popcorn, peanuts and souvenirs. After the show, we went back to the surrey. Mama had brought a big basket of fried chicken, ham and biscuits, potato salad, pies and cakes, and two jugs of lemonade. She spread it all out on a cloth on the ground under a shade tree for supper.

I was too excited to eat, so I went back to the midway. I didn't have but one nickel left, but Mr. Gerst gave me a whole half-dollar. I made a beeline for the old mill. I got in one of the boats with some big boys and girls, and when we got into the dark part they were hugging and kissing and acting silly. I still wanted one of those knives, so I spent another fifteen cents, but, again, I got nothing. I walked up and down the hill, watching the games of chance, the organ-grinder with a monkey, and rode the ferris wheel. By now, I was getting hungry, and the smell of cooking hamburgers and onions was too much, so I spent 15 cents for a hamburger, a piece of pie and a glass of muscadine punch. I was full, but I only had a nickel left.

I rejoined the family and we all went back to the grandstand to see the night show. A big crowd had come to the hill to see the fireworks.

And after that, they started for the midway or the streetcars, or to their buggies and surreys. They all seemed happy and were having a good time, but by now I was tired, worn out and sleepy.

At breakfast the next morning, I heard Papa tell Mama that the day had cost them $5.60.

Note: Sixty-eight Years Later

One of the boring attitudes of us oldsters is the strong contention about the superlatives of our age. To hear us, everything of our day was better. We were more disciplined—and on and on. The older we get, the further we had to walk to school, etc.

However, there is good proof that we are right about our annual State Fair.

The old Tennessee State Fair was the big event of the year. Next to Christmas and Easter, both the old and the young looked forward to the Fair more than any other date.

In those days, it was, in fact, a *State* Fair—regulated by a State Fair Board, subsidized by the state and managed by the very capable J. W. Russwurm.

For its day, the buildings, exhibit facilities and grandstand were of the best.

The beautiful one-mile dirt racetrack, the scene of the Cumberland Derby, before pari-mutuel betting became illegal, attracted the great trotters and pacers of the country for harness racing. "Pop" Geers, the greatest driver of them all, won many races here. The horse barns were kept like homes. Harness racing was a daily fixture.

The old State Fair was simple, plain and family-like, good and wholesome—something for everybody. There was none of the rush, impatience, razzle-dazzle, cheating, vandalism, violence, danger and expensiveness of the events today.

The old State Fair provided wholesome fun and relaxation, clean entertainment, education, opportunity to see the new things of the day, and a reward for excellence in farming, housekeeping, business and domestic achievement.

This was sufficient for the time.

It served as a family attraction for Nashville when she was known as the "Athens of the South"—and was full of Southern pride.

Nashville and World War I

By 1915 the horrors of the Civil War and the Reconstruction days were being forgotten. The Confederate veterans were becoming the "thin gray line," in fact. Since that national ordeal, the following third and fourth generations of young America were now enthralled with the emergence of their country as a world power.

The swift conclusion of the Spanish–American War had sent this notice to the Old World. The Industrial Revolution had awakened the country to its potentials. Europeans were passing through Ellis Island in droves. The country was at peace—and busy. Our new quality of life and freedom had attracted the attention of the world.

Nashville was yet a conservative, traditional Southern town, comfortable and satisfied with its easy-going habits and customs and a sense of self-sufficiency. It was growing, but its progress was not interfering with its peace and standards. It had won the status of the "Athens of the South" and was proud to be the capital of the Volunteer State and the home of Andrew Jackson.

War had broken out in Europe in August of 1914 but President Woodrow Wilson had issued a proclamation of neutrality for the United States. However, to most Americans, and especially to us here in an inland city of the South, this conflict belonged to a world far removed from us. However, the United States was becoming increasingly embroiled in the war as the atrocities continued.

On April 6, 1917, the United States declared war on Germany.

When the country mobilized for the war, the Volunteer State and Nashville rolled up the sleeves and became caught up in intense na-

Early wharf scene.

tional spirit as they recoiled from the continuing reports of German ruthlessness and cruelty.

For the next few years life in America—and Nashville—would change. Our blood would boil—we would face the international challenges of a power hungry enemy. We would see our mother country in extreme peril. Our strength and fortitude would be tested. Our resolve to go to the assistance of our friends and to defend against the threat to

America grew to fever heat. Our determination to help "make the world safe for democracy" was now set in concrete.

The young men and boys of Nashville and Davidson County marched to the recruiting stations to preserve the reputation of the Volunteer State. Mothers and fathers cried and suffered as they left—but they were proud and prayed as they went to work to "do their bit." Service flags began to appear in the windows of Nashville homes. We began to sing to ease the ordeal. "Over There," "Tipperary," "Johnny Get Your Gun," and other new war songs came from every phonograph and band.

By now, the young American soldiers were sailing from our ports to the tune of "Goodbye Broadway, Hello France." Mothers, daughters, sisters and sweethearts were busy with Red Cross canteens to assist, comfort and entertain the soldiers passing through Nashville at the Union Station and in nearby camps. DuPont was building the powder plant at Old Hickory. The L&N Railroad was building Radnor yards to facilitate the growing shipment of war material. Nashvillians were exceeding their quotas in the purchase of Liberty Bonds and in their con-

Aerial view of Radnor Yards.

tribution to the Red Cross and Salvation Army, both of which were shouldering great responsibility at home and on the front.

Colonels Harry Berry and Luke Lea had organized the 115th and the 114th field artillery units consisting mainly of Nashville and Tennessee boys. These, together with other units of the Thirtieth Division with southern boys, had gone to France.

Mothers and fathers began to scan the War Department's daily listing of the dead and wounded. We learned about trench warfare and first heard of no-man's-land. We thrilled at reports of the exploits of Captain Eddie Rickenbacker, were bitter over the fate of nurse Edith Cavell, and were outraged over the mass murder of the Canadian soldiers by the first use of poison gas by the Germans at Ypres. We now became familiar with the ugly "peach-seed" gas masks being furnished to the American forces. We now hated the Hindenberg Line and Count von Luckner (the Sea Wolf), the German U-Boat commander who was sending so many to the bottom of the sea.

Now we began to see the blue stars on the service flags turn to gold as parents began to receive the dreaded telegrams from the War Department, which began with "We regret to inform you. . . ." The most horrible cost of the war was coming home.

Do you remember:

"Mid the war's great curse, stands a Red Cross nurse. She's the rose of No-man's-land" and—

"In Flander's fields, the poppies blow. Between the crosses, row on row."

Do you remember the canvas and woolen wrap-around leggings, the overseas caps, Sam Browne belts and army shoes and ponchos? How about the different colored hat cords to denote the branch of service? Can you still sing "The White Cliffs of Dover"? Do you recall the special thrill of Tennesseans when the world learned of the heroic action of Sergeant Alvin C. York of Pall Mall, Tennessee—and the attempt of Colonel Luke Lea to kidnap the kaiser?

Finally we came to learn that the tide was turning.

The "Huns" were retreating—the "Krauts" were beginning to feel American steel and Old Glory. The tricolor and the Union Jack were flying over increasing amounts of recaptured areas of Europe.

The smell of victory was in the air. On November 11, 1918, Germany surrendered. That night I climbed upon the lower ledge of a building on the corner of Third Avenue and Union Street so I could see over the tremendous and surging crowd gathered in uptown Nashville to celebrate the end of the war. It was impossible to walk in the crowd. They walked, they came in wagons, buggies, surreys, on horseback and some in the few automobiles in Nashville at the time. They screamed and yelled until they were too hoarse to be heard. They waved flags, they cried, they shouted and they prayed. I don't believe that there had ever been, or that there will ever be again, such a heart-felt and joyous outpouring of triumph, relief and thankfulness on the part of Nashvillians, as I saw that night.

My brother and all the others who had volunteered from Flat Rock came back—except one—our friend and neighbor Alpheus White.

His name is inscribed in bronze on the rolls of the dead in the ro-tunda of the War Memorial Building together with others from the Vol-unteer State who gave their lives for our country.

Nashville had done its part—and more.

Christmastime, 1920

It is Thursday before Christmas in 1920. It is cold in Nashville, but it looks like we will not have a white Christmas.

This has been an eventful year for the country. The Tennessee boys are all home from Europe after serving in World War I, and they are settling down to normal life—some looking for jobs. The ailing presi-dent, Woodrow Wilson, has received the Nobel Peace Prize, but has lost his fight for the League of Nations. Warren G. Harding has been elected to succeed him with Calvin Coolidge as vice-president. Women voted for the first time. Station KDKA carried the first national broad-cast. National Prohibition has taken effect. Judge Kennesaw Landis has become the first commissioner of baseball. Jack Dempsey knocked out Jess Willard for the championship. An airplane has crossed the Atlantic for the first time, and air mail service has been started between New York and San Francisco. Anticommunist sentiment is raging and many are being deported to Russia. Postwar employment is a big problem. The 1920 census places the population of the United States at 106,021,537. For the first time the rural population of the country is smaller than the urban. The Bolshevik army has captured Georgia in the Caucasus, as the Russian Revolution rages, and the Japanese are slaughtering Koreans.

Nashville is growing. They have started to build the Commerce Union Bank Building at Fourth and Union. The old buildings are being razed to build the War Memorial Building. It looks like the age of the automobile is at hand. They are fast replacing the horse and wagon on our streets. Construction has started on our first concrete thoroughfare—Woodmont Boulevard.

F. Arthur Henkle has conducted the first Nashville Symphony Orchestra on the stage of the Princess Theatre. Sergeant Alvin York is being toasted all over the nation as the outstanding hero of World War I. Dr. John J. Mullowney has been named as the new president of Meharry College. Senator McKellar is being applauded for his opposition in the Senate to the cancellation of war debts owed to the U.S. by the Allies.

Today's *Banner* says that Monk Sharp's Ramblers beat Bryson College 40–17 and carries a poem by Grantland Rice titled "Clan to Clan." It also carries the announcement of Governor Albert Roberts that he would issue Christmas pardons and of the city judge that he would free everyone from the city jail for Christmas. Major Stahlman says that he has two tons of turkeys ready for the *Banner* employees.

Other articles in today's *Banner*: Dr. George Holcomb married to Miss Ruth Hyde; a story by O. Henry called "The Ransom of Red Chief"; fifty thousand dollars worth of bonds and securities taken from the Bank of Smyrna found floating down the Cumberland at Ashland City.

O. K. Houck advertises pianos for $335; the White Front Market has spiced round at 25 cents per pound; rump roast at 17$\frac{1}{2}$ cents; steak for 25 cents; and sliced bacon at 35 cents. The cost of the *Banner* is ten dollars per year. The price of a Ford touring car has gone up to about seven hundred fifty dollars.

The *Banner* asks that its subscribers remember the paperboys today as they distribute the calendars. The Elks, Shriners and Knights of Columbus are all set for their Christmas parties for the orphanages and underprivileged children. The bells and band of the Salvation Army are on the streets and the "Big Brothers" are ready with their baskets for the poor. The Nashville churches are all preparing for their annual services.

The cold weather is causing some trouble with freezing pipes and car radiators are freezing up and bursting. People are putting denatured alcohol in the radiators.

Schools are out for the holidays and lots of boys and girls have gone to the woods to cut Christmas trees. The old City Market is a beehive of activity as many buy hams, spiced round, cranberries and foodstuffs for the Christmas tables. The stores are all decorated and the Christmas spirit is everywhere.

Families are being united and the kitchen is the busiest place in the homes. Most fruitcakes have been baked and are now soaking in a little bourbon. Housewives are busy today baking and cooking turkey, ham, cakes and pies and other goodies.

Some oranges are available, but the stores are selling lots of nuts, raisins, candies and fruits. You can hardly get into Mitchell's or Candyland for candies because of the crowds—and because of the slow giftwrapping.

Lots of men are cussing the first Christmas of Prohibition. The bootleggers are having a field day with their "white lightning"— six dollars a gallon. Some poor devils will be drinking Jamaica ginger or bay rum. Some are disgusted with boiled custard as a substitute for the usual Christmas spiked eggnog.

Another busy place is Joe Roller's bicycle shop. Many stores are giving their calendars to customers. The Union Station is busy with the trains bringing people home for the holidays and others leaving for homes elsewhere.

Many children gather before the front windows of Phillips-Buttorff, Caster-Knott, Lebeck's and other stores to see the Christmas toy displays, and parents are coming out of the stores with sacks of toys. Hiding them in the homes 'til Christmas is a problem. Older children are after the red-hot item, the new crystal radios. The boys are buying fireworks.

The paper is carrying two pages of letters to Santa from small children. Some are pitiful. The streetcars are crowded and cold, and you can hardly find your way through the Transfer Station—but no one seems to care, and all seem tired but in a jolly mood. Mothers probably wish that the children had been kept in school until Christmas Eve so they would not be underfoot while they are scurrying around the kitchen. They will have some cookies ready for the carol singers when they come around tonight. At a late hour they will go to bed tired but knowing that they have lots to do for the next two days. But it is Christmas time—MERRY CHRISTMAS TO ALL!

P.S. In this week's *Saturday Evening Post* there is a poem by Fairfax Downey:

> There was a hole in our town,
>   and it was wonderous wide.
> The traffic barely managed to
>   get by on either side.
> And when they'd finished with the hole
>   and covered up the main,
> Contractors jumped upon the street
>   and dug it up again.

Also an ad for the new Oliver Typewriter—$49.

The movies this week are starring Pauline Frederick, Mary Pickford, Mary Miles Minter, Jack Pickford, Phyllis Haver, Billie Burke and William S. Hart.

A Saxon roadster sells for $675.

They are saying that radios will be available for homes this year and even predicting that people will be traveling by land and sea in airplanes instead of on ships and trains.

Merry Christmas to all.

Prohibition

It has now been fifty years since the repeal of Prohibition and the return of legal liquor, wine and beer. Nashvillians who remember the days of the "dry" era are becoming fewer in number.

The states of New York, Maine, Kansas and others had attempted prohibition laws as early as 1845, but all of them failed. A "dry" state could not protect itself against sister "wet" states. World War I was to give enormous impetus to the prohibition movement. The need to conserve food led to limited or prohibited use of grains for brewing and distilling. This resulted in aid to the organized efforts, for the sake of public order and decency, and later as medical men studied alcoholism—for the sake of health—to induce people to abstain. By then the great voices and efforts of Frances Willard, Cardinal Manning, Lyman Beecher and other leaders—and the persistent efforts of the temperance organizations—had begun to hold the American ear and attention. The churches were in the vanguard of the prohibition movement. The resistance of the wealth and resultant power of the liquor interests was crumbling under the social assault.

Nashville, originally a steamboat town and rather liberal in the old Southern fashion toward liquor, had known its saloon days, its Tennessee distilleries, its own brewery and had been a free-drinking community, with no more and no less of the alcohol problems of the country. However, the rural people of the state were responding to the evils of liquor and the movement toward Prohibition. They controlled the legislature. So it was that Tennessee joined the parade toward the barring of alcohol before the advent of national Prohibition.

The Tennessee "bone-dry laws" were enacted in 1917. They made it illegal to receive, possess, transport or to sell intoxicating liquors, wines or beer. Acts barring the manufacture came a few years later. The 18th Amendment to the Constitution of the U.S., enacted in 1919, prohibited the manufacture, sale, importation or exportation of alcoholic beverages. The Volstead Act to enforce Prohibition was passed over the veto of President Wilson. The nation became legally "dry."

The young American soldiers of World War I had left "dry" America for "wet" Europe in the midst of the pressures and deprivations of war. Many of them came home to resent Prohibition. The evils of Prohibition were beginning to show in lawlessness, gang warfare, murder, profiteering and politics. The debate over which was worse—liquor or Prohibition—started. It was to continue until 1933, and after that until today, unresolved.

For a quarter of this century, therefore, we of the age saw and knew the experiment. We saw the smuggling of liquor from Cuba, Mexico and Canada become a colorful and big business. We saw bootlegging become profitable locally. We saw illicit stills opening up in all the hills and mountains of Tennessee. We came to know the speakeasy, the rum-runner, the pocket bootlegger, and the blockade-runner. We drank "light beer" (less than one-half of one percent alcohol); we saw the development of a general disrespect for law and a rather keen sense of challenge in the violation of the liquor laws. The thirst for that which was now forbidden was increased. It was now contended that Prohibition had greatly increased the use of alcohol.

Violations of the liquor laws—city, state and federal—were clogging the court dockets and enforcement was becoming very costly to the American taxpayers. Underworld figures like the Capones, Schultzes, and others were becoming dangerous to the nation.

In Nashville and Tennessee, as was the case elsewhere, we saw a change come over our community and its people. The struggle for solutions became more intense. The division of opinions became hostile.

Remember the revenuers who raided stills and the moonshiners who operated them? Those who drank pure grain alcohol and the poor devils who died from drinking denatured alcohol? The fruit jar drinkers? Elderberry and dandelion wine and peach brandy? Home brew? Wine from Paradise Ridge? Remember the jake legs—those who drank Jamaica ginger and paregoric for cheap drunks? Bathtub gin? "White mule" or "white lightning"? Did you ever go to Five Points behind the Fairgrounds or to the Allied, Automobile, Ridgetop or Plantation clubs? Remember Harry Lehman, Sol Cohen, Jim Raines, Harriman Cherry, Wes Ingram, "Buck" Riat and Donnelly Davenport?

Remember the Hoptown Special—the train that brought so much liquor to Tennessee from Kentucky before national Prohibition?

Remember the WCTU, the antisaloon league and the campaigns of Noah Cooper and Bishop Dubose? How about the peepholes on the doors of speakeasies, the so-called "private clubs" and the flasks of the college boys? The secret compartment in the automobiles of the blockade runners? Raids by Gus Kiger, Leo Flair, Joe Marsherello, Van Tiene, Badacour and other officers? T. Allison's camp? Mickey Baines? Remember the bottle carried in the rumble seat?

The church remained adamant in its insistence on complete abstinence and based its campaign for Prohibition on morality and health. Its leaders were brave and persistent. The liquor and brewing interests, reeling from their losses from Prohibition, carried on their fight for survival.

The young, and especially the veterans of World War I, argued for their "individual rights." Labor clamored for repeal. Politicians cited the new lawlessness and growing disrespect for law and order. The government was losing revenue from the illicit manufacture and liquor traffic. The Great Depression was to bring greater pressure for repeal. The New Deal was to bolster the clamor for more "personal liberty" and "individual rights." By now the American people had decided, rightly or wrongly, that Prohibition was a mistake. A repeal resolution was passed by Congress in March 1933, and in nine months, in December 1933, it was ratified by 35 states and became the 21st Amendment. Tennessee later passed a series of careful and slower enactments repealing the rigors of Prohibition.

It was not until Prohibition that liquor appeared on university campuses or that many women were known to drink. To some extent it became a "dare," an "experience" for the young to drink. It made it a little fashionable to drink at the speakeasy. Liquor began to be served at parties and in homes. This was to carry over in the "brown-sack" and "personal bottles."

However, repeal was to bring in cocktail bars, fashionable drinking, driving under the influence, youth addiction, alcoholism as a national disease and—according to many experts—the use of drugs. There was crime under Prohibition and there is now more crime under repeal.

The debate continues, but one thing is sure, it all depends upon the morality, the discipline, the will and the temperance of the individual; you don't have to drink.

The thirty years from 1917 through 1947 saw World War I, Prohibition, Depression, the New Deal and World War II. Together they turned the country upside down and shook it to its foundations. Many of its customs, habits, traditions and values changed. It was to get up and move forward in many new directions. It was never to be the same. It was a miracle that the fundamental cornerstones remained in place, that we survived the upheavals and held our course as a democratic people as well as we did.

We were victorious in the wars, we overcame the Depression, we moved forward after the New Deal; but the problem of liquor is still with us—and closer to all of us.

Whether Prohibition was a fool's errand or repeal opened up a fool's paradise is still open to debate.

The Electoral College, March 1933

Together with the late Claude Stephenson of Centerville and Bob Gallimore of Dresden, I arrived by train in Washington, D.C., on March 2, 1933.

The presidential electors from Tennessee had cast their votes at the Capitol in Nashville for Franklin D. Roosevelt for president and John N. Garner for vice-president as the result of the election in November 1932. Roosevelt and Garner held 472 of the 531 electoral votes. We had been summoned to Washington for a formal meeting of the entire Electoral College, a banquet where we were to meet Mr. Roosevelt, Mr. Garner and the new cabinet, and for the inaugural ceremonies. Senator Kenneth McKellar had procured a room for me across the hall from his suite in the Mayflower Hotel.

As we left the train it seemed that everyone in the country was converging on the capital. The station, the streets and sidewalks, restaurants, hotels and public buildings were so crowded you could hardly walk. The city was in a complete uproar. I have never experienced such wild excitement.

After a difficult taxi ride to the Mayflower, we entered what seemed to be complete bedlam. It was easy to recognize senators, congressmen, generals, admirals, governors and public officials, whose faces were familiar from the press, swarming all over the place.

The next afternoon, March 3, there was a formal meeting of the College after which we were taken in special cars to the Willard Hotel for the formal dinner for the presidential electors.

Mr. James A. "Big Jim" Farley, chairman of the Democratic National Committee, presided. In the center of the ballroom, the U.S. Navy band furnished the music. To each side of Mr. Farley were seated those who had been chosen for the Roosevelt cabinet, including Cordell Hull of Tennessee. The national anthem was sung by John Charles Thomas, the famous Metropolitan Opera star. The main address was to be by Claude Bowers, one of the great political leaders of the time. The prayer was by the famous Reverend "Father" Charles E. Coughlin.

Also seated on the rostrum was Ruth Bryan Owen, later a congresswomen and ambassador. She was the daughter of the late William Jennings Bryan, "the silver-tongued orator" and former candidate for president. Some time before, Mr. Bryan had died in Dayton, Tennessee, after participating as a prosecutor of John Scopes in the famous "Monkey Trial."

In the course of introducing the electors by states, Mr. Farley came to introduce our delegation from Tennessee. As we stood, Mrs. Owen came down to our table and pinned a white carnation on each of us, in memory of her father.

He then introduced the new cabinet members.

When the dinner was completed and Mr. Bowers had spoken, the room went wild with the entry of Mr. Roosevelt and Mr. Garner. They were introduced and the standing, cheering, shouting ovation lasted for a full fifteen minutes until the president-elect himself had to quiet the house. He and Mr. Garner spoke briefly and were escorted out after he had announced that the electors had been assigned seats at the next day's inaugural ceremonies directly in front of the platform, saying that we were the most recently selected representatives of the American people. As we left the Willard, we found that thousands of people had jammed the streets outside to get a glimpse of the new president and "Cactus Jack" Garner.

We had been given our passes to the ceremony seats as well as passes to the Senate and House of Representatives.

Sure enough, the next morning when Mr. Stephenson and I arrived in front of the capitol grounds early, we had seats on the front row immediately in front of and under the deck where the oaths would be administered and the address of President Roosevelt would be delivered, approximately 30 feet away. Before a tremendous crowd Mr. Roosevelt came to the platform on the arm of his son, James.

The scene is carved in my memory, as the event is in history.

It was a solemn moment when he raised his hand to take the oath administered by Chief Justice Charles Edwin Hughes and then he began to speak:

"Let me assert my firm belief that the only thing we have to fear is fear itself—nameless, unreasoning, unjustified terror which paralyzes needed effort to convert retreat into advance."

What was the new president speaking of?

On October 20, 1929, the American stock market had crashed. The American economy was in shambles. However, economists, lawyers and political leaders, groping for an explanation, believed that the American economy was still sound and that the market would soon recover. Some said that it was only a "momentary psychological aberration." Secretary Mellon was saying that the stock market debacle was "just an illness that would soon run its course and cure itself." Actual statistics revealed the problem to be much deeper but most tried to ignore them. They showed tremendous unemployment and an alarming decrease in construction activity.

President Hoover had signed an income tax reduction bill on December 16, 1929. By October, the president announced that 4.5 million Americans were out of work but said that he was unwilling to concede that the government should provide direct assistance to the needy. The proportion of urban over rural inhabitants was increasing fast. The president signed the Hawley-Smoot Tariff Act on June 17 raising import duties, contending that it would help bankrupt farmers. On December 11, the Bank of the U.S. closed its doors on 400,000 depositors. By 1932 the unemployment reached 13 million. The population of the U.S. was 123,202,624. The steel industry was paralyzed. The reverend James Cox had headed a group of 18,000 unemployed on a march on Washington. The veterans led the "Bonus Army" of 15,000 on a march against the Capitol. President Hoover had ordered federal troops under General Douglas MacArthur to drive them out. The wages of railroad workers had been reduced 10 percent. Men were killed by police when they fired on rioters at the Michigan Ford plant. The average farmer earned only $341 after expenses during 1932. Industrial production had almost halted. Fortunes had been lost. People were hungry and desperate. Men formed lines to get jobs that paid only 20 cents per hour. Over 5,000 national banks had failed. Two hundred had failed in a period of two weeks just before the inauguration.

The pretended assurance that "prosperity was just around the corner" was now met with contempt and curses.

During and since the November election this man Roosevelt had caught the imagination of the suffering populace. In him they thought they saw hope of deliverance. Republicans and Independents joined the victorious Democrats, in the hope that he would succeed. They had put all their trust in him. The promise of the New Deal caught fire.

At last, America got up off its knees to help Roosevelt get started.

As I left the scene I could see a transformation in the crowd. He had changed the mood of the entire nation. The new president had the American people "in his vest pocket." The New Deal was started.

It was a matter of hours before we could make our way through the tremendous crowds back to the Mayflower. I distinctly remember how different they seemed to be. There was a different mood. They were smiling—they looked like they had just found something good.

Upon reaching the Mayflower, I made my way through the crowd to the cigar counter to get some cigars. It took some time for the clerk to get to me. While he was giving me my change, something heavy fell against the back of my legs. The force of the contact almost knocked me down. When I looked around it was the late Senator Huey Long (the Kingfish of Louisiana). He was drunk and helpless. His bodyguards hurried him away.

On the next morning, March 5th, my friend the late Joe Holman, the well-known Nashville architect, came to my room before breakfast. He had flown up from Miami, Florida, for the inauguration and on the way up, as they were flying over North Carolina, the president of one of the largest corporations in America, which was in grave financial trouble, had opened the plane door and jumped out—to commit suicide. Joe had witnessed the tragedy. He was terribly excited and concerned as he told me that an army of insurance investigators were in the hotel to question him about the tragedy for a large number of insurance companies. We spent about three hours with them. We then had lunch and later in the afternoon, we heard that the new president had (temporarily) closed every bank in America. Notices were posted in the hotel that no checks were to be received or cashed. I had a round trip railroad ticket. Joe had no ticket to Nashville nor any cash. Claude Stephenson and I had to pool our cash to get Joe back to Nashville.

As I alighted from the train at the Union Station, somehow I believed that the country would go to work and rebuild itself, that it had rediscovered its strength.

Little did I know that we would only have seven years in which to do it in order to be ready to meet another threat to our national existence.

A crazed Austrian paperhanger was coming upon the scene in Berlin and the war lords of Japan were secretly looking at the entire Pacific with cunning and greedy eyes.

Today, fifty years later, as I look back I reflect on the generosity of Providence to the United States of America.

The Woodland Street Bridge.

CHAPTER 9

Memories Are Made of This
The Medley Continued

W HEN ONE TURNS memory loose to wander back and through and in and out of the yesteryears, it starts an unpredictable and disconnected chain of persons, places and events. Some are pleasant and some are unpleasant.

The following is an example:

Did you ever catch a ride on a steam "willapus-wallapus" that was rolling the crushed rock on a street, or ride on a "drag" which was pulled by a horse?

Did you ever prime a well pump or a T-model Ford to make it start?

Remember that after you killed a chicken you dipped it into hot water to make the feathers easy to pull out? Did you really believe that billygoats would eat tin cans, or that thing about frogs and warts? Remember those small collar buttons that came back in shirts from the laundry?

How about the vestibules and the signs on the rear cars of the Dixie Flyer and the Pan-American? Did you ever ride in a barouche, or wear a pair of hob-nailed boots?

Did you ever go to Borum's Camp, Setter's Lake or T. Allison's Camp, or to Doc Mannion's place? Remember the Sunday dinners at Horn Springs? Did your parents grow sunflowers in the backyard?

Have you forgotten Horseshoe Curve on the old road to Joelton?

Remember how they used to ice the old refrigerated railroad cars on the side tracks at the Noel Ice Company?

Have you forgotten those awful little cone-shaped paper cups in a holder by water fountains that you had to fill 10 times to get a small drink of water? How about peanut butter glasses?

Did you have a bag in which you carried your pee-wees, toofers, crockers, glasses, imitations, steelies and agates? Have you forgotten the "Boston ring" marble game? Remember the "plumb line"? Did you play for fun, or "for keeps"?

Remember folding paper 10 or 15 times to cut out paper dolls holding hands?

What do you think that young sophisticated teen-agers who pay $15 to $30 for a ticket to a rock concert would say if you suggested that they go on a marshmallow roast instead—or that instead of a beer bust, they go on a hayride? Of course, we had the further choice of a candy-pulling, the Epworth League meeting, a lawn festival, or just sitting on the front porch swing. The later got real interesting after the parents got sleepy and left their chairs to retire. And there was always the ice cream parlor, with its chocolate and nut sundaes, banana splits, chocolate, strawberry and vanilla sodas, and "dopes" (Coca-Colas).

Remember your mother threading the bobbin on the old foot-propelled Singer sewing machine?

Remember, "Fox in the morning" and the answer, "Goose in the evening," and "All who ain't ready, can't hide over"?

It seems to be stylish today to wear patched and ragged pants. Don't you wish it had been that way when we had to wear them?

Yesterday's paper announced that a ticket to Michael Jackson's so-called "concert" would cost young people $30. Times sure have changed. Seventy years ago $30 would have bought:

Tickets to 100 picture shows—$5
10 haircuts—$1.50
60 ice cream cones—$3
60 soft drinks—$3
60 bags of popcorn—$3
50 hamburgers—$5
20 bags of peanuts—$2.50
20 bags of fudge—$2
and $5 left over.

I knew a man who earned $30 then for working as a bookkeeper, 10 hours each day for a six-day week, and he raised five children and bought a home.

What would you have said if you could have earned $35 for cutting grass for a small lawn?

Did you envy the boy who could "skin the cat" five times, chin the bar ten times, and walk on his hands?

You young carpenter's helpers—did you know what queen posts, rafters, straining pieces, beams, struts and studs were?

Remember the McEwen roll-towel services in public places?

Have you forgotten that, when the metal tag came off the end of your shoelace, you would have to wet the end of the string to get it through the eye?

Did you ever lose the metal rim off a wagon wheel, or have a piece of the hard rubber tire come off your buggy or surrey wheel?

Remember when popular drugstore items were Castoria, Stark's headache powders, C. C. pills, Dr. Caldwell's syrup of pepsin, Black

Draught, tincture of arnica, turpentine, magnesium blocks, senna leaves, Lydia E. Pinkham's Compound and Tanclac?

When the realities and demands of the present jerk you back from reminiscence, then old memories begin to fade again.

Did you know:

That Nashville was the first city in the South to attempt a water-works system? It was started in 1830 and completed in 1833, at a cost of $55,000.

That General Andrew Jackson held more offices of trust and honor than were ever held by any other citizen of the republic?

Public Prosecutor, 1790.

Member of first constitutional convention of Tennessee, 1796.

First representative from Tennessee in Congress, 1796.

U.S. Senator from Tennessee, elected twice, 1797 and 1823.

Judge of Superior Court of Law and Equity, 1798.

General in the Tennessee militia, 1802.

Conqueror of the Creek Indians, 1813-1814.

Major general, U.S. Army, 1814.

Victor, Battle of New Orleans, June 8, 1815.

Governor of Florida, 1821.

President of the U.S., elected twice, 1828 and 1832.

He resigned more offices than were ever held by any other citizen.

He was the only president, except Washington, to appoint during his term the entire U.S. Supreme Court, and the only president to pay off the entire national debt.

Do you remember: Gloria flour, Rising Sun flour, chautauquas, Fish brothers in the Arcade, and Shinola shoe polish?

Ladies, do you remember the Nashville corsetieres of 60 years ago: Mrs. Louise Brandon, Charis of Nashville, and Kelly Corset Company?

Did you ever use the expressions "skidoo," "ski-daddle," "get a move on," "sniggle-fritz," "fiddle-faddle," "spidunk," "snopy-quop," and "fiddle-de-dee"?

Remember when iris blooms were called "flags," and when men did not comb their hair down over their foreheads to look sophisticated or to hide a receding hair line?

Would your grandchildren know what you meant by "loblollies"?

Have you forgotten that at one time pot liquor (pot likker) and pone cornbread tasted as good as today's vichyssoise or other gourmet soups?

Remember the music of: "I'll Be Seeing You," "Blueberry Hill," "Smiles," "Fascination," "Autumn Leaves," "Bluebird of Happiness,"

"Peg O' My Heart," "Spanish Eyes," "For Me and My Gal," "The Nearness of You"? All beautiful, real music that did not have to be supported by flashing lights, weird costumes, loud instruments, body twisting or references to sex, liquor or cocaine?

Have you forgotten "Lasses" White as "Skunktown Jones," singing "Don't Cadillac Me," in his minstrel show? In the same show our local "Skeets" Mayo appeared as "Quinine Bitters." How about Paris, Tennessee's great Bert Swor as "King of Spades," singing "California," in the old Al G. Fields' minstrels?

Sixty years ago this month the big silent-screen picture shows were featuring:

Charlie Chaplin in *The Pilgrims*; Mae Murray in *Jazz Mania*; Bebe Daniels in *Glimpses of the Moon*; Douglas Fairbanks in *Robin Hood*.

Remember the colored, round and hard candy balls called "jawbreakers"? How about R.J.R. (R. J. Reynolds) smoking tobacco, which was popularly known as "Run, Johnny, Run"?

Remember Liggett's Corner, the Western Front, and the Red-Light District? How about Al Menah Temple's "Shimmying Lizzie" Ford? Or these old Courthouse characters: Dick Lindsey, Felix Wilson, Sr., Tom Hill, Romans Hailey, Chris Kreig, West Morton, W. B. Cook, Joseph West, Joe McCord, Dan Phillips, Bill Lingner, Dick McClure, W. C. Dodson, R. L. Wright and Bud Minton?

Did you ever watch one of the Shelby Avenue soapbox derbies, or the Hippodrome dance contests?

You country boys, have you forgotten swinging bridges, cow paths, rabbit nests, killdees and IXL pocket knives?

Didn't we used to call Vaseline petroleum jelly?

Remember when men's pants had watch pockets?

You old wrestling and baseball fans: Do you remember when "Chief" Marvin challenged the entire Yankee baseball team at the Andrew Jackson Hotel while they were here for a pre-season game with the Vols at the Dell and really whipped about three of them before the police got there?

Whatever became of collar buttons? Remember when a stubborn buttonhole made you drop one and it always rolled under the bed or dresser, and you had to get down on your knees to retrieve it—and cuss?

Have you forgotten hod carriers and how they carried mortar to bricklayers? How about motorcycle sidecars? Did you like root beer?

Did you know that when your country friend said, "I holped him," that he was using a dialect word recognized by Webster?

Did you smoke Pall Mall cigarettes?

A 1910 copy of *The Exhaust*, the publication of the then Nashville Automobile Club, carried the following advertisements for automobiles in Nashville:

Tennessee Auto Co.—Pierce-Arrow, Oldsmobile-Flanders, and the Thomas Flyer; Chester Motor Co.—Cadillac; Deeds & Hirsig—Hudson, Chalmers; Imperial Motor Co.—Packard; Marathon Sales Co.—Marathon; Hager & Elliott—Peerless, Marman, Elliott; Southern States Sales—Stevens; Cohen Car Co.—Maxwell; Whiteman & Kirkpatrick—Electrics; and Ivo Glen—Overland.

The last Stanley Steamer was made in 1922. The publication also carried an announcement of the commencement of the construction of the Memphis to Bristol Highway by Governor Malcolm Patterson.

Have you forgotten "cut-outs" on early automobiles?

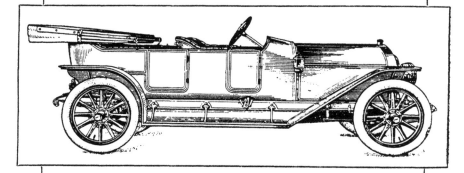

MARATHON

Not Simply a Car   **But Car Service**

Marathon cars are made throughout in our big plant by skilled mechanics and under the critical supervision of experts. They are the culminating results of the best practice in automobile engineering, together with various improvements suggested by time and a constant effort to better our product, therefore in the 1911 Marathon line we offer what we believe to be the highest development of the Motor Car. In durability, grace of design, efficiency—in all the desirable features of automobile construction, these cars stand pre-eminent at the price.

Southern Motor Works
Nashville, Tennessee

Remember the old iron cage elevators—and tongues on wagons, shoes, bells, buckles and boards of lumber? Whatever became of licorice plugs? Have you forgotten Sophie Tucker singing "My Yiddish Mama"—and her trademark—the large white silk handkerchief?

How about these old popular pieces of music: "Day In and Day Out"; "The Acheson, Topeka and the Santa Fe"; "You, and the Night and the Music"; "Just the Way You Look Tonight"; "I Can't Give You Anything but Love"; "Someone to Watch Over Me"; "Who Could Ask for Anything More?"; "A One-Man Woman"; "They Can't Take That Away from Me"; "Accentuate the Positive"; "Jeepers Creepers"; and "Come Rain or Come Shine."

Remember ice cream sodas at Chubby's; the Englehardt brothers, who were cigar makers; Hagey's grocery—and Rabbit's on Church Street?

Did you know these: "Bubber" and "Jakie" Jonnard, "Shaky" Kain, "Dutch" Uhlian, "Gawky" Nichol, "Son" Bostick, "Artie" Hoffman, "Gussie" Gerst, "Cam" Faircloth, "Nate" Craig, "Loosh" Connell, "Bull" Giddens, "Snaky" Haltom, "Tim" Rassberry, "Jake" Petway, "Pug" Dillon, "Abbie" Arnette, "Slick" Vester, "Rooster" Carr, "Papa John" Truett, "Buck" Fuller, "Al" Kuhn, "Hap" Sudekem, "Doll" Randolph, "Kit" McConnico, "Buttons" Satterfield, "Pick" Robinson, "Cherry" Metz, "Slockey" Kelly, "Hack" Hackworth, "Drag" Benson, "Jap" Thompson, "Sump" Anderson, "Windy" Wilson, "Bo" Bess, "Lou" Lusky, "Lem" Baker, "Skipper" Scarborough, "Bowser" Chest, and "Greasy" Hanley?

Did you ever sleep on a corn-shuck mattress? Why did the old butter molds always leave an oak leaf imprinted on country butter?

Remember how the electric sparks would fly when the streetcar trolley jumped the line?

They have removed the old Sycamore Lodge at Shelby Park. Those walls could tell some interesting stories—remember yours?

The wrecking bar is ready to knock down the walls of the Old Ladies Home on West End Avenue. They have heard thousands of memories of girlhood dreams.

Remember the signs on uptown streets that warned of a $5 fine for spitting on the streets? The plug tobacco cutters? The one of iron with the Naughty Imp thumbing his nose? The crock jugs we used to take to the store to buy bulk vinegar? When your mother made chow-chow and hung it up in a cloth sack to drip before putting it in jars? Cowcatchers on steam railroad engines? The paths that led through the "commons," as we called vacant and uncultivated land? Poor-man's gates? The revolving postcard racks in old drugstores? Rit dyes? When bathtubs stood on four legs? McEwen's towel service? Popcorn and peanut wagons? Boston men's garters and those brass bells that decorated the horns of hames placed over horse collars?

Remember runaways, where frightened horses would break out of control of the buggy or wagon driver? The rumbling and hissing of the old steam radiators and how we hung on to every word of Roosevelt and Churchill over radio during World War II?

Did you know Albert Vaughan, who was brought back from Belgium as a small boy by Ted Vaughan after his service in World War II? He took the Vaughan name, grew up in East Nashville and later became a U.S. Secret Service agent.

Did your dog sleep under the house?

How many things used to be kept in cigar and shoe boxes and in fruit jars?

Can you recall all the passenger stops on the streetcar lines you rode? How about the passenger train stops between Nashville and other cities?

Have you forgotten the Sunrise Automobile Club on top of old Nine Mile Hill? How about that early automobile enthusiast, Billy Bordeiser? Do you remember that he was a friend of Barney Oldfield, the first American race car driver and a very popular Nashvillian?

Remember Clara Bow, the Omph Girl, and movie actors William and Dustin Farnum?

Did you sing "Casey Jones," "I'll See You in My Dreams," "Red Wing," "I'm Alabamy Bound," "Shuffle Off to Buffalo," "Keep the Home Fires Burning," "What Do You Want to Make Those Eyes at Me for When They Don't Mean What They Say," "I'm Forever Blowing Bubbles," "I Want a Girl Just Like the Girl That Married Dear Old Dad," and "I Want to Be Happy, But I Won't Be Happy, 'til I Make You Happy Too."

Remember the band playing, "There'll Be a Hot Time in the Old Town Tonight"?

Do you recall the twelve o'clock whistle, when all the factories, foundries and businesses blew steam whistles at noon?

Before the day of plastics, remember celluloid combs, moving picture film, etc.? Have you forgotten chamois skins? Did you ever ride in a two-wheeled pony cart? Were you afraid to cross swinging bridges?

Remember theme papers?

Did you ever know what cruppers, checkreins and martingales were?

Remember hand cars?

Did you ever trade at Page & Sim's or Leickhardt's drugstores on the Square, or the Fun Shop on Deaderick?

Remember when men and women had just one set of head hair?

Did you ever have to have knee patches sewed on your short pants, especially during marble season?

Did you know Reeves Handley, Wilkes Northern, Bennett Corley, Dudley and George Gale, Roy Norwood, Burton Wilkerson, T. Willie Conners, Bill Gerst, Chris Kreig, Bill Lingner, "Fats" McCullough, West Morton, John Todd, Al Armstrong, Dr. Neal Rutland, John Noel, Ed Sulzbacher, Harry Husband, Arch Bishop, or Jay Stephenson—all popular figures on the streets of old Nashville?

Did you ever see a flea circus?

Remember the St. Bernard Coal Company and Hooper Love—and when they changed from the horse-drawn coal wagons to motor trucks?

Did you ever ride in a tallyho?

What ever became of top spinning and bead stringing? Did your mother save Octagon soap coupons? Remember when the city used to be decorated for conventions, reunions and the Fourth of July, with red, white and blue bunting and festoons—and when we would have public speakings at set places around the city and county during election campaigns? Have you forgotten how, before the days of junk and advertising mail, advertising and announcements were by flyers or handbills, hand delivered in the communities?

Remember hotel call boys who paged people? The Phillip Morris advertisements?

How about the annual Glendale Park Easter egg hunt, and the Easter sunrise services at Centennial and Shelby parks?

Have you forgotten how, when we were small, we counted out to see who was "it" in games?

Can you finish these: "One'ry, ore'y, ickory, ann . . ." "One, two, buckle your shoe . . ." "Engine, engine, number 9 . . ." "One, two, three, . . ." or, "One for the money . . ."?

How about the button game? Hully, gully, how many?

These games, which gave us fun, would seem, I am afraid, rather silly to the sophisticated, and maybe spoiled, little ones of today. They belonged to the day of gingham dresses, bloomers, plaited hair, stockings, button shoes, short pants, waists, and soda water caps, lemonade and tea cakes, roasted marshmallows and popcorn, chores and lessons, and paddles and switches.

Dream on, old timer.

Do you recall the old songs: "For Me and My Gal," "Side by Side," "All Alone," "Beautiful Doll," "I Found a Million Dollar Baby," and "Tea for Two"? How about Fanny Brice singing "My Man" and Marilyn Monroe singing "Diamonds Are a Girl's Best Friend"?

I know that you remember Miss Sara playing sheet music for prospective customers at the French Music Store.

Clyde W. "Fats" McCullough and his Harley-Davidson motorcycle—early 1920.

Did you ever learn "pig Latin"? Remember tumble bugs? How about the Fox Movietone news in picture shows?

Old Nashville gave colorful handles to the names of colorful people. The number of these which you remember will depend upon your age: "Rabbit" Curry, "Cap" Alley, "Blinkey" Horn, "Tot" McCullough, "Steamboat" Johnson, "Boots" Richardson, "Bugs" Litterer, "Monk" Sharp, "Sister" Kykes, "Dopey" Sneed, "Slats" Schlater, "Skeets" Mayo, "Kid" Wolfe, "Gabby" Street, "Tub" Sullivan, "Spike" McClure, "Jew" Sam, "Baby" Ray, "Shorty" Yates, "Sleepy" Bainbridge, "Butch" Plique, "Pluto" Jones, "Tookie"

Homer C. "Gabby" Street.

Gilbert, "Spot" Burton, "Pinkey" White, "Coon" Creswell, "Toots" Tignor, "Moon" Mason, "Doody" Redford, "Hobby" Horn, "War Horse" Rogers, "Preacher" Gann, "Dizzy" Dismukes, "Tuck" Russell, "Jelly" Drennon, "Cotton" Swint?

"Dingham" Bell, "Rooster" Whitley, "Gus" Bloudau, "Cocky" Groomes, "Buttermilk" Shelton, "Polly" Woodfin, "Titsy" Carter, "East" Hyde, "Pete" Carter, "Hoot" Lowery, "Lefty" Durr, "Daddy" Chadwell, "Tip-Toe" Stevens, "Push" Howard, "Si" Parrish, "Big-Tap" Wright, "Slick" Welsh, "Tige" Garrett, "Deacon" Douglas, "Papa John" Gordy, "Little Evil" Jacobs, "Cocky" Adcock, "Yellow" Briggs, "Red" Sanders, "Jeezbo" Avery, "Slim" Embry, "Skinny" Stumb, "Pie" Hardison, "Doc" Manion, "Pony" Redd, "Dog" Ward, "Cat" Sawyers, "Sally" Walker, "Blue" Green, "Runt" Troutman, "Honey" Martin, "Blackie" Goodman, "Pop" Varner, "Pup" Wright?

"Tank" Ferguson, "Goose" Warren, "Rosie" Rosenfield, "Pos" Elam, "Speedy" Rawlings, "Nig" Allen, "Cowboy" Jones, "Dutch" Morrisey, "Shorty" Yates, "Britches" Jones, "Nubby" Johnson, "Mulie" Vaughn, "Hap" Motlow, "Boo" Sneed, "Gun" Puryear, "Big Boy" Leibengute, "Rocky" Argo, "Punk" Puryear, "Spooney" Noon, "Piggie" Dodd, "Hog" Levy, "Hek" Wakefield, "Scotty" Neil, "Smokey Joe" Warren, "Tree-Top" Jones, "Hank" Fort, "Wee" Jones, "Tootsie" Bess, "Plunk" Gould, "Buster" Boguskie, "Hinky" Sloan, "Fatty" Lawrence, "Rube" McKinney, "Hot" Shaffer, "Crip" Warwick, "Pooper" Bomar, "Slo" Barnes, "Wonder" Harris, "Fuzzy" Warner, "Pup" Doggett, "Butts" Geny, "Pap" Strigle, "Cracker" Patton,

"Windy" Malone, "Scoop" Hudgins, "Chili" Hardin, and "Chick" Davitt? And then there were—"Bodiddly," "Goodjelly," "Highpocket," and others.

Remember Tip-Top bread, O-J No. 11 canned goods, Saxon soap, Grandma's Wonder flour, Kingham's bacon, salt pork, pork butts, hogs' heads, souse, calves' brains, duck, goose and guinea eggs, lamb fries, and salt mackerel, melts, and sorghum molasses?

Have you forgotten poke bonnets? Remember your mother's knitting and embroidery needles? Did you call peanuts "goobers"? Did you have prickly heat or eat ripe mulberries? Remember when margarine was called "oleo"? Remember playing tag? Did your grandpa like his hot toddy and dunk his toast? Remember whipcord pants? Girls, remember when it was very daring and forward to wear a décollete' dress?

Remember corn shuck door mats, the March kite season, putting fireflies in a bottle, climbing trees, raising pigeons, gathering eggs, baiting the mousetraps and winding the mantel clock before going to bed?

Remember that kind Mr. Jones who ran the billiard parlor in the old Maxwell House Hotel—a good friend to everyone?

Here are a few more memory testers for older Nashvillians:

Remember dog and pony shows?

Did you help collect scrap aluminum for the war effort during World War I? How about the "Indian princess" who rode the white horse that dived from a platform into a tank of water at Glendale Park?

How many times have men's neckties, coat lapels and pants legs changed from narrow to wide, and vice-versa, during your lifetime?

Did you use hair grease or oil to pompadour your hair?

Have you forgotten those glass locomotives that contained mints, which were sold at the Union Station?

Remember when women would not dare to allow their clothing to reveal the natural contour of their backsides?

Remember this:

> Pack up your troubles in your old kit bag
>   and smile, smile, smile.
> While you've a lucifer to light your fag,
>   smile boys, that's the style.
>
> There's no use in worrying, it never
>   was worthwhile.
> So, pack up your troubles in your old kit bag
>   and smile, smile, smile.

Remember Mrs. Weaver Harris and her "El Chico" group of musicians? How about the bobby-sox craze and Hank Fort's, "I Didn't Know the Gun Was Loaded"?

Whatever became of chicken coops and roosts?

Remember the railroad ticket office at Fourth and Church where the L&C Tower is today? How about the York Riding Academy on Lynwood Boulevard; the James-Sanford Collection Agency, or the magistrate's courts on Deaderick Street? Remember Hap Cassedy's parking lot at Sulphur Dell? Did you ever see the turntable at the N&C Railroad shops? Remember the pony buggies with basket seats and tassled umbrellas? How about cowbells?

Do you recall how men used to gather at the neighborhood fire halls in the evenings just to shoot the breeze, argue politics, and learn some new gossip and jokes?

Did you ever bank a fire in the grate before going to bed on a cold winter night?

Remember when colored kite paper sold for two sheets for a penny? How about the red Indian Chief thick writing tablets with rough paper, for a nickel?

Did you have one of those thumb bells on your bicycle? Remember the Merchant's Delivery Company's fleet of trucks?

Did you ever ride in a wagon when the driver had to scotch the back wheels to keep the wagon from crowding the horses while going down a steep hill? Remember motorcycle sidecars, and rubber water pistols?

One of the unnoticed improvements in the quality of life has been the smoothing of the surfaces over which we walk. Remember when the part of our shoes which wore out first was the toe? Remember the metal taps we used to have the cobbler tack onto the toes of the shoes?

Did you ever help to stoke the fire in a tobacco barn where the tobacco was being fired, or in a meat smokehouse where hams and bacon were being cured? Remember how the smoke that didn't get in your eyes escaped from the buildings?

Remember those little wooden horns with a small rubber balloon on the end? You would blow the balloon up and, as it released the air, it would blow the horn.

Remember how the car washers would be waiting to clean the coach windows of the Dixie Flyer, the Pan-American, and the Hummingbird when they pulled into Union Station to take on passengers?

Did you ever play drop the handkerchief? Did you ever knock on the door and run after leaving a sassy valentine at a neighbor's house?

Remember singing, "It Ain't Gonna Rain No More"? Could your

school teacher see out of the back of her head? Remember how garters cut your legs? How about when walking policemen were referred to as "flatfoots," professional boxers were called "prizefighters"—and the day of the motorman and conductor, engineer and fireman, switchman and car-knocker, the trashman, the ice man, the milkman, the fish man, the dressmaker, the pack-peddlers, the market man, the music teacher, the preacher, the horse doctor, the blacksmith, the soda-jerker, the hash-slinger, the paper boy, the tooth doctor, the sawbones, the shoe-shine boy, the grocery man, the wagon driver, the well-driller, the closet-cleaner, the rag man, and the shoemaker?

Remember white door knobs, pin cushions, razor straps, corset stays and strings, rock hammers, monkey wrenches, crosscut saws, back braces for children, gold teeth, peg legs, hearing horns and celluloid shields for vaccinations?

Did you have a canvas or leather book strap?

See if your grandchildren know how to fold and make a paper dunce cap, to make a kite or a flipper. I don't think that they would care for a bean bag.

Remember bar pins, breast pins and coral necklaces?

What ever became of hobble skirts?

Do you remember when the toothpick holder was always on the dinner table?

Have you forgotten the different colored cords on the wide-brimmed hats worn by the soldiers during World War I before the advent of "overseas" or "cootie" caps? They were blue for infantry, yellow for cavalry and red for artillery. How about the service pins with a red border, white field and a blue star for each son in the military service worn by "war mothers" and a flag of similar design that hung in the windows?

Did you see the movie *Salome* which featured Nazimova?

Have you forgotten the large wooden barrels with the wooden faucets that held bulk vinegar at the grocery store? How about those little cylinder dime banks?

In the old days the only weed control we knew was—to pull them.

Remember souvenir fly swatters and corkscrews?

Wonder why we thought it was fun to walk railroad or streetcar rails.

Did you have to split kindling, get in the coal and lay the fire?

Did you have one of those wire popcorn poppers? Did you ever clip the wings of chickens to keep them from flying out of the chicken yard, cut off the tails of little ten-day-old bull puppies, trim a horse's mane or saw off the points of cows' horns?

Do you remember what a fetlock was? How about getting cockle-burrs out of a cow's tail and sticktights off your pants legs?

Did you ever see a cow with five teats or an albino skunk? Did you ever have a skunk to get up under your house, or get too close to one yourself? That has been an excuse for many a country boy to miss school.

Do you remember demijohns? How about calf muzzles? Did you ever ride in a victoria? Have you forgotten tortoiseshell combs or tete-a-tete, (forward and backward or S-shaped) sofas? Could you operate an apple cider press? Remember when the coal companies gave away thermometers as souvenirs?

Did you ever stop to listen to the little string band playing on the sidewalk in front of the Elks' Club? Have you forgotten "servidoors," those hotel room doors into which drycleaning, laundry and packages could be deposited from the outside to be received by the occupant from the inside?

Remember Huggins' Baby Bunting stick candy, Neuhoff's hams and Alloway's dressed chickens and Tip Top bread? Did your father or grandfather dunk his toast or doughnuts into his morning coffee?

You old country boys—did you know the difference between bar,

Delivery truck, Huggins Candy Company.

snaffle and curb bits? How about the bull tongue and the double shovel? Remember riding on horsedrawn drags?

Did you use an agate or an emma as your taw in a marble game?

Whatever became of butter paddles?

Could you tell the difference between blackberries and dewberries?

Surely, you did not like horehound candy; but what became of those different colored little cream candy teddybears?

Remember when mufflers became "scarfs" and when men wore spats and capes? I asked one of the grandchildren if he had ever seen a cape. He answered, "Yes, Canaveral, Cod and Girardeau."

And now, I would like to have some hot crackling bread and butter, a glass of cold buttermilk and a big bowl of homemade peach ice cream.

Jubilee Hall, Fisk University.

CHAPTER 10

Thanks for the Memory
Concluding Thoughts

I T HAS BEEN MY HOPE that some of these excursions in memory back to old Nashville would provide some escape from the more uncomfortable realities of the day, especially for those of us with whom they have not entirely faded. If some of the younger generations find an exaggerated expression of pride in some of the references, they will come to understand as they grow older and reflect on their past.

Nashville: The Best Hometown I Know

We have, at times, dealt with the better memories, but our lives were also touched with some community disasters and tragedies. As our parents and grandparents knew of the Civil War days of the eighteen-sixties and the horror of the cholera epidemic of the eighteen-seventies, we experienced catastrophes in the first half of the twentieth century: The bursting of the city reservoir on Eighth Avenue in 1912; the train wreck at Dutchman's Curve in 1918; the horrible winter of 1917 with the flu epidemic and loss of life among Mexican laborers at Old Hickory; the cyclone of Bakertown and Antioch; the East Nashville fires; the East Nashville cyclones; the deprivation and sufferings of the Depression in the thirties; World Wars I and II; flooding, before the Cumberland was controlled.

While each of these brought deaths, property loss and suffering, they were small in magnitude as compared to the tragedies of some sister cities during the same period. Considered as a whole, Nashville has been comparatively fortunate in this respect.

Nashville has been courageous and generous before all these misfortunes. It has not faltered but has moved quickly to face what had to be done to alleviate the consequent suffering and to rebuild. It has always emerged stronger and better for its bitter experiences.

It may be that we have lived in the Golden Age of Nashville, the United States and the world.

We have actually witnessed the introduction of a new mode of life with electricity, the telephone, the automobile, the airplane, plastics, aluminum, radio, television, asphalt, domestic appliances, telecommunications, electronics, synthetics, refrigeration, merchandising, transportation . . . and now computers.

More than any one of these, but by reason of all, a new quality of life has come.

It may be that all this has brought with it less discipline, too much appetite for pleasure and ease, and less inclination to work. Perhaps all this can be blamed for unrest, violence, lack of respect for law, lack of patriotism and national appreciation.

However, no people in the world enjoy the opportunity for peace, prosperity, and civil tranquility as much as we Nashvillians—and Americans.

All this is right here in our Nashville, and we can have it if we have our health and are willing to work. Nashville abounds with American opportunity and good fortune.

On the whole, our citizens are good people. A strong native stock has been joined by others from many places and countries to strengthen our potential. As America has welcomed those from other lands, Nashville has extended an open and unprejudiced invitation to all who would cast their lots with us and seek a better life.

Nashville has always had a big heart. It has looked after its poor, its afflicted, its old and its unfortunate. Hardly ever has a drive, a campaign, or any effort to assist the unfortunate failed.

Unfortunately, as the city has grown, the number of the indolent, lazy, and dependent by choice has increased. This will always be a problem beyond cure and, consequently, a necessary evil which does not attract nor deserve sympathy.

Nowhere in the world does a young boy or girl have a greater opportunity than here in Nashville. The gate to a good life is wide open. The chance for a quality education is abundant. The provision for encouragement and ambition abounds. The old society not only welcomes but yearns for the recruitment of the successful and ambitious. It has always and will continue to reward and honor those who work hard and do right.

If in these articles I have dipped my pen too deep into the wells of sentiment and emotion, I hope the readers will understand that it results from the fact that I love and respect the community which has been so generous to me and mine, and which offers the same opportunity to every boy and girl, regardless of how and where he or she was born.

Nashville: A Challenge to Youth

As I conclude this series on memories of old Nashville, I fear that some of our young friends may feel that I have, at times, been unfair in

Centennial Exposition—1896.

Centennial Committee Reunion, 1904 (note replica of the Parthenon in background).

Fort Negley site.

1937 flood scene in the area that is now James Robertson Parkway below the State Capitol.

comparisons, evaluations and conclusions. It will be recalled that I cautioned in the beginning that, as we grow old, we are prone to overvalue our own days and experiences.

However, there is some justification for the complaints of our older friends that our advancing years have brought us into a youth-oriented age, that the world is geared to the necessities, opportunities and pleasures of young people. Frankly, I am afraid that this results in some jealousy on our part, aggravated by an attendant sense of loneliness. Certainly, we are pleased with the advantage this gives our own children, but we all wonder what we could have done with these advantages. However, it pains us to see the enticements that dilute and dissolve the family units.

We think that we have lived in the Golden Age, but we worry about whether its new quality of life will destroy the will to work, the thrill of achievement, the sense of social obligation, the national spirit and the moral responsibility of our grandchildren. We are concerned that they have had it too easy.

This fear is aggravated by the realization of our own lost opportunities, mistakes, errors and failures, by the memories of what we might or could have done. The only consolation is the fact that our grandparents worried over the same things. And, as we sit wondering and worrying, perhaps we are underestimating the sense, ability, strength and intentions of our young people and their capacity to face the challenges of their future. Perhaps we are still looking at them as our little boys and girls, still dependent upon us. Maybe we are not understanding that they, too, have grown up with these changes and have prepared themselves for them, while we were still worrying about them getting hurt, or getting sick, or getting in the "wrong company," as children. Perhaps we have discounted the fact that the new world has made them smarter, stronger and better prepared than we think. Maybe we have made the mistake of measuring them, their abilities and their moralities with yesterday's yardsticks. We would be the first to admit that we thought that our grandparents made this mistake.

Tomorrow will depend on them, as today depended upon us. We demonstrated to our questioning parents that we could handle the changing responsibilities and we are forced to believe that our children will meet the tests of tomorrow.

Our respect for their preparedness is mingled with some degree of awe at the world they face, but it is excited by the wonders which lie ahead of them. That awe is an indefinable sense of the dreadful and the sublime. As our youthful ardors have been cooled down by time, we made the mistake of thinking that our young people start from the limits of our subdued experience. They start, as we did, from youthful expectations. They are encouraged by challenge and will not be sneered down or repressed by caution or fear.

They will come to have the same apprehensions about their grandchildren, and the same confidence in them.

The world cannot be energized, supplied and supervised from the rocking chair, whether it be occupied by the aged and infirm or by the indolent and unconcerned. It is the young, the strong, the active and the alert who must man the controls. We have no right to prescribe the limits of their ardors, ambitions, elections and conclusions. Certainly, we have no right to limit to our experiences their progress, inventions, innovations and explorations. We can and should advise and counsel, but we cannot limit their futures to our past.

The youth of Nashville will respond to all of these challenges as the youth of yesterday did.

Index of Names

Index of Businesses, Institutions, and Locations